Power of Will

Frank C. Haddock

Alpha Editions

This edition published in 2019

ISBN : 9789353978983

Design and Setting By
Alpha Editions
email - alphaedis@gmail.com

As per information held with us this book is in Public Domain.
This book is a reproduction of an important historical work.
Alpha Editions uses the best technology to reproduce historical
work in the same manner it was first published to preserve its
original nature. Any marks or number seen are left intentionally
to preserve its true form.

The Power-Book Library.
Volume One.

Power of Will

By Frank Channing Haddock, M.S., Ph.D.

Author of "Power for Success," "Culture of Courage," "Practical Psychology," "Business Power," "Creative Personality."

A Practical Companion Book for Unfoldment of the Powers of Mind.

In Three Parts:
EMBRACING
The Theory and Practice of a Growing Will;
Direct Control of the Personal Faculties;
and Success in the Conduct of Affairs.

Two-hundred-fifty-fifth Edition
(18,000 copies)

1918

The Pelton Publishing Company,
Meriden, Conn.

(L. N. Fowler & Co., 7 Imperial Arcade, Ludgate Circus, London.)

PREFACE

THIS book comes to you as a Well-wisher, a Teacher, and a Prophet.

It will become a Teacher if you will honestly try to secure mental reaction upon it; that is, if you will resolve to THINK — to Think *with* it and to Think *into* it.

It will be Prophet of a higher and more successful living if you will persistently and intelligently follow its requirements, for this will make yourself a completer Manual of the Perfected Will.

But remember! This book cannot think for you; THAT IS THE TASK OF YOUR MIND.

This book cannot give you greater power of Will; THAT IS FOR YOURSELF TO ACQUIRE BY THE RIGHT USE OF ITS CONTENTS.

This book cannot hold you to persistence in self-culture; THAT IS THE TEST OF YOUR WILL.

This book is not magical. It promises nothing occult or mysterious. It is simply a call to practical and scientific work.

If you will steadfastly go on through the requirements marked out, this book will develop within you highest wishes of welfare for self, it will make you a teacher of self, it will inspire you as a prophet of self brought to largest efficiency.

ALL NOW RESTS WITH YOU!!

PREFACE TO THE REVISED EDITION

"POWER OF WILL" has been a pioneer in its chosen field — the only book of its kind, the only kind of its class, the only class in the world. A number of writers, literary and otherwise, have since followed the pathway thus pointed out, some of them exhibiting scant regard for magnanimity, that virtue which, seemingly demanded by the much-exploited "New Thought," is without spiritual littleness and is ever fair in acknowledgments. The author bids all such, Take and confess if they are true knights of the larger age, but, an' they cannot stand so high, Take for their own that which birth forbids creating, since our world life is so great, and in its abundance every mind may claim to live, even that of the humblest parasite. "Many a frog masquerades in the costume of a bird."

The kindness with which the book has been received, its literary deficiencies being overlooked in view of its practical purpose, and the evidences given by students that the work has helped many to a larger growth and a better self-handling, have inspired the present revision.

The volumes of the Power-Book Library have sought always to be clear, plain, practical, sane and helpful, and neither chicanery nor suspicious "occultism" has to the author been conscious in mind or mood or work.

The study of these books will vastly multiply the power of the man or woman, with or without a school education. Scholarship does not necessarily mean power, but the Library promises personal power whether the student be educated or uneducated, provided he is of average intelligence.

To all who follow the instructions, there will unfold, in the measure of effort and capacity, the four great fundamentals — Will-Power, Mind-Power, Magnetism and Practical Ability. This is a positive assurance.

As the present edition goes to press there is an army of over 100,000 students of "Power of Will." This is a record unequalled by any other book of a similar nature in the history of literature. With thousands of warm letters of praise from people in all walks of life who are being helped to a quick realization of their most cherished ambitions, the author feels that his long labor in preparing the following lessons has not been in vain.

And so, good fortune attend both the book and the student.

STATEMENT OF GENERAL PRINCIPLES

1.— The goal of evolution is psychic person.
Person acts behind the mask of body.
The basic idea of person is self-determined unfoldment.
The central factor in such unfoldment is Will.
Will is a way person has of being and doing.
A certain complex of our ways of being and doing constitutes mind.
Mind operates on two levels: one on that of awareness, the other on that of the subconscious.
In the subconscious realm of person the evolutionary phases of heredity, habit, established processes, exhibit.
In the field of awareness the phase of variation, both by reason of external stimulus and by reason of psychic freedom, appears.
But organized person is inherently restless. The Will exhibits the law of discontent. Restlessness of organism develops Will.
Person unfolds by control and use of Will.
The Will must take itself in hand for greatest personal completeness.

2.— Personal life is a play between powers without and powers within the central function of Will.
Personal life ends in subjection to such external powers, or rises to mastery over them.

3.— The Will grows by directed exercise.

    Exercise involves the use of its own instruments — body, mind, the world.

    The only method which can strengthen and ennoble Will is that which puts into action itself in conjunction with its furniture.

    This method, persistently followed, is certain to give to the Will mighty power, and to enlarge and enrich person.

THE SCIENCE OF OUR PRESENT IDEAL

THE goal of the book before you may be presented by the following quotations from "Brain and Personality," by William Hanna Thomson, M.D.:

"A stimulus to nervous matter effects a change in the matter by calling forth a reaction in it. This change may be exceedingly slight after the first stimulus, but each repetition of the stimulus increases the change, with its following specific reaction, until by constant repetition a *permanent alteration in the nervous matter stimulated occurs,* which produces a fixed habitual way of working in it. In other words, the nervous matter acquires a special way of working, that is, of function, by habit.

"From the facts which we have been reviewing, we arrive at one of the most important of all conclusions, namely, that the gray matter of our brains is actually plastic and *capable of being fashioned.* It need not be left with only the slender equipment of functions which Nature gives it at birth. Instead, it can be fashioned artificially, that is, by education, so that it may acquire very many new functions or capacities which never come by birth nor by inheritance, but which can be stamped upon it as so many physical alterations in its proplasmic substance.

"This well-demonstrated truth is of far-reaching significance, because it gives an entirely new aspect to the momentous subject of Education." It would seem to be perfectly evident that the more direct the efforts of education become, that is to say, the more surely attention is concentrated upon the alteration for improvement of nervous matter and the development of mental powers rather than to the mastering of objective studies, many of which must prove of little benefit in actual life, the more nearly will education approach its true goal — power in self and ability for successful handling of self with all its powers. This is the method of The Power-Book Library, the ideal of which is — not mastery of books, but sovereign use of the growing self. "Most persons conceive of education vaguely as only mental, a training of the mind as such, with small thought that it involves *physical changes in the brain itself* ere it can become real and permanent. But as perfect examples of education as can be named are ultimately dependent upon the sound condition of certain portions of the gray matter which have been 'educated' for each work." "The brain must be modified by every process of true special education.

"*We can make our own brains,* so far as special mental functions or aptitudes are concerned, if only we have *Wills strong enough to take the trouble.* By practice, practice, practice, the Will stimulus will not only organize brain centers to perform new functions, but will project new connecting, or, as they are technically called, association fibres, which will make nerve centers work together as they could not without being thus associated. Each such self-created brain center requires great labor to make it, because nothing but the prolonged exertion of the personal Will can fashion anything of the kind." And, since the use of any

The Science of Our Present Ideal

human power tends to its growth, such labor as that suggested in the pages of this book cannot fail both to develop brain centers and also to unfold mind's power *in* Will.

"It is the masterful personal Will which makes the brain human. By a human brain we mean one which has been slowly fashioned into an instrument by which the personality can recognize and know all things physical, from the composition of a pebble to the elements of a fixed star. It is the *Will alone which can make material seats for mind,* and when made they are the most personal things in the body.

"In thus making an instrument for the mind to use, the *Will is higher than the Mind,* and hence its rightful prerogative is to govern and direct the mind, just as it is the prerogative of the mind to govern and direct the body.

"It is the Will, as the ranking official of all in man, who should now step forward to take the command. We cannot over-estimate the priceless value of such direction, when completely effective, for the life of the individual in this world. A mind always broken in to the sway of the Will, and therefore thinking according to Will, and not according to reflex action, constitutes a purposive life. A man who habitually thinks according to purpose, will then speak according to purpose; and who will care to measure strength with such a man?

"In short, the world has yet to learn, once for all, that men are not to be justified nor condemned by such superficial things about them as their opinions. Set the will right first, and men's opinions will follow suit, as soon as they have opportunities for knowing better; but the will remaining perverted, not the opportunities for knowing of an eternity will avail.

"In fact man reigns here below only because he is responsible, and it is his will alone which makes him responsible.

"Not a few of those whom they have known started out apparently well equipped, so far as mental gifts and opportunities for education and of social position could enable them to go far and ascend high. But one by one they lagged and suffered themselves to be outstripped by others, whom perhaps few suspected at the start would reach the first rank before them, because they appeared so much inferior in mental powers to the men whom ultimately they outdistanced wholly. *Will direction explains it all.* What is the finest mental machine in this life without will power!

"That majestic endowment (the Will) constitutes the high privilege granted to each man apparently to *test how much the man will make of himself.* It is clothed with powers which will enable him to obtain the greatest of all possessions — self-possession. Self-possession implies the capacity for self-restraint, self-compulsion and self-direction; and he who has these, if he live long enough, *can have any other possessions that he wants.*"

And so — in the foregoing — you discover the reason and need for training your power to will. "It is the will that makes the man."

Your brain matter is your sole workshop for success in this world — and possibly the next too. What you do with this mysterious substance — the lines of action which you open up in it — the freedom with which thought processes are allowed to operate — the skill and swiftness with which you transform the mind's

The Science of Our Present Ideal

energy into visible reality — *all rests with your will.*

You have in your brain an inexhaustible wealth. You can so develop your power of will that it will command the luxuries, the accomplishments, the marked successes, which potentially lie dormant in every human being.

Well spake the philosopher who said: "You are the architect of your own career." But the real wonder-worker that builds your life structure in this world is — POWER OF WILL.

CONTENTS

CHAPTERS

		PAGE
PART I.— THE WILL AND SUCCESS.		1
CHAPTER I.	The Will and its Action	3
CHAPTER II.	Tests of Will	17
CHAPTER III.	The Conduct of Life	33
CHAPTER IV.	Diseases of the Will	49
CHAPTER V.	Training of the Will	65
CHAPTER VI.	Training of the Will, continued: A Study of Moods	79
CHAPTER VII.	Some General Rules	97
PART II.— THE WILL AND SENSE-CULTURE.		111
CHAPTER VIII.	Suggestions for Practice	113
CHAPTER IX.	Exercises for the Eye	127
CHAPTER X.	Exercises for the Ear	141
CHAPTER XI.	Exercises in Taste	153
CHAPTER XII.	Exercises in Smell	161
CHAPTER XIII.	Exercises in Touch	169
CHAPTER XIV.	Exercises for the Nerves	177
CHAPTER XV.	Exercises for the Hands	189
CHAPTER XVI.	Exercises in Steadiness	197
CHAPTER XVII.	General Health	205
PART III.— MENTAL RÉGIME.		215
CHAPTER XVIII.	Exercises in Attention	217
CHAPTER XIX.	Attention in Reading	229
CHAPTER XX.	Attention in Thinking	239
CHAPTER XXI.	Exercises in Memory	253
CHAPTER XXII.	Exercises in Imagination	267
CHAPTER XXIII.	Some Diseases of the Imagination	285
PART IV.— DESTRUCTION OF HABIT.		291
CHAPTER XXIV.	Destruction of Immoral Habits	293
CHAPTER XXV.	Correction of Other Habits	317

Contents

	PAGE
PART V.— CONTACT WITH OTHER PEOPLE.	339
CHAPTER XXVI. The Will in Public Speaking	341
CHAPTER XXVII. Control of Others	355
CHAPTER XXVIII. The Child's Will	369
CHAPTER XXIX. The Symmetrical Life	391

PREFATORY MATTERS.

"O Living Will"	2
"The Will is the Man"	16
"Balance"	32
"Sense Joys"	48
"Be Master"	64
"Heed Not Thy Moods"	78
"The Great Psychic Flower"	96
"The King"	110
Resolution	112
"The Riddle"	126
"The Soul and the Ear"	140
"Taste"	152
"The Fragrance"	160
"Self and Worlds"	168
"Harmony"	176
"The Hand"	188
"Bubbles"	196
"Health"	204
"Thy Self"	214
"What Seest Thou?"	216
"Who Reads?"	228
"Thought"	238
"Remembered"	252
"How Came Imagination?"	266
"Who Hath Wisdom?"	284
Quotation from Field	290
"We Live By Sacrifice Alone"	292
"'Tis Wise Surrender Crowns the King"	316
"Speech"	338
"Eloquence"	340
"Knighted"	354
"The Will of the Child"	368
"Sir Anyman"	390

The Master Spirit

The Master Spirit needeth none
　Of brawny force to probe its skill:
It hath the Secret of the Sun,
　That cosmic power, Magnetic Will.

Part I—The Will and Success

"*O living Will, thou shalt endure
When all that seems shall suffer shock.*"
— TENNYSON.

POWER OF WILL

CHAPTER I

THE WILL AND ITS ACTION

"THERE has been altogether too much talk about the secret of success. Success has no secret. Her voice is forever ringing through the marketplace and crying in the wilderness, and the burden of her cry is one word — *will*. Any man who hears and heeds that cry is equipped fully to climb to the very heights of life. . . . If there is one thing I have tried to do through these years it is to indent in the minds of the men of America the living fact that when they give *Will* the reins and say 'Drive!' they are headed toward the heights." — *Dr. Russell H. Conwell.*

The human Will involves mysteries which have never been fathomed. As a "faculty" of mind it is, nevertheless, a familiar and practical reality. There are those who deny man's spiritual nature, but no one calls in question the existence of this power. While differences obtain among writers as to its source, its constitution, its functions, its limitations, its freedom, all concede that the Will itself is an actual part of the mind of man, and that its place and uses in our life are of transcendent importance.

Disagreements as to interpretations do not destroy facts.

The Will is sometimes defined as the "faculty of conscious, and especially of deliberative action." Whether the word "conscious" is essential to the definition may be questioned. Some actions which are unconscious are, nevertheless, probably expressions of the Will; and some involuntary acts are certainly conscious. All voluntary acts are deliberative, for deliberation may proceed "with the swiftness of lightning," as the saying goes, but both deliberation and its attendant actions are not always conscious. A better definition of the Will, therefore, is "THE POWER OF SELF-DIRECTION."

This power acts in conjunction with *feeling* and *knowledge,* but is not to be identified with them as a matter of definition. Nor ought it to be confounded with *desire,* nor with the *moral sense*. One may feel without willing, and one may will contrary to feeling. So the Will may proceed either with knowledge or in opposition thereto, or, indeed, in a manner indifferent. Oftentimes desires are experienced which are unaccompanied by acts of Will, and the moral sense frequently becomes the sole occasion of willing, or it is set aside by the Will, whatever the ethical dictates in the case.

PRESENT DEFINITIONS

The Will is a way a person has of being and doing, by which itself and the body in which it dwells are directed.

It is not the Will that wills, any more than it is the perceptive powers that perceive, or the faculty of imagination that pictures mental images.

The Will is "the Soul Itself Exercising Self-direction."

The Will Is the Man

"By the term Will in the narrower sense," says Royce, "one very commonly means so much of our mental life as involves the *attentive guidance of our conduct.*"

When person employs this instrumental power, it puts forth a *Volition*.

A Volition is the willing power in action.

All Volitions are thus *secondary mental commands* for appropriate mental or physical acts.

Obedience of mind or body to Volitions *exhibits the power* of the Will.

No one wills the impossible for himself. One cannot will to raise a paralyzed arm, nor to fly in the air without machinery. In such cases there may be desire to act, but always mind refuses to will — that is, to put forth a Volition, which is a secondary command — when obedience, of the mind itself, or of the body, is known to lie beyond the range of the possible.

The Will may be regarded as both *Static* and *Dynamic*.

In the one case it is a *power of person* to originate and direct human activities; in the other case, it is *action of person* for these ends.

Thus, one is said to be possessed of a *strong* Will (the *static*) when he is capable of exerting his mind with great force in a Volition or in a series of Volitions. The *quality* of his Will is manifest in the force and persistence of his Volitions or his acts. The manifested Will then becomes *dynamic;* his Volitions are the actions of the mind in self-direction.

Hence, the Will is to be regarded as an *energy,* and, according to its degree as such, is it weak, or fairly developed, or very great.

"It is related of Muley Moluc, the Moorish leader,

that, when lying ill, almost worn out by incurable disease, a battle took place between his troops and the Portuguese, when, starting from his litter at the great crisis of the fight, he rallied his army, led them to victory, and then instantly sank exhausted, and expired."

Here was an exhibition of stored-up Will-power.

So, also, Blondin, the rope-walker, said: "One day I signed an agreement to wheel a barrow along a rope on a given day. A day or two before I was seized with lumbago. I called in my medical man, and told him I must be cured by a certain day; not only because I should lose what I hoped to earn, but also forfeit a large sum. I got no better, and the evening before the day of the exploit, he argued against my thinking of carrying out my agreement. Next morning when I was no better, the doctor forbade my getting up. I told him, 'What do I want with your advice? If you cannot cure me, of what good is your advice?' When I got to the place, there was the doctor, protesting I was unfit for the exploit. I went on, though I felt like a frog with my back. I got ready my pole and barrow, took hold of the handles and wheeled it along the rope as well as ever I did. When I got to the end I wheeled it back again, and when this was done I was a frog again. What made me that I could wheel the barrow? *It was my reserve-Will.*"

Power of Will is, first, mental capacity for a *single volitional act:* A powerful Will, as the saying is, means the mind's ability to throw great energy into a given command for action, by itself, or by the body, or by other beings. This is what Emerson calls "the spasm to collect and swing the whole man."

The mind may, in this respect, be compared to an

electric battery; discharges of force depend upon the size and make-up of the instrument; large amounts of force may be accumulated within it; and by proper manipulation an electric current of great strength may be obtained. There are minds that seem capable of huge exercise of Will-power in single acts and under peculiar circumstances — as by the insane when enraged, or by ordinary people under the influence of excessive fear, or by exceptional individuals normally possessed of remarkable mental energy. So, power of Will may, as it were, be regarded as capable of accumulation. It may be looked upon as an energy which is susceptible of increase in quantity and of development in quality.

The Will is not only a dynamic force in mind, it is also secondly, a power of *persistent adherence to a purpose,* be that purpose temporary and not remote, or abiding and far afield in the future; whether it pertain to a small area of action or to a wide complexity of interests involving a life-long career. But what it is in persistence must depend upon what it is in any single *average* act of Volition. The Will may exhibit enormous energy in isolated instances while utterly weak with reference to a continuous course of conduct or any great purpose in life. A mind that is weak in its average Volitions is incapable of sustained willing through a long series of actions or with reference to a remote purpose. The cultivation, therefore, of the Dynamic Will is essential to the possession of volitional power for a successful life.

" A chain is no stronger than its weakest link."

Development of Will has no other highway than absolute adherence to wise and intelligent resolutions.

The conduct of life hinges on the Will, but the Will

depends upon the man. Ultimately it is never other than his own election.

At this point appears the paradox of the Will: —

The Will is the soul's power of self-direction; yet the soul must decide how and for what purposes this power shall be exercised.

It is in such a paradox that questions of moral freedom have their origin. The freedom of the Will is a vexed problem, and can here receive only superficial discussion. The case seems to be clear enough, but it is too metaphysical for these pages.

PRESENT THEORY OF WILL

"The Will," says a French writer, "is to choose in order to act." This is not strictly true, for the Will does not choose at all. The person chooses. But in a general or loose way the Will may be now defined as a power to choose what the man shall do. The choice is always followed by Volition, and Volition by appropriate action. To say that we choose to act in a certain way, while abstaining from so doing, is simply to say either that, at the instant of so abstaining, we do not choose, or that we cease to choose. We always do what we actually choose to do, so far as mental and physical ability permit. When they do not permit, we may *desire*, but we do not *choose* in the sense of willing. In this sense choice involves some *reason*, and such *reason* must always be *sufficient* in order to induce person to will.

A Sufficient Reason is a motive which the person approves as ground of action. This approval precedes the act of willing, that is, the Volition. The act of willing, therefore, involves choice among motives as its necessary precedent, and decision based upon such selection. When the mind approves a motive, that is, constitutes it Sufficient Reason for its action in willing, it has thereby chosen the appropriate act obedient to willing. The mind frequently recognizes what, at first thought, might be regarded as Sufficient Reason for Volition, yet refrains from putting forth that Volition. In this case other motives have instantaneously, perhaps unconsciously, constituted Sufficient Reason for inaction, or for action opposed to that immediately before considered.

We thus perceive four steps connected with the act of willing:

1. Presentation in mind of something that may be done;
2. Presentation in mind of motives or reasons relating to what may be done;
3. The rise in mind of Sufficient Reason;
4. Putting forth in mind of Volition corresponding to Sufficient Reason.

As Professor Josiah Royce remarks in "Outlines of Psychology," "We not only observe and feel our own doings and attitudes as a mass of inner facts, viewed all together, but in particular we attend to them with greater or less care, selecting now these, now those tendencies to action as the central objects in our experience of our own desires." "To attend to any action or to any tendency to action, to any desire, or to any passion, is the same thing as 'to select,' or 'to choose,' or 'to prefer,' or 'to take serious interest in,' just that tendency or deed. And such attentive (and *practical*) preference of one course of conduct, or of one tendency or desire, as against all others present to our minds at any time, is called a voluntary act." This is in effect the view of the author taken ten years before the writing of the first edition of the present work.

A motive is an appeal to person for a Volition. "A motive cannot be identified with the Volition to act, for it is the reason of the Volition. The identification of motives and Volitions would involve us in the absurdity of holding that we have as many Volitions as motives, which would result in plain contradiction." And, it may also be remarked, "a motive is not an irresistible tendency, an irresistible tendency is not a desire, and a desire is not a Volition. In short, it is impossible to identify a Volition or act of Will with anything else. It is an act, *sui generis.*"

But while motives must be constituted Sufficient Reasons for willing, the reason is not a *cause;* it is merely an *occasion.* The *cause* of the act of Will is the person, free to select a reason for Volition. The *occasion* of the action of Volition in mind is solely the motive approved.

Motives are conditions; they are not causes. The testimony that they are not determining conditions stands on the validity of the moral consciousness. The word "ought" always preaches freedom, defying gospelers and metaphysicians of every pagan field.

FREEDOM

Moreover, the phrase "*freedom of will*" is tautology, and the phrase "*bondage of will*" is contradiction of terms. To speak of the freedom of the Will is simply to speak of the Will's existence. A person without power to decide what he shall do is not a complete organism.

Will may not exist, but if there is any Will in mind, it is free.

The Will Is the Man

Will may be weak, but within the limitations of weakness, freedom nevertheless obtains.

No bondage exists in the power of person to will *somewhat*. Bondage may obtain in the man, by reason of physical disorders, or of mental incapacity, or of moral perversion, or, perhaps, of environment. For the Will " does not sensate: that is done by the senses; it does not cognize: that is done by the intellect; it does not crave or loathe an object of choice: that is done by the affections; it does not judge of the nature, or value, or qualities of an object: that is done by the intellect; it does not moralize on the right or wrong of an object, or of an act of choice: that is done by the conscience (loosely speaking); it does not select the object to be chosen or to be refused, and set it out distinct and defined, known and discriminated from all others, and thus made ready, after passing under the review of all the other faculties, to be chosen or refused by the Will: for this act of selecting has already been done by the intellect."

The operations of the sense perceptions, of the intellect and of the moral powers may thus be inadequate, and there may be great difficulty in deliberating among motives, and even inability to decide which motive shall rule, but these weaknesses obtain in the mind or the man, they do not inhere in the Will. This does not surrender the freedom of the Will by shifting it from a faculty the definition of which makes it free to the person which may or may not be free, because any bondage of person has before it actual freedom as the result of development, education and moral influences. The action of Will is not determined by motive but by condition of person, and, to a degree, except under the oppression of disease, the person may always raise any motive to the dignity of Sufficient Reason.

Most people experience some bondage to evil, but the bondage of evil lies in the fact that the evil self tends to select a motive whose moral quality is of a like character. Accountability springs from this — that evil has been permitted to establish that tendency. "A force endowed with intelligence, capable of forming purposes and pursuing self-chosen ends may neglect those rules of action which alone can guide it safely, and thus at last wholly miss the natural ends of its being."

As Samuel Johnson says: "By trusting to impressions a man may gradually come to yield to them and at length be subject to them so as not to be a free agent, or, what is the same thing in effect, to *suppose* that he is not a free agent."

"As to the doctrine of necessity, no man believes it. If a man should give me arguments that I did not see, *though I could not answer them,* should I believe that I did not see?"

Hence the sway and the value of moral character in the arena of Will.

A person of right character tends to constitute right motives Sufficient Reason for Volitions.

The Will, therefore, is *under law,* for it is a part of the universal system of things. It must obey the general laws of man's being, must be true to the laws of its own nature. A lawless Will can have no assignable object of existence. As a function in mind it is subject to the influences of the individual character, of environment and of ethical realities. But in itself it discloses that all Volitions are connected with motives or reasons, that every Volition has its suffi-

The Will Is the Man

cient Reason, and that no Volition is determined solely by any given reason. To suppose the Will to act otherwise than as required by these laws is to destroy its meaning. A lawless Volition is not a free Volition, it is no Volition. Lawless Volition is caprice. Capricious Volitions indicate a mind subject to indeterminate influences. When an individual is in such a state, we say that he is a slave, because he is without power to act intelligently for a definite purpose and according to a self-chosen end.

Will is not free if it is not self-caused, but to be self-caused, in any true sense, it must act according to the laws of its own being. Law is the essence of freedom. Whatever is free is so because it is capable of acting out unhindered the laws of its nature.

The Will cannot transcend itself. It is not necessary that it should transcend its own nature in order to be free. A bird is free to fly, but not to pass its life under water. A bird with a broken wing cannot fly; nevertheless flight is of the freedom of bird-nature. And limitations upon bird-nature are not limitations upon such freedom. Induced limited states of individual minds cannot set aside the free ability of Will to act according to its fundamental nature.

The following, written of Howard the philanthropist, is a good illustration of the Will (*a*) as static, (*b*) as dynamic, (*c*) as an energy, (*d*) as controlled by the mind, (*e*) as free, and (*f*) as determined by character — what the individual makes himself to be:

"The (*c*) energy of his (*a*) determination was so great, that if, instead of being habitual, it had been (*b*) shown only for a short time on particular occasions, it would have appeared a vehement impetuosity; but, by being unintermitted, it had an equability of manner which scarcely appeared to exceed the tone of a calm constancy, it was so totally the reverse of anything like turbulence or agitation. It was the calmness of an intensity, (*d*) kept uniform by the nature of the human mind forbidding it to be more, and by the (*f*) character of the individual (*e*) forbidding it to be less."

Howard was an illustration of Emerson's meaning when he said: "There can be no driving force, except through the conversion of the man into his Will, making him the Will, and the Will him." Human nature is a huge commentary on this remark. Man's driving force, conquering fate, is the energy of the free Will.

Said Dr. Edward H. Clarke: "The Will or Ego who is only known by his volitions, is a constitutional monarch, whose authority within certain limits is acknowledged throughout the system. If he chooses, like most monarchs, to extend his dominions and enlarge his power, he can do so. By a judicious exercise of his authority, employing direct rather than indirect measures, he can make every organ his cheerful subject. If, on the other hand, he is careless of his position, sluggish and weary of constant vigilance and labor, he will find his authority slipping from him, and himself the slave of his ganglia."

That you have a great world of opportunity awaiting your determination to possess it, is evidenced by this stirring view from the pen of C. G. Leland: "Now the man who can develop his will, has it in his power not only to control his moral nature to any extent, but also to call into action or realize very extraordinary states of mind, that is faculties, talents, or abilities which he never suspected to be within his reach. . . . All that Man has ever attributed to the Invisible World without, lies, in fact, within him, and the magic key which will confer the faculty of sight and the power to conquer is the *Will.*"

We have now finished our brief survey of the theory of Will-power. The idea has been to make clear to you the place which Will-power occupies in your life — to stimulate you to an immediate, determined, and pleasurable, nay — profitable training in this kingly force within your possession.

What this book shall accomplish for the reader depends solely upon himself.

"THE WILL IS THE MAN"

The Will is God, the Will is man,
 The Will is power loosed in Thought;
In Will th' Unfathomed Self began,
 In Will the lesser mind is wrought:
  Nothing is will-less entity:
  All one — to act, to will, to be.

He only is who wills to live
 The best his nature prophesies:
Master of fate, executive
  Of self — a sovereign strong and wise.
   Art thou a pigmy? Courage, soul!
   For thee, as all, the kingly goal.
                                — The Author.

CHAPTER II

TESTS OF WILL

"THE seat of the Will seems to vary with the organ through which it is manifested; to transport itself to different parts of the brain, as we may wish to recall a picture, a phrase, or a melody; to throw its force on the muscles or the intellectual processes. Like the general-in-chief, its place is everywhere in the field of action. It is the least like an instrument of any of our faculties; the farthest removed from our conceptions of mechanism and matter, as we commonly define them."— *O. W. Holmes.*

The developed Will manifests itself, as has been suggested, in two general ways:

First. In an energetic *single act;* here it may be called the *Dynamic Will.* The Will so acting is not necessarily ideal. "Rousseau," says Carlyle, "has not depth or width, nor calm force for difficulty; — the first characteristic of true greatness. A fundamental error, to call vehemence and rigidity strength! A man is not strong who takes convulsion-fits, though six men cannot hold him then. He that can walk under the heaviest weight without staggering, he is the strong man."

Secondly. In a *series of acts* conducted with force

and related intelligently to a given end; here the *Static Will discharges* in dynamic actions its store of accumulated power.

Acts of Will may be described as Explosive, Decisive, Impelling, Restraining, Deliberative, Persistent.

These forms of Will are exhibited in connection with Physical, Mental, Moral states of the man.

Remembering that the Will is always the mind's power of self-direction, we now suggest certain

GENERAL FUNCTIONS OF WILL

I. — The strong Will is master of the body.

II. — The right Will is lord of the mind's several faculties.

III. — The perfect Will is high priest of the moral self.

I

The strong Will is master of the body, directing it according to the dictates of desire or reason. Hamlet's grave-digger determines his own physical vocation. The hero Dewey and his sailors send their bodies into Manilla Bay and forbid flight, while shot and shell are falling. Martyrs give their bodies to be burned. Paganini directs his fingers to execute marvels upon the violin. The trained athlete is the director of an assembly of physical powers as difficult of original control as the mob that threatened Beecher at Liverpool. Ignatius uncovered brute Will when he said: "It is the part of a good athlete to be flayed with pounding, and yet to conquer." The psychic investigator of the modern college makes every physical element and power a tool, a prophet, a revelator of mental reality.

Mastery of the body is frequently seen in remarkable instances of *physical control.* All voluntarily acquired habits are examples. Though a given habit becomes automatic, it yet represents a long and persistent application of Will, and, as often, perhaps, the present exercise of Volition directing and maintaining actions that are apparently unconscious. The singer's use of his voice exhibits trained impulse; the musician's manipulation of his fingers, habituated movements; the skilled rider's mastery of his limbs in most difficult feats and unexpected situations, spontaneous response to mind; the eloquent orator, celerity of muscular obedience to feeling. In all these and similar cases the Will must act, co-ordinating particular movements with general details of Volition with the ultimate purpose in view. Indeed, the specific activities that make up the complex physical uses of the human body in all trades of skill demand supervision of the Will as an adequate explanation. The person may not be conscious of its sovereign acts, but it is the power upon the throne.

Underlying those states of the soul of which it is immediately aware are conditions not formulated in consciousness, which nevertheless constitute its highest powers. If these exhibitions of "second nature" involved no immediate action of Will, the very exercise and training of Will which look to their attainment would, so far forth, defeat the end in view; — they would weaken rather than develop Will.

The Unconscious or Subconscious Mind plays a vast rôle in human life. The reader is referred to the author's work "Practical Psychology" for further study of that important subject.

The mind, again, has the power to summon, as it

were, a special degree of *intensity of Will*, and to throw this with great force into a particular act. This may be done during a repetition of the act, while the repetition is going on "automatically," as it is said. Does such intensity imply that no Will has hitherto been exerted? We know that in such cases we put forth a more energetic Volition.

The human eye may be made to blaze by the application of Will-power to the act of gazing.

The hearing may be made more acute by willing that all other sensations shall be ruled out of consciousness.

By focusing the attention upon the terminal nerves the sense of touch is vastly quickened, as, for example, in the case of the blind.

Muscular effort accomplishing a certain amount of work while Will is but lightly applied, becomes terrific when the whole man wills himself into the act.

Certain stimulations of mind, as fear, or love, or hate, or hope of reward, or religious excitement, or musical influence, or insanity, rouse the Will at times to vast proportions in its feats with muscle and limb.

The Olympic contests and modern exhibition games, rescues from fire or wave, woman's defense of her offspring, prolonged exertion of political speakers and evangelists, and herculean achievements of enraged inmates of insane hospitals, furnish examples.

So, also, the Will accomplishes wonders through its *power of inhibition.* Under fear of detection the hiding criminal simulates the stillness of death. Pride often represses the cry of pain. In the presence of the desperately ill, love refuses the relief of tears. Irritated nerves are controlled under maddening conditions. Certain nervous diseases can be cured by the

Will. Habits of the body, such as facial twitching, movements of the hands or limbs, etc., are controlled, and mannerisms of private and public life are banished. Sounds are shut out of consciousness in the act of reading. Strong appetites are denied indulgence. Pronounced tendencies in general physical conduct are varied. Attitudes of body are assumed and maintained at the cost of great pain.

Even more than is ordinarily supposed, the body is the servant of the Will. The curious thing here is that so little attention is given to the training of Will in this capacity.

II

The right Will is the lord of the mind's several faculties. A familiar example is seen in the act of *attention*. Here the soul concentrates its energies upon a single object, or upon a number of objects grouped together. A striking example may be noted in the fact that "we can smell either one of two odors, brought to the nostrils by means of paper tubes, in preference to the other, by simply thinking about it." This is a good illustration of abstraction induced by the Will. The degree of exclusiveness and force with which the mind engages itself upon a single line of action represents the cultivation of the persistent Will. If the Will is strong in this respect, it is probably strong in what is called "*compound attention,*" or that considering state of mind in which it holds deliberative court among motives, facts, principles, means and methods relating to some possible end of effort or goal of conduct.

Thus the person wills intense consciousness of physical acts or states. One, for example, who studies profoundly the relation of physiology to psychology, exhibits great powers in willed attention, embracing largest sensations, and taking note of minutest variations with the greatest nicety. The child in learning to walk manifests admirable ability in this regard. Vocal exercises demand utmost attention of mind to musical notes, their effects upon the ear, and the manner and method of their attainment and execution. Musical instruments are also mastered in this way alone. All use of tools and instruments makes large demand upon the Will, and in proportion to their delicacy, complexity, and the difficulty of handling properly, is this demand increased. " Great skill, great Will," may be written as the general law in this regard.

So, also, as previously suggested, the power of the eye, ear and end nerves is frequently increased by application of mental energy thrown forcibly into the sense-perception involved.

The action and capacity of the lungs may be developed by intelligent attention, a style of walk may be cultivated, and habits of speech entirely reorganized. Where pronounced ability in such cases has been acquired, the cost of willed attention has been enormous.

A test of Will may be further seen in the degree of attention exerted in reading. Much is dignified as reading that is not so. In true reading the mind is focused upon the printed page. Kossuth said, " I have a certain rule never to go on in reading anything without perfectly understanding what I read." That was true reading.

Equally concentrated must be the mind of the artist in painting, and that of the musician in mastering a difficult composition. An artist who painted three hundred portraits during a year, said: "When a sitter came, I looked at him attentively for half an hour, sketching from time to time on the canvas. I wanted no more. I put away my canvas and was ready for another sitter. When I wished to resume my first portrait, I took the man and sat him in the chair, when I saw him as distinctly as if he had been before me in his own proper person." A similar story is related of the sculptor David. Wishing to execute the bust of a dying woman without alarming her, he called upon her as a jeweler's man, and in a few moments secured a mental portrait of her features, which he afterward reproduced in stone. So Blind Tom listened with "rapt attention" to a complicated musical composition, and instantly repeated it, exactly as played before him, including errors. In part, concentrated attention is the secret of genius.

In *sustained thinking* the Will manifests one of its noblest aspects. The mind must now plunge into the depths of a subject, penetrate by driving force into its minutest details, and follow out the ramifications of its utmost complexities, concentrating upon fact, reality, relation, etc., with great power, and comparing, conjoining, separating, evolving, with tireless persistency. Napoleon was gigantic in all these particulars. Senator Carpenter, of Wisconsin, used to seclude himself in his law library the night before some important case was docketed for trial, and feel, think and care for nothing else until morning, utterly absorbed in the mastery of its problems. So Byron was wont to immure himself with brandy and water and write for many consecutive hours in the elaboration of his poems. "The success of Hegel is in part explained by the fact that he took a manuscript to his publishers in Jena on the very day when the battle of that name was fought, and to his amazement — for he had heard or seen nothing — he found French veterans, the victorious soldiers of Napoleon, in the streets. Mohammed falling into lone trances on the mountains above Mecca, Paul in Arabia, Dante in the woods of Fonte Abellana, and Bunyan in prison, form eloquent illustrations of the necessity of mental seclusion and concentration in order to arrive at great mental results."

It is familiarly known that one of the secrets of concentration is *interest* in the matter in hand. But the mind's *interest may be enhanced* by persistent assertion of its power of Will. Study, resolutely continued, bores into the subject considered, and, discovering new features, finally induces absorbed attention of an increased degree. School-work furnishes many illustrations of this reward of Will. The mind may be wrought up, by long attention to matters of thought, to a state of great activity. As with mechanical contrivances, so with Will; initial movements of mind, weak at first, acquire by continuance an enhanced power. "We can work ourselves up," as one has said, "into a loving mood, by forcing the attention and the train of ideas upon all the kindness and affection that we have experienced in the past." Similarly in regard to other emotions and states of the soul. The activity of reasoning is no exception. It is a mistake to suppose that great intellectual achievements are products alone of what is called "inspiration." The processes of reasoning, composing, speaking, all exhibit the power of Will to develop interest and beget a true inspiration as well as to hold the mind in the grip of a subject. Lord Macaulay thus sought facility in the preparation and writing of his History. Anthony Trollope made it a rule, while writing a work of fiction, to turn off a fixed number of pages each day, and found his rule not a hindrance, but a help. In jury trials advocates talk on for hours against some supposedly obstinate juryman, and legislative halls frequently witness "speaking against time." In both cases the orator's mind develops special and unexpected interest and power.

The strength of the Will is, again, notably shown in the action of *memory*. Mental energy usually "charges" the soul by the process of "memorizing." But some facts are blazed into the abiding self, as it were, by the power of great interest. The storing act of mind in education, as it is commonly understood, requires Will in a very especial sense. Listless repetition of lessons accomplishes little. Attention, concentration, the forcing of interest, must take this kingdom by a kind of violence. A phrase like, "Remember! yes, remember!" suggests the victorious attitude of mind. Macaulay, fearing that his memory might fail, deliberately set himself to the task of its test and further development. William H. Prescott, who wrote his histories with greatly impaired eyesight, trained his memory so thoroughly that he could perform mentally the work required for sixty pages before dictation. Francis Parkman and Charles Darwin acquired prodigious memories under similar difficulties. Some minds are naturally endowed with great powers in this respect, but the really useful memories of the world exhibit the driving and sustaining action of Will.

Memory is always involved in *imagination*. The mind which is a blank as to its past can form no memory pictures. In its noblest character, the imagination exhibits compulsion, purpose, control. Milton must summon in luminous array the majestic images of Paradise Lost. Does Angelo see his immortal shapes without the direction of Will? Do the phantoms of the ideal world come unbidden to the arena of thought? Undoubtedly fantasies and hallucinations may troop across the plains of mental vision in capricious freedom, as when Luther saw the devil, or Goethe beheld in his sister's home a picture by Ostade; and these may frequently tyrannize over the mind with terrible power, as when Kipling's civilian of India became "possessed" by the "Phantom 'Rickshaw." But the hallucinations of disease often yield to treatment of physical improvement and resolute Will. It is significant that Goethe, relating the experience above referred to, says: "This was the first time that I discovered, in so high a degree, the gift, *which I afterwards used* with more complete consciousness, of bringing before me the characteristics of this or that great artist, to whose works I had devoted great attention." That the power of creating such luminous mental vision can be acquired by strenuous Will may be doubted; but there are minds that have frequent flashes of clear pictorial innersight, in which objects seem to appear with all the vividness of sunlit reality, although they can never command this experience at will. If possessed, the gift, as Goethe calls it, is, however, subject to summons and control, as seen in his case and in that of many artists. A secondary quality of mental vision, in which ideas of things, more or less vague and confused, and similar assemblages of objects, arise, is, by common testimony a matter of determined cultivation. Professions which require regular public speaking, as of the ministry or the law; the massing of facts before the mind, as in the trial of jury cases; the form-

According to Your Will

ing of material shapes and their organization into imaginary mechanisms, as in invention; the grasp of details and comprehensive plans, as in large business enterprises and military operations; — all furnish illustrations of the truth that not original endowment alone, but energetic exercise of Will, is requisite to success. Ideas, relations, objects and combinations may be made more vivid and real by resolution of mind and persistent practice. Failures in these fields are frequently due to the fact that the Will does not force the mind to see things as details and as complex wholes. The strong Will enables the mind to recall, with growing intensity, objects, mechanisms, assemblages of facts and persons, outlines of territory, complex details and laws of enterprise, and airy fancies and huge conceptions of the worlds of real life and of ideal existence. The imagination is the pioneer of progress — in religion, industry, art and science; but as such it is not a lawless necromancer without deliberate purpose. The spirit that summons, guides and controls it is the soul's mysterious power of self-direction. And this power is equally susceptible of being so developed as to indicate selection and exclusion of clamoring images.

Hence it would seem that *the mind may train and develop its own power of willing.* When cultivation and improvement of Will are sought, we may say, "*I will to will with energy and decision! I will to persist in willing! I will to will intelligently and for a goal! I will to exercise the Will according to the dictates of reason and of morals!*" Some men are born with what are called "strong Wills." If these are to be reasonable Wills as well, they must be trained. For the most part Will would seem to develop and to acquire something of the " sweet quality of reasonableness," under life-processes which are more or less unconscious and unpurposed so far as this end is concerned; nevertheless, the exigencies of "getting on" are constant and unappreciated trainers. Discipline knocks men about with ruthless jocularity. "A man who fails, and will not see his faults, can never improve." Here is a grim-visaged, and oftentimes humorous schoolmaster who gives small pity to his pupils. They must needs acquire some power of Will or demonstrate themselves, not human, but blockheads. Much of life's suffering is due to the fact that force of Will is neither developed nor trained by conscious intelligent effort, and is more often devoid than possessed of rational moral quality. This is a curious thing — that the Will is left, like Topsy, "to grow up." Why value this power, yet take it "catch-as-catch-can"? Why hinge success upon it, yet give it so little conscious attention? Why delegate its improvement to the indirection of "hard knocks," and disappointment cankering resolution, and misfortune making water of life's blooded forces, and all manner of diseases destroying the fine fibre of mind's divine organism? Why neglect the Will until consequence, another name for hell, oftentimes, has removed "heaven" by the diameter of the universe?

James Tyson, a Bushman in Australia, died worth $25,000,000. "But," he said, with a characteristic semi-exultant snap of the fingers, "the money is nothing. It was the little game that was the fun!" Being asked once, "What was the little game?" he replied with an energy of concentration peculiar to him: "Fighting the desert. That has been my work. I have been fighting the desert all my life, and I have won! I have put water where was no water, and beef where was no beef. I have put fences where there were no fences, and roads where there were no roads. Nothing can undo what I have done, and millions will be happier for it after I am long dead and forgotten."

"The longer I live," said Fowell Buxton, whose name is connected in philanthropy with that of Wilberforce, "the more certain I am that the great difference between men, between the feeble and the powerful, the great and the insignificant, is ENERGY — INVINCIBLE DETERMINATION — a purpose once fixed, and then Death or Victory. That quality will do anything that can be done in this world; — and no talents, no circumstances, no opportunities will make a two-legged creature a MAN without it." The power, then, of such resistless energy should with resistless energy be cultivated.

"When the Will fails, the battle is lost."

III

The perfect Will is high Priest of the moral self. Indeed, a true cultivation of Will is not possible without reference to highest reason or ideas of right. In the moral consciousness alone is discovered the explanation of this faculty of the soul. A great Will may obtain while moral considerations are ignored, but no perfection of Will can be attained regardless of requirements of highest reason. The crowning phase of the Will is always ethical.

Here is the empire of man's true constitution. Resolute Will scorns the word "impossible." The strong Will of large and prolonged persistence condemns whatever is unreasonable. Nobility of Will is seen in the question, "What is right?" Napoleon exhibits the strong continuous Will. Washington illustrates the persistence of moral resolution. Jesus incarnates the Will whose law is holiness.

The Will that possesses energy and persistence, but is wanting in reasonableness and moral control, rules in its kingdom with the fool's industry and the fanatical obstinacy of Philip the Second. "It was Philip's policy and pride to direct all the machinery of his extensive empire, and to pull every string himself. . . . The object, alike paltry and impossible, of this ambition, bespoke the narrow mind." Thus has Motley described an incarnation of perverted wilfulness.

If the "King" will not train himself, how shall he demand obedience of his subjects, the powers of body, mind and spirit? This is the "artist" of whom Lord Lytton sang: —

> "All things are thine estate; yet must
> Thou first display the title deeds,
> And sue the world. Be strong; and trust
> High instincts more than all the creeds."

A recent writer along these lines puts it pithily when he says: "In respect to mere mundane relations, the development and discipline of one's will-power is of supreme moment in relation to success in life. No man can ever estimate the power of will. It is a part of the divine nature, all of a piece with the power of creation. . . . The achievements of history have been the choices, the determinations, the creations, of the human will. It was the will, quiet or pugnacious, gentle or grim, of men like Wilberforce and Garrison, Goodyear and Cyrus Field, Bismark and Grant, that made them indomitable. They simply would do what they planned. Such men can be no more stopped than the sun can be, or the tide. Most men fail, not through lack of education or agreeable personal qualities, but from lack of dogged determination, from lack of dauntless will."

Yet it is always the *righteous* will which accomplishes the more lasting victories — the will which demonstrates that all who grant its demands will be sharers in a mutual advance and profit. The use of will power regardless of other-interest — riding rough shod over everything in its path — is headed for a precipice.

BALANCE

Full waves, full tides, swing in from out the vast,
  Lapping and dashing, breasting up the marge;
Yet ever gently turned, or backward cast
  In sullen wrath. The steadfast shore comes large.
    Here meet two infinites, equal, face to face,
    In wage titanic for all time and space.

To urge right onward — this the Will's high course;
  And this — to stand, a soul of adamant.
The sea recedes: force triumphs over force;
  Crumbles the shore: the waves their vict'ry chant.
    Lo, at the heart of Power's war untimed
    Emerges soul — undaunted and sublimed.
    —The Author.

CHAPTER III

THE CONDUCT OF LIFE

"RESOLVE is what makes a man manifest; not puny resolve, not crude determinations, not errant purpose—but that strong and indefatigable Will which treads down difficulties and danger, as a boy treads down the heaving frost-lands of winter; which kindles his eye and brain with a proud pulse-beat toward the unattainable. Will makes men giants."—*Ik Marvel*.

The thing that is, and creates human power, as the author remarks in "Business Power," is the Will. Theoretically, the Will is the man. Practically, the Will is just a way the man has of being and doing. The Will is man's inherent nature-tendency to act—to do something. This tendency to act in some way must act on itself—take itself in hand, so to speak, in order that it may act intelligently, continuously, and with a purpose. Will is itself power; but unfolded, controlled and directed power in man is Will self-mastered, not man-mastered nor nature-mastered. The man-mastered and nature-mastered Will goes with the motive or impulse which is strongest. The self-mastered Will goes with the motive which the self makes greatest, and with mere impulse in very slight degree so far as the life of intelligence is concerned.

The self-mastered Will can do anything—within reason; and reason in this connection should be conceived in its highest human sense. The function of Will is like that of steam. It must be powerful, under control, and properly directed. The power of Will may be developed, but only through controlled and directed action. The control may be acquired, but only through willed and directed action. The direction may be determined, but only through willed and controlled action. When Will is self-developed, self-mastered, self-directed, it only needs proper application to become practically all-powerful.

FORMS OF WILL

In the conduct of life every form in which the normal Will manifests itself is demanded for success. These forms are: The Persistent Will; The Static Will; The Impelling Will; The Dynamic Will; The Restraining Will; The Explosive Will; The Decisive Will.

The *Static Will,* or Will in reserve, constitutes original source of energy. As heat, light, and life are rooted in the sun, so are varied Volitions sent forth from this central seat of power, exhibiting the *Dynamic Will.*

The *Explosive Will* illustrates the mind's ability for quick and masterful summoning of all its forces. The sudden rush of the whole soul in one compelling deed seems sometimes next to omnipotence.

Persistence of Will involves "standing," *sto — stare — sistere,* and "through" — *per;* "standing through." The weakness of otherwise strong men may be revealed in life's reactions. "Having done all, to stand," furnishes many a deciding test. This phase of Will is not exhausted in the common saying, "sticking to it," for a barnacle sticks, and is carried hither and thither on a ship's bottom. Persistence involves adherence to a purpose clean through to a goal.

The *abiding mind* necessitates the *Impelling Will*. The Impelling Will suggests an ocean "liner," driving onward, right onward, through calm and storm, for a determined goal. Sixty years of that kind of direct motion must summon Will to all its varied activities.

It is curious, too, that the noble quality of Willpower observed in impelling persistence, depends upon the paradox of restraint. An engine without control will wreck itself and its connected machinery. The finest racing speed is achieved under bit and mastery. In man the power that drives must hold back. The supremest type of man exhibits this as a constant attitude. Success in life depends upon what the writers call the Will's power of inhibition. Here we have the *Restraining Will*.

At times the character of Will is also manifest in its ability to forbid obedience to a thousand appealing motives, and even to bring all action to a full stop and "back water," in order to a new decision, a new immediate or ultimate goal. Hence life is full of demands for quick decisions and resistless massing of resources squarely upon the spur of exigency. This suggests the *Decisive Will*.

Such are some of the forms of Will which are required for the conduct of affairs, whether ordinary or extraordinary. Even a slight analysis of the matter would seem to suggest that there can be no tonic like the mental mood which resolves to will.

Here is a treatment from deepest laboratories of the soul insuring health. A purposeful mind says, sooner or later, "I RESOLVE TO WILL.*" After a time that phrase is in the air, blows with the wind, shines in star* and sun, sings with rivers and seas, whispers with dreams of sleep and trumpets through the hurly-burly of day. Eventually it becomes a feeling of achievement saturating consciousness. The man knows now the end, because all prophecies have one reading. He has begotten the instinct of victory.

It is not as a blind man, however, that he walks. His ineradicable conviction sees with the eye of purpose. If his purpose is approvable at the court of conscience, all roads lead to his Rome.

One Aim Victorious

Men fail for lack of *Some Aim*. Their desires cover the entire little field of life, and what becomes theirs does so by accident. Multitudes of people are the beneficiaries of blundering luck.

Everywhere *Some Aim* would make "hands" foremen, and foremen superintendents; would conduct poverty to comfort, and comfort to wealth; would render men who are of no value to society useful, and useful men indispensable.

The man who is indispensable owns the situation.

The world is ruled by its servants. The successful servant is king.

But better than *Some Aim*, which, because it need be neither long-headed nor long-lived, is a player at a gaming table, is *One Aim*, by which all fortune is turned schoolmaster and good fortune is labeled "reward by divine right." The true divine right of kings is here alone.

The soul that resolves to will *One Aim* makes heavy and imperious call on the nature of things.

For, while many understand that the individual must needs adjust himself to life, few perceive the greater law, that *life is forever engaged in a desperate struggle to adjust itself to the individual.* It is but required of him that he treat life with some degree of dignity, and make his election and plea sure by putting mind in the masterful spell of some *One* ultimate *Aim* to which all things else shall be subordinated.

Some Aim has luck on its side; *One Aim* has law.

Some Aim may achieve large things, and occasionally it does; *One Aim* cannot fail to make the nature of things its prime minister.

Life does not always yield the *One Aim* its boon in exact terms of desire, because men often fall at cross-purposes with endowment; but life never fails to grant all the equities in any given case.

In the long run every man gets in life about what he deserves. The vision of that truth embraces many things which the objector will not see. The objector mistakes what he desires for what he deserves.

Hence the importance of self-discovery in life's conduct. It is probably true that every man has some one supreme possibility within his make-up. The purposeful Will usually discovers what it is.

Buried talents are always " fool's gold."

One thing settled — the *Ultimate Aim* — and talents begin to emerge by a divine fiat.

The revelation of power may, indeed, be made while Will roams in quest of a purpose, but, that purpose found, Will looks for its means and methods; and discovers them within.

William Pitt was in fact born with a definite aim in life. "From a child," says a recent writer, " he was made to realize that a great career was expected of him, worthy of his renowned father. This was the keynote of all his instruction."

General Grant is said to have been called "Useless Grant" by his mother. He discovered himself at Shiloh, after some pottering with hides and leather which was not even preliminary. But Grant always "stuck to the thing in hand," so far as it was worth while doing so. When war brought his awareness of self to the point of definite meaning, he found every detail and the largest campaigns eminently worth the while of a Will which had at last uncovered its highway. "The great thing about him," said Lincoln, "is cool persistency of purpose. He is not easily excited, and he has got the grip of a bulldog. When he once gets his teeth in, nothing can shake him off."

The *One Aim* is always a commentary on character. It is not difficult to see why life needs *Some Aim*. Why it should concentrate upon *One Aim* suggests the whole philosophy of human existence. Nero had *One Aim*, and it destroyed the half of Rome. Alexander the Great had *One Aim*, and he died in a debauch. The *One Aim* may involve selfishness, crimes, massacres, anarchy, universal war, civilization hurled to chaos. *One Aim* assassinated Garfield, ruined Spain, inaugurated the Massacre of Saint Bartholomew, gave birth to the "unspeakable Turk," devised a system of enmity against existing orders and institutions, threatens to throw Europe into revolutionary carnage, and, in a thousand ways, has power to light the pyre of civilization's destruction. *One Aim* is no more descriptive of Heaven than it is of Hell.

The climax of Will, therefore, is possible under moral considerations alone. Character, which is the sum total of a man's good (moral) qualities, furnishes a third phrasing for Will's purpose, the *Righteous Aim*.

THE HIGHEST AIM

Will with *Righteous Aim* creates character. Character, with *Righteous Will*, creates *Noblest Aim*. Character, with *Noblest Aim*, creates *Righteous Will*. The relation between the man, the aim, the Will, is dependent and productive. There is really no high justification for *One Aim* if it be not best aim. Life is ethical. Its motives and its means and its achievements justify only in aims converging to its utmost moral quality.

It is here that possession of Will finds explanation, as elsewhere remarked. Below man there is no supreme sovereignty of Will; all is relative and reflex. But this sovereignty furnishes its reason in moral self-development, in moral community-relations, in moral oneness with Deity.

So true is it that *righteousness alone justifies the existence of the human Will,* that the finest development of the power comes of its moral exercise. Above the martyr who founds a material government the world places with eager zeal that soul who establishes by his death a kingdom of religion.

The Static Will furnishes energy in abnormal life. The Explosive Will murders. The Persistent Will may exhibit in obstinacy and national crimes. The Impelling Will is sometimes hugely reckless. The Restraining Will has its phases in "mulishness" and stupidity. The Decisive Will is frequently guilty of wondrous foolhardiness. Idiocy, insanity, senility, savagery and various forms of induced mania represent the Will in disorder, without a master, and working pathos fathomless or tragic horror.

If, then, we ask, "Why *One Aim* in life?" the

names of Socrates, Buddha, Charlemagne, Alfred the Great, William of Orange, Gladstone, Washington, Wilberforce, Lincoln, may be offset by those of Caligula, the Medici, Lucretia Borgia, Philip the Second. Asking, "Why the *Righteous Aim?*" troop before the mind's expanding eye all holy heroes and movements "i' the tide o' time"; and no counterpoise appears, for all is great, all is good.

Moral purpose, however, is no prestidigitator. The Will, set on all good things for ultimate goal, is still merely the mind's power of self-direction. All requisites for strong Will anywhere are demands here. Inasmuch as the moral aim involves the whole of life, Will, making for it, requires the ministry of cultivated perceptions: seeing things as they are, especially right things; developed sensibilities: sensitive toward evil, capacious for good; a large imagination: embracing details, qualities, consequences, reasons and ultimate manifold objects; active, trained and just reasoning faculties: apprehending the incentive, utility and inspiration of truth; and deep and rich moral consciousness: nourishing the Will from inexhaustible fountains of legitimate self-complacency.

In other words, the moral Will, which alone is best Will, demands of its owner constant and adequate consideration, of plan, of means, of methods, of immediate and ultimate end.

The successful conduct of life is always hinged upon "This one thing I do." Where such is really the law of conduct, the world beholds an aroused soul. "The first essential of success," said a great bank president, "is the fear of God."

A live man is like a factory working on full time. Here is creation; every power at labor, every function charged with energy, huge action dominating the entire situation, and yielding valuable products. This man puts his body into the thing in hand, mightily confident. His mental being does not detail itself off in "gangs," but swarms at it with that tirelessness which makes enthusiasm a wonder. His intuitions flash, impel, restrain, urge resistlessly, decide instantly — presiding genii of limited empires. Reasoning faculties mass upon questions vital, and hold clear court, till justice be known. If he be right-souled man, he emerges, Will at the fore, from Decalogue and Mountain Sermon daily, squaring enterprise with the Infinite.

The *whole man,* swinging a great Will, *conserves himself.*

Why must there be discussions on selfishness and self-interest? A sound soul is always a best soul. A selfish soul is never sound. But a sound soul must continue sound. Altruism begins with the self. Society needs the whole man — all there is of him, and always at his best. Hence the nature of things makes it law that a man shall endeavor to make the most of himself in every way which is not inimical to soundness. This is the first principle of holiness — wholeness — soundness. As that is worked into conduct, the second principle appears — Service.

For the service of a sound soul the Universe will pay any price.

And here again emerge some old and common rules. It is function of Will to resolve on preservation of bodily health, mental integrity and growth, and moral development. In the eye of that high resolution no detail is without importance. A trained Will regards every detail as a campaign.

DRUDGERY AND THE WILL

Power of Will is an accretion. Force is atoms actively aggregated. The strong Will is omnivorous, feeding upon all things with little discrimination. Pebbles, no less than boulders, compose mountains. The man who cannot will to stick to trifles and bundle them into importants, is now defeated. The keynote of success is drudgery.

Drudgery stands at every factory door, and looks out of every store window. If drudgery be not somewhere in a book, it is not worth the reading. Inspiration stands tip-toe on the back of poor drudgery. The antecedents of facile and swift art are the aches and sorrows of drudgery. The resistance of angels collapses only after Jacob has found his thigh out of joint, and yet cries: "I will not let thee go!" Jesus had to climb even Calvary.

An English Bishop said truly: "Of all work that produces results, nine-tenths must be drudgery." Really great poets, prose-writers and artists verify this remark. Edmund Burke bestowed upon his speeches and addresses an immense amount of painstaking toil. Macaulay's History cost almost incalculable labor. The first Emperor of Germany was an enormous worker. Indeed, taking the world "by and large," labor without genius is little more incapable than genius without labor.

Kepler, the astronomer, carried on his investigations with prodigious labor. In calculating an opposition of Mars, he filled ten folio pages with figures, and repeated the work ten times, so that seven oppositions required a folio volume of 700 pages. It has been said that "the discoveries of Kepler were secrets extorted from nature by the most profound and laborious research."

It was the steadiness of Haydn's application to his art which made him one of the first of modern musicians. He did not compose haphazard, but proceeded to his work regularly at a fixed hour every day. These methods, with the extremest nicety of care in labor, gave him a place by the side of Mozart, who, while possessed of the genius of facility, was nevertheless thoroughly acquainted with drudgery.

And there can be no drudgery without patience, the ability to wait, constancy in exertion with an eye on the goal. Here is a complex word which readily splits into fortitude, endurance and expectation. It is kaleidoscopic in its variations. In the saint's character patience is a lamb; in that which builds an industry or founds an empire, it is a determined bulldog.

"Genius is patience," said Davy; "what I am I have made myself." Grant was patient: "Once his teeth got in, they never let go." The assiduous Will is first principle in achievement, whether of men or nations. The indefatigable purpose is prophet of all futures.

But the "King on his Throne" (your Will) is no dull monarch of obstinacy. Reason defies inertia. "We say that Will is strong whose aim," remarks Th. Ribot, "whatever it be, is fixed. If circumstances change, means are changed; adaptations are successfully made, in view of new environments; but the centre toward which all converges does not change. Its stability expresses the permanency of character in the individual."

All things come to the net of this rational indefatigability. As Carlyle says of Cromwell: "That such a man, with the eye to see, with the heart to dare, should advance, from post to post, from victory to victory, till the Huntington Farmer became, by whatever name you might call him, the acknowledged strongest man in England, requires no magic to explain it. For this kind of man, on a shoemaker's bench or in the President's chair, is always 'Rex, Regulator, Roi'; or still better, 'King, Koenig,' which means Can-ning, Able-man."

And this same adaptive pursuit of the main thing has made of Cromwell's and Carlyle's England the First Power in Europe. As William Mathews has said: "The 'asthmatic skeleton' (William III.) who disputed, sword in hand, the bloody field of Landon, succeeded at last, without winning a single great victory, in destroying the prestige of his antagonist (Louis XIV.), exhausting his resources, and sowing the seeds of his final ruin, simply by the superiority of British patience and perseverance. So, too, in the war of giants waged with Napoleon, when all the great military powers of the continent went down before the iron flail of the 'child of destiny,' like ninepins, England wearied him out by her pertinacity, rather than by the brilliancy of her operations, triumphing by sheer dogged determination over the greatest master of combination the world ever saw."

It was identically this that led, in American history, to the surrender of Cornwallis to Washington, and to the last interview with Lee, a great soul, an heroic Christian fighter, a consummate "Can-ning man, Able-man."

To a Will of this sort defeats are merely new lights on reason, and difficulties are fresh gymnastics for development of colossal resolve, and discouragements are the goading stimuli of titanic bursts of energy.

"By means of a cord, which passes from his artificial hand up his right coat-sleeve, then across his back, then down his left coat-sleeve to the remainder of his left arm, an American editor has achieved success. He is enabled to close the fingers of his artificial hand and grasp his pen. By keeping his left elbow bent, the tension of the string is continued, and the artificial fingers hold the pen tightly, while the editor controls its course over the paper by a movement of the upper arm and shoulder. By this means, without arms, he has learned to write with the greatest ease, and more rapidly and legibly than the average man of his age who has two good hands. For ten years, he has written with this mechanical hand practically all of the editorials, and a very large amount of the local and advertising matter that has gone into his paper."

"Suppose," said Lord Clarendon to Cyrus W. Field, talking about the proposed Atlantic Cable, "you don't succeed? Suppose you make the attempt and fail — your cable is lost in the sea — then what will you do?" "Charge it to profit and loss, and go to work to lay another."

To suppose the iron Will to fail is to suppose a contradiction of terms.

Perhaps no historic character has more perfectly illustrated this element of success than William of Orange, to whom Holland the Wonderful owes more than to any other son in her brilliant family. "Of the soldier's great virtues," writes Motley, "constancy in disaster, devotion to duty, hopefulness in defeat — no man ever possessed a larger share. That with no lieutenant of eminent valor or experience, save only his brother Louis, and with none at all after that chieftain's death, William of Orange should succeed in baffling the efforts of Alva, Requesens, Don John of Austria, and Alexander Farnese — men whose names are among the most brilliant in the military annals of the world — is in itself sufficient evidence of his warlike ability."

These men, great and world-famed, were, however, men only. They were but Intellects working with the "King on his Throne." It is a statement which points every other man to his ultimate goal that they achieved through that common endowment, power of Will.

The conduct of life hinges on the strength and quality of Will more than any other factor. The cry for "opportunity" is essentially weak; opportunity crowds upon the imperious Will. The mediocrity of men is too largely of their own creation.

Gladstone, with large faith in the "commoners," said truly:

"In some sense and in some effectual degree, there is in every man the material of good work in the world; in every man, not only in those who are brilliant, not only in those who are quick, but in those who are stolid, and even in those who are dull."

Every normal educated man, deep in his heart believes that by the proper conduct of his life he can become great — or at least win a measure of success that puts him far ahead of the mediocre millions. But as "rest and inertia" is the law of matter, he gradually gives in to this law and is shackled by it. He becomes, speaking "in the large," too lazy to forge on toward the higher goals. It is here that incessant use of will power is required.

"The education of the will should be begun, contradictory as it may seem, by assuring yourself you can do what you wish to do, and assuring yourself on the principles of auto-suggestion. Of course no amount of will-power can accomplish impossible aims. . . . By 'what you wish to do' we mean the ambitions proper to your intelligence and place in life. Not to set yourself an impossible task, is half the battle. A mighty will with no intelligence behind it is foiled everywhere; and without scruple it becomes a menace to the world's peace. So 'choose right,' and move forwards."

SENSE JOYS

To see not with a gladsome eye,
  Nor own the vibrant ear;
To sense no fragrance drifting by,
  To feel no lover near:
Of such dread loss, oh what choose I
  Were either loss my fear?

Now all these gifts of soul a-thrill,
  With taste for bread and wine,
And one good servant, Master Will,
  And the wide world, are mine!
Lo, riches vast my coffers fill,
  And life's a joy divine!

—The Author.

CHAPTER IV

DISEASES OF THE WILL

"'MECHANICAL obedience' (in the treatment of disease — and of mind as well as of body) is but one-half the battle; the patient must not only will, he must believe. The whole nature of man must be brought to the task, moral as well as physical, for the seat of the disease is not confined to the body; the vital energies are wasted; the Will, often the mind, are impaired. Fidelity of the body is as nothing if not reinforced by fidelity of the soul." — *Dr. Salisbury.*

The Will may become diseased. Disease is "want of ease," that is, of comfort, arising from the failure of functions to act in a normal manner. It is, then, "any disorder or depraved condition or element," physical, mental or moral.

A disease of the Will may be defined as a more or less permanent lack of action, normal, (*a*) to the individual, (*b*) to sound human nature in general. When a person's Will is more or less permanently disordered with reference to his normal individual activity, we have a case for medical treatment. When a person's Will is more or less permanently disordered with reference to the normal human standard, we have a case for education.

It is now to be observed that a diseased condition of the Will may result —

First, from a diseased mind;

Secondly, from an illy-developed mind;

Thirdly, from causes resident in the Will considered as a "faculty" of mind. Strictly speaking, a disease of the Will is a disease of the self, inasmuch as it is the self that wills. But there are phases of the Will, practically to be regarded as diseases, which manifest themselves in the midst of otherwise normal conditions of mind, and these are, therefore, mentioned under the third division above.

CLASSES OF DISEASED WILL

I

Class First: Diseases of Will coming under the head of diseased mind are shown in *insanity*. In almost all cases of mental variation from the normal standard, the Will is more or less affected. This follows because insanity is "a *prolonged* departure of the individual's normal standard of thinking, feeling and acting." The standard is that of the *individual*, not that of normal human nature. Always the action of the Will depends largely upon the individual's way of thinking and feeling. Insanity often clearly defines, and thus separates from, diseases of Will in the so-called normal mind. In cases of insanity the Will, considered as power in mind to put forth some kind of Volition, may remain with more or less strength, but is either weakened or controlled by physiological conditions or false ideas. The "King" is here dethroned. In diseases of Will which are subject to education not medical, the "King" remains in his

As is the Mind, so is the Will

normal position as ruler, but is weak, or erratic, or permanently irrational as to the standard of average human conduct.

II

Class Second: There are some cases of diseased Will in the *illy-developed mind* which show paralysis of power, all other functions remaining normal. Thus, a sudden great emotion may paralyze the volitional action, such as fear, or anger, or joy. Inability to will may also obtain temporarily in reverie or ecstasy, or as seen in curious experiences common to most people when the self wishes to act, but seems for the time unable to put forth the necessary Volition. Such paralysis runs all the way from momentary to prolonged or total. In the latter cases we have again subjects for medical treatment, as when one person was two hours in trying to get his coat off, or was unable to take a glass of water offered.

Whether the difficulty in cases of illy-developed mind is physiological, or a mere lack of belief in one's power to will a given act, the outcome is the same. For the time-being, the Will is dead, or the mind, as to willing, is in a state of dead-lock. It cannot put forth a Volition in the desired direction. Hence it is evident that feeling, desire, thinking, judgment, conscience, are not always determinative of Will-action. The action of mind in willing is as distinct as the action of mind in imagining, recalling, reasoning, or apprehending right and wrong. For example, why, in a state of indecision as to getting up of a cold winter morning, do you suddenly find yourself shivering on the floor and wondering how it happened that you are out of bed? It needs but to fix that state of irresolution or inability for a period, to show the mind in a dead-lock of the Will.

Willing is a matter of mental states. The illy-developed self may will neither correctly nor strongly. Whether or not it can do so depends upon many things which are discussed in the Third Part of this book. Of the mind in general it is said that "willing, in intensity ranges up and down a scale in which are three degrees — wishing, purposing and determining. Weak Volition wishes, resolute Volition purposes, while strong Volition acts." But Volition does not wish; this is an act of mind. As one has said: " I may desire meat, or ease from pain; but to say that I will meat or ease from pain is not English." Weak Volition is the Will exerting itself weakly. Strong Volition indicates mental energy in the act of willing. Resolute Volition is strong Volition continued. The facts in this connection are as follows:

When the state of mind is predominantly that of desire merely, its act in willing may be weak or indecisive. When the mind greatly approves a given desire and determines that to be purpose, its Volition becomes strong. The energy with which itself or the body obeys Volition, and if the purpose is remote, continues to obey, measures the intensity of the willing act.

Now, what are called diseases of the Will under our second division, are simply ill-conditions of the self immediately going out in the act of willing, or of the mind engaged in the realm of the sensibilities, the imagination, the reasoning faculties and the moral consciousness, as realities capable of influencing the action of the Will.

For "the ultimate reason of choice is partly in the

character, that is to say, in that which constitutes the distinctive mark of the individual in the psychological sense, and differentiates him from all other individuals in the same species," and partly in possible ideals, following which he may more or less change that distinctive character.

"It is the general tone of the individual's feelings, the general tone of his organism, that is the first and true motor. If this is lacking the individual cannot exercise Will at all. It is precisely because this fundamental state is, according to the individual constitution, stable or fluctuating, continuous or variable, strong or weak, that we have three principal types of Will — strong, weak and intermittent, with all intermediate degrees and shades of difference between the three. But these differences, we repeat, spring from the character of the individual, and that depends upon his special constitution." And it is precisely because "this fundamental state is, according to the individual constitution," subject to education and improvement, so that, if fluctuating, it may become stable, if variable it may become continuous, if weak, it may become strong, that this book is written.

A good Will may or may not act quickly: that depends upon the individual's constitution; but it is marked by power when it does act.

A good Will may or may not persist: that depends upon the constitution and the dictates of personal wisdom; but when personal wisdom succeeds in influence, the Will holds steadfastly to the thing in hand.

The highest type of Will reveals "a mighty, irrepressible passion which controls all the thoughts of the man. This passion *is* the man — the psychic expression of his constitution as nature made it." Historic examples are seen in Cæsar, Michael Angelo, Napoleon.

In the next lower grade the above harmony between the outer conduct and the inner purpose is broken by various groups of tendencies, working together, but opposing the central purpose. The man is switched off the main track. Francis Bacon was called "the greatest, the wisest and the meanest of mankind," having diverged from the highest line of rectitude, and Leonardo da Vinci, following Art, yet yielded to the seductions of his inventive genius, and produced but one masterpiece.

A third grade is seen where two or more main purposes alternately sway the individual, none ruling for long, each influencing the conduct in turn. Dr. Jekyll and Mr. Hyde are two beings in one person, each possessing a strong Will for himself, but unable to cope with the tendencies of the other. A multiplication of such diverting purposes denotes a still further degradation of the Will.

Lastly appear those types of diseased Will peculiar to insanity.

III

Class Third: In this division we have before us, not the mind as acting, but the willing-act of the mind. Whether the Will be exercised rightly or wrongly, wisely or foolishly, is not now the question in hand. That question refers simply to Will-power, or the naked Will; just as, if an individual's muscular power were in question, the morality or the wisdom of its use might be variously estimated, itself being swift or slow, weak or strong, capable of endurance or easily exhausted. The Will is what it is, regardless of the direction or the quality of its exercise.

Disease of Will, as considered in the *third class,* is limited to two general forms: *want of power* and *want of stability.*

But these general divisions resolve themselves into more *specific cases,* as follows:—

1. *Want of Volitional Impulse.* A state of mind in which the impulse to will is wanting is illustrated in the cases already cited, in which one could not get his coat off; or in cases of reverie, ecstasy, etc., where the mind is so fully absorbed by some fanciful condition as to be momentarily incapable of willing contrary thereto.

Cure: Of insane cases, medical treatment; of those of reverie, ecstasy, and the like, good health, full life, vigorous action. For the mind that suffers the deadlock of Will there is no other remedy than actual, concrete life, and practical, strenuous activity.

Cultivate the Moods of Resolution and Decision. (See Chapter VI.)

2. *Inability to Decide.* Some people never attain to a clear view of any situation; they cannot see the essential details; they cannot weigh motives; they cannot forecast the future; they are wanting in courage as to possible consequences; their imagination is good for evils, but not for benefits; hence they can never, or rarely, come to a definite, decisive determination. They drift; they do not act according to specific determinations; they are creatures of momentary impulse; they are *automata,* so far as concerns the ordinary affairs of life, and, in its extraordinary crises, they are as helpless as driftwood.

Cure: Cultivate the habit of concentrated attention to the thing in hand, pro and con; resolve to will, anyhow, somehow, with the best light rapidly examined, confident that such resolution, under the lessons of experience, will ultimately come out best for individual interests.

"Sometimes a person encounters emergencies where he must make a decision, although aware that it is not a mature decision, approved by the whole cabinet of his mental powers. In that case he must bring all his comprehension and comparison into active, instant exercise, and feel that he is making the best decision he can at the time, and act. Many important decisions of life are of this kind — off-hand decisions.'

And especially ought it to be remembered that " calling upon others for help in forming a decision is worse than useless. A man must so train his habit as to rely upon his own courage in moments of emergency."

Act always on the straight line.

Cultivate the Mood of Decision.

3. *Weakness of Volition.* The failures of life, which are innumerable, are largely due to this disorder of the Will. Whether it be owing to a want of feeling, desire, imagination, memory or reason, it seems to be universal. The energetic person is the exception. Thus, a writer on Mental Philosophy has described a historic example of this prevalent disease; speaking of Coleridge:

"There was probably never a man endowed with such remarkable gifts who accomplished so little that was worthy of them — the great defect of his character being the want of Will to turn his gifts to account; so that, with numerous gigantic projects constantly floating in the mind, he never brought himself even seri-

As is the Mind, so is the Will

ously to attempt to execute any one of them. It used to be said of him, that whenever either natural obligation or voluntary undertaking made it his duty to do anything, the fact seemed a sufficient reason for his *not* doing it."

So De Quincey, the celebrated victim of the opium habit, said in his " Confessions ":

"I seldom could prevail upon myself to write a letter; an answer of a few words, to any that I received, was the utmost that I could accomplish; and often that not until the letter had lain weeks, or even months on my writing-table."

Such are historic examples of Will-power so weak as to be practically nil. They are common in life, although seldom in so marked a degree as in the above cases. This disease is the basis of all grades of poverty..

Cure: Cultivate the sustained mental attitude — " I Resolve to Will! " The Resolute Mood ought to be kept constantly before and in the mind, with *inability to will* as the *paramount reason* for *determining now to will* with the greatest energy.

Cultivate the Mood of Energy.

4. *Fickleness of Will.* In this case the man is persistent so far as he goes, but he never goes far in any one direction. In certain main or underlying lines of activity he may show great apparent steadfastness, as in pursuing the means of a livelihood, but these lines are necessitated and automatic or habitual, not really the subjects of his Volitions. There are those, too, who exhibit not even the dumb adherence of labor, but fly from scheme to scheme, whether main or in-

cidental, as birds fly from tree to tree, with no long-continued purpose, during the whole course of life. In this class, the Will is subject to every new impulse.

Cure: The cautious beginning; the resolute pursuit of the undertaking to the end. Minds thus afflicted should learn to attend to one thing at a time, not in the sense that only a single iron should be kept in the fire, but that the iron should not be put there without due deliberation, and that once in, it should receive undivided attention so long as required by the end in view. Generally speaking, every supposed reason for a change of action should be made a determining reason for not changing. The extra schemes need not be given up; it is not necessary for any person to settle down to the mere drudgery of existence; but, while following the course of bread-winning, the mind should determine, *resolve,* SWEAR, to work each theory or scheme to the end thereof.

Cultivate the Mood of Continuity.

5. *Want of Perseverance.* There is a marked difference between this condition of Will and that of fickleness. Will is fickle because it yields to sudden or new impulses. Want of perseverance is due to the fact that the *Will wears out* in any given direction. It then becomes like a tired muscle; the mind refuses or fails to volitionate with reference to an old purpose. Its characteristic phrase is, "I am tired of the thing," or "I can't hold out in the effort." Resolution has simply run down; the Will has become exhausted.

Cure: The resolution to refrain from yielding permanently to such momentary exhaustion; patience with

As is the Mind, so is the Will 59

the mind's present inertia; vigorous search, carried on round-about, for new points of view and new interest. The saying, "I am tired of it," indicates simply a temporary lack of interest; willed interest has failed; but a new view or another mental attitude may inspire spontaneous interest; hence, the matter should be held over until the search for new interest has awakened a spontaneous action of the Will, which will almost invariably follow. This cure is infallible; but it is by no means easy.

Cultivate the Moods of Understanding, Reason and Continuity.

6. *The Explosive Will.* Any explosion indicates want of equilibrium. Great temper, unpremeditated crime, volcanic Volitions, are sudden releases of energy revealing an overcharged or unbalanced nervous tone. With some men power is always in what may be called a chemico-psychical state of instability. The Will leaps to its decisions like an animal upon its prey, or rushes into action like a torrent from a broken reservoir of water. There are exigencies of life which demand such eruptive outgoes of Volition, but they are rare; and if this kind of Will is characteristic, it surely indicates want of self-control. The true Will is a constitutional monarch, and is never ruled by mob influences or despotic motives. The Will must control itself, or it is unfit to reign. It may decide quickly and irresistibly, but without violent loosing of its powers. Ordinarily all violence signifies weakness.

Cure: A healthy tone of the individuality; calmness cultivated, so as to be maintainable in the direst extremity of feeling; a forecasting and vivid realization of the reaction, sure to follow, and which will equal the outburst; a vigorous repression, at the moment of temptation, of all feelings, letting them out in some unimportant side-issue; a determination to recall past experiences, and to profit thereby.

Cultivate the Mood of Reason and Righteousness.

7. *Obstinacy.* We have here an excess of Will as set upon some particular act or state. There are so-called cases of obstinacy which exhibit a curious want of Will-power, but true obstinacy is firmness of Will carried beyond the dictates of reason or right. The obstinate man always believes himself to be right in the matter at hand. His weakness is his refusal to consider. He is willful, not because he is perverse, but because he does not perceive the need for further investigation; the case is with him all settled, and it is rightly settled; he alone is right, all others are obstinate in their difference or their opposition. George the Third and Philip the Second take first rank among incarnations of obstinacy.

Cure: The most minute, as well as the broadest, attention to reasons for or against; greater weight given the judgment of others; the spirit of concession cultivated; determination to swallow pride and yield to wisdom.

Cultivate the Spirit of Concession.

8. *The Headstrong Will.* The chief characteristic of this disease may be seen in the expression, "I don't care." With neither patience, sentiment nor reason, it rushes the man on to a given act or a line of con-

duct, unmindful of warning, regardless of self-conviction. It is not only a case of obstinacy, but of heedlessness as well. It is the Will self-hypnotized by senseless desire. Napoleon on the way to Moscow is the Headstrong Will.

Cure: Cultivation of humility; review of past experiences; resolute heed to the advice of others; elevation into the field of thought of deepest personal convictions; slow, crucifying attention to opposing motives and reasons.

Cultivate the Mood of Reason.

9. *Perversity.* The perverse Will is obstinate, but peculiarly set in wrong directions. The Will that is obstinate merely may be fixed by wisdom and right (self-conceived), but perversity of Will shows itself in twisting the dictates of both, notwithstanding the mind's recognition of the same. Thousands of men are perversely willful when they fully know that the course they are pursuing is foolish and injurious. The Will is here strong, but it is used in a manner that is consciously wrong.

Cure: Cultivation of memory as to past experiences, and of imagination as to future; resolution to study previous consequences and to profit by them; determination to force attention upon the opinions of others; persistent and candid examination of one's own character and of the basic principles of human conduct — which are few in number and easily mastered and committed to memory; a condition of mind open to conviction kept steadily before thought; each matter thought out, step by step, mere wish, as much as possible, being put out of the way, and the question, What is right or best? substituted; willingness held fast to give up when convinced.

As an assistance, the mind should change its point of view, get into a new atmosphere of life, and bring about other physical conditions.

Cultivate the Moods of Reason and Righteousness.

10. *Lack of Confidence in Will.*—"This cause is due to a lack of knowledge of the Will, for the reason that a true knowledge of the will would mean immense confidence in its powers. But, of itself, it is so important that it merits to be put down as a special cause.

Many will-maladies would disappear if only we trusted in the will. Its native force is so great, its recuperative power is so sure, and its resources so unlimited that it is capable of achieving wonderful results. All that is needed is a firm confidence in it. It is, as we have said, our highest and most perfect faculty. It is the best thing we have, and the most effective weapon that we wield. It alone can develop itself. As we saw, it cannot be trained or perfected from without. It alone can cure its own diseases. The one essential thing is, however, that we should place trust and confidence in it."

Cultivate confidence and belief in your own Will.

11. *In general,* the Will may be said to be diseased when the mind cannot patiently attend; when the mind cannot clearly and persistently exercise memory; when the mind cannot clearly and persistently exercise the imagination; when the mind cannot clearly and persistently exercise the powers of reasoning; when the mind will not call up, and reason in regard to, great

moral principles. Because of these failures arise weakness, indecision, fickleness, want of perseverance, violence, obstinacy, headstrong willfulness and perversity.

Cure: Resolute cultivation of the willing-mood, and faithful observance of all exercises suggested in Part III.

BE MASTER

Be master! Of thy work:
Mayhap 'twill irk
Or nerve or bone
To capture crown and throne;
Still,— master be
Splendidly!

Be master! Of thy place:
In sooth, the case
Must test thy soul —
Ne'er weakling wins the goal;
Still,— bankrupt go
Lord "Power" to know.

Be master! Of one art:
'Twill strain thy heart
And drain life's best
To prove this kingly quest;
Still,— court the dream —
Stand thou supreme!

— The Author.

CHAPTER V

TRAINING OF THE WILL

"THE great thing in all education is to make our nervous system our ally instead of our enemy.

"For this we must make automatic and habitual, as early as possible, as many useful actions as we can, and as carefully guard against growing into ways that are likely to be disadvantageous.

"In the acquisition of a new habit, or the leaving off of an old one, we must take care to launch ourselves with as strong and decided an initiative as possible.

"Never suffer an exception to occur till the new habit is securely rooted in your life.

"Seize the very first possible opportunity to act on every resolution you make, and on every emotional prompting you may experience in the direction of the habits you aspire to gain."— *Professor William James.*

The power of person in Will may be trained and developed, as has been suggested. By this statement is meant, not only that it may be exercised and strengthened by the various agencies of command, encouragement, and instruction in the school-room, but that ability to originate a purposeful action, and to continue a series of actions with an end in view, may be cultivated and disciplined by personal attention thereto, and by specific exercises undertaken by the individual. The *need of such development* and training is evident from the following facts:

"Not unfrequently a strong volitional power originally exists, but lies dormant for want of being called into exercise, and here it is that judicious training can work its greatest wonders."

In many persons Will-power is confessedly weak, life being very largely, so to speak, automatic. And in multitudes the Will exhibits the disorders mentioned in the chapter on "Diseases of the Will."

It is singular that so little would seem to have been written on this important subject, and that the training of the Will should now receive, as it does, such scant attention in modern educational methods. In works on psychology and education, paragraphs may be found here and there indicating the importance of Will-training, but they are curiously deficient in suggestions of methods referring the matter to personal effort.

"The education of the Will is really of far greater importance, as shaping the destiny of the individual, than that of the intellect. Theory and doctrine, and inculcation of laws and propositions, will never of themselves lead to the uniform habit of right action. It is by doing, that we learn to do; by overcoming, that we learn to overcome; by obeying reason and conscience, that we learn to obey; and every right action which we cause to spring out of pure principles, whether by authority, precept or example, will have a greater weight in the formation of character than all the theory in the world."

Education of the mind's powers should not be left to hap-hazard methods. If the end of education is the evolution of these powers, methods of the direct gymnasium order are in demand. And, as all mental faculties are mutual in interaction, any scientific method which seeks, by specific gymnasium exercises, the development of one faculty, must result in cultivation of others, whether immediately or remotely related thereto.

Principles in Will-Training

1. Any direct effort to cultivate the perceptive powers must affect the growth of memory, imagination and reason.

2. Any direct effort to cultivate the memory must affect the growth of the perceptive powers, imagination and reason.

3. Any direct effort to cultivate the imagination must affect the growth of the perceptive powers, memory and reason.

4. Any direct effort to cultivate the reasoning powers must affect the perceptive powers, memory and imagination.

5. Any direct effort to cultivate the moral faculties must affect the growth of the perceptive powers, memory, imagination and reason.

6. And any direct effort to cultivate the perceptive powers, memory, imagination, reasoning or moral faculties must affect the growth of the Will.

Yet the application of definite and scientific methods to the discipline and growth of the perceptive powers, the imagination, the memory and the reason seems to be largely wanting in all the schools.

In what school to-day are classes formed for the education of the power of observation? Where is scientific attention given to the cultivation of the imagination? What college schedules any definite number of hours to the strengthening and training of the memory? Probably nowhere in the world are there any specific efforts made to increase and train the power of the Will.

It is the claim of the present work that the Will may be made stronger by the employment of proper methods. And this, (*a*) as a static power through deliberated and intelligent exercises; (*b*) as a dynamic energy continuing through a series of acts by deliberate and intelligent determination that such shall be the case.

CULTIVATION OF THE WILL MAY BE ACCOMPLISHED:

First, by systematic exercises which shall tend to strengthen it as a faculty.

Activity of the brain reacts upon the particular faculty engaged,— to speak more specially, upon the particular brain element engaged,— modifying it in some unknown way, and bringing about a subsequent "*physiological disposition*" to act in a particular manner.

Thus, musicians acquire enormous facility in the use of hands and fingers. So, people who have lost their sight are able to picture visible objects independently of external stimulation, having acquired "a disposition so to act through previous exercises *under* external stimulation."

As the seat of the Will is the whole person, so the exercise of willing brings about its own physiological disposition. "The different parts of the brain which are exercised together, acquire in some way a disposition to conjoint action along lines of 'least resistance,' that are gradually formed for nervous action by the repeated flow of nerve-energy in certain definite directions."

"Lines of least resistance" may be formed by constant action of mind in willing, in certain ways and for certain ends.

"The Cerebrum of man grows to the modes of thought in which it is habitually exercised."

But the development of Will not only involves establishment of facility along easiest channels, but an *increase in power* within the person as determining to choose motives and to put forth Volitions. The willing-act becomes more facile, and it also becomes stronger. Increase of power is not relative alone; it is equally positive.

"The Will grows by exercise. Each form of its activity becomes more perfect by practice. *And the lower forms of exercise in bodily movement prepare the way, to some extent at least, for the higher exercises.*"

So it is that habits may be voluntarily or unconsciously formed, and old habits may be voluntarily abandoned. All such results involve the Will. Their attainment does not weaken Will, but rather strengthens its application to general conduct. "It is well for our actions to grow habituated to a considerable extent. ... In this way nerve-energy is economized and the powers of the mind are left free for other matters. ... At the same time ... much of our life consists in modifying our movements and adapting them to new circumstances. The *growth of Will* implies thus a *two-fold process:* (*a*) the deepening of particular aptitudes and tendencies, that is, the fixing of oft-repeated action in a definite and unvarying form; (*b*) the widening of these active capabilities by a constant variation of old actions, by new adaptations, or special combinations suited to the particular circumstances of the time."

Secondly, the Will may be cultivated by *general improvement of the mind as a whole,* giving it greater force while putting forth Volitions, and larger continuity in a series of Volitions having an end in view, because of increased mental power and wiser treatment of various motives; and this especially if, in all intellectual growth, the purpose of stronger Will-power be kept constantly in mind.

"The Will can never originate any form of mental activity." But it can select among the objects of consciousness, and in thus utilizing the powers of mind can improve the latter. Its efforts to do so will invariably improve itself: by cultivating attention, by shutting out subjects of thought, by developing natural gifts, by instituting correct habits of thinking and of living.

Exercises for a general development of mind must present a variety of motives for consideration with a view to the act of willing, both for the formation of aptitudes, and for the symmetrical development of the Will as a function. This involves:—

1. The *perceptive faculties,* which may be quickened, thus increasing the vividness of motives and inducing Volitions;

2. The *emotions,* the intelligent cultivation of which widens the range of motives and imparts to the mind facility and force in selection of reasons for action;

3. The *imagination,* which represents, according to its strength and scope, various remote and contingent,

as well as immediate, reasons for choice of motives, and adherence to the same;

4. The *deliberative faculty*, which requires cultivation in order adequately to weigh the force and value of motives;

5. The *intuitive faculty*, which, without being able to furnish its reasons, frequently impels or prohibits choice, and may wisely be cultivated by intelligent obedience, but needs strict and constant attention to prevent the reign of impulse. Thus, women are wont to follow intuitions of expediency, and business men are often guided by a similar " feeling " or " judgment." So, also, Socrates possessed what he called his " Daimonion," an inner voice which forbade certain actions, but never affirmatively advised an act or a course of conduct. Such " intuitions " may be searched out and examined for the underlying reasons, and this effort will usually bring to light some hidden cause for the impulse to act or refrain from action.

Thirdly, the Will may be cultivated by *development of the moral character.*

" The greatest man," said Seneca, " is he who chooses right with the most invincible determination."

Self-development involves the moral quality and symmetry of the soul as sustaining relations to its fellows and to Deity. The cultivation of Will in its highest values, therefore, depends upon its exercise in a moral sense. This involves every conscious mental function in action with reference to a moral end. A developed moral consciousness modifies consideration of motives through perception, memory, imagination, reason and " intuition," and increases the force and continuity of that act of the mind by which it constitutes any motive a Sufficient Reason.

Moral development cultivates the Will: —

1st, by bringing to the fore truest motives and goals in the conduct of life;

2dly, by presenting in mind for its consideration new motives, and motives of an unfamiliar nature;

3dly, by enabling self to deliberate with greater clearness, forethought and wisdom among all possible motives for action;

4thly, by prohibiting certain acts or lines of conduct, and by destroying injurious habits;

5thly, by instituting self-control of the highest order;

6thly, by inspiring a constant search for truth, and obedience thereto;

7thly, by inciting to noblest planes of being and holding before consciousness the great alternatives of human destiny for ultimate good or evil.

Luther said to Erasmus: " You desire to walk upon eggs without crushing them." The latter replied: " I will not be unfaithful to the cause of Christ, at least so far as the age will permit me." An untruthful Will in a scholar's brain.

" I will go to Worms," shouted Luther, " though devils were combined against me as thick as the tiles upon the housetops!" A Will which might have become disordered or illy-developed but for the mighty moral character of the reformer.

All human powers are interdependent and interactive. What has righteousness to do with Willpower? Answer: What has Will-power to do with righteousness? Will makes for righteousness; righteousness makes for Will.

A morally growing life establishes "lines of least resistance," with consequent aptitudes and habits which more or less react upon personal power to will. Above all, at least in this connection, it widens the field of active capabilities and develops new adaptations and tendencies by presenting larger and more varied worlds of motive and conduct, with an ultimate end having reference to the individual and his relations to others, which end always appeals to the Will, calling it into activity, and so adding to its power.

The *same truth may be reached from a material starting-point.*

The basis of human life is physical. The original ground of impulse in the volitional nature deals with sense-impressions. In a healthy body these impressions are normal, that is, true. When both body and mind are in a healthy condition, that is to say, are normal and true, they will invariably co-operate, the one with the other.

Instinct co-ordinates with vital chemistry in normal animal life. Such life is true; it is a full realization of itself; it exhibits truth; hence the instincts are right, because the physical basis is right and co-operates with animal intelligence. Instinct and animal intelligence in turn co-operate with the physical nature to maintain its normality or truth.

In man, mind ought to co-ordinate similarly with his physical life. Conversely, the physical life ought to co-ordinate with mind. Physical health signifies right, that is, truthful, physical sensations. And truthful, that is, normal, physical sensations tend always to produce right or normal action of mind, just as normal or right action of mind tends to produce good health — truthful physical sensations. When sound mind co-operates with correct sense-impressions, the result is health, normality, truth in the whole man.

Mind is sensation plus perception, plus Will, plus

memory, plus imagination, plus reason, plus consciousness — self-consciousness, sub-consciousness, moral consciousness.

If mind is deficient in any of these respects the personality is not normal. The end of each function is nothing more nor less than exhibition of truth; perception of things as they are, memory of facts as they have existed, imagination of reality in true relations, conclusions correctly deduced from correct premises and correct observation, convictions based in the actual moral nature of things, sane ideas of self, vigorous action of sub-consciousness, habituating in activities conducive to self-interest, working of objective consciousness for mental freedom. Then there is a perfect co-ordination among all the elements of human nature and character. This co-ordination produces, and it is, health, normality, truth.

Out of such a truth-condition of being comes always the highest form of Will-power. The Will is an exhibition of the character, the individual constitution. Righteousness — which is right-wiseness toward all powers and all realities — becomes, then, the sole true developer and trainer of the human Will. The unrighteous mind is sure to exhibit disease or disorder of the Will, because the act of Will, as already seen, involves presentation of motives, deliberation among the same, constitution of Sufficient Reason, putting forth of the volitional act, and mental or bodily obedience thereto; and the mind which lacks in right-wiseness cannot properly deliberate among motives, will miss from its field the best motives, and thus cannot wisely constitute Sufficient Reason. Hence, such inability continuing, exercise of Will must surely establish habits of weak or disordered Volition, as well as

"The Will Grows by Exercise"

Volitions put forth in wrong directions, so that in time all disorders must become chronic and settle into types of Will that fail to manifest normality and truth.

Observe: The law-abiding physical life is absolutely best; all below weakens Will. The truth-showing mental life is absolutely best; all below disorganizes the Will. The righteous moral life is absolutely best; all below destroys the dynamic power of Will.

Will-power issuing from good physical, mental and moral health, wherein right co-ordination obtains, gives to life's endeavors resistless force, and finds training in all intelligent activity. The more it toils, the more it resolves. No obstacle can deter it, no defeat dismay.

Said John Ledyard, the Explorer: "My distresses have been greater than I have owned, or will own, to any man. I have known hunger and nakedness to the utmost extremity of human suffering; I have known what it is to have food given me as charity to a madman; and I have at times been obliged to shelter myself under the miseries of that character to avoid a heavier calamity. Such evils are terrible to bear, but they have never yet had the power to turn me from my purpose." But observe:—

"He is spoken of as a man of iron Will, sure to make his way, to carry his point, and he thinks himself a man of strong Will. He is only an egotist, morally unable to resist, or even to hesitate at, any evil whereby his selfish aim is assured."

"Energy, without integrity and a soul of goodness, may only represent the embodied principle of evil. It is observed by Novalis, in his 'Thoughts on Morals,' that the ideal of moral perfection has no more dangerous rival to contend with than the ideal of the highest strength and the most energetic life, the maximum of the barbarian — which needs only a due admixture of pride, ambition, and selfishness, to be a perfect ideal of the devil."

"Nothing schools the will, and renders it ready for effort in this complex world, better than accustoming it to face disagreeable things. Professor James advises all to do something occasionally for no other reason than that they would rather not do it, if it is nothing more than giving up a seat in a street car. He likens such effort to the insurance a man pays on his house. He has something he can fall back upon in time of trouble. A will schooled in this way is always ready to respond, no matter how great the emergency. Julius Cæsar, Oliver Cromwell, George Washington, and all other world-famous men have been the possessors of wills that acted in the line of the greatest resistance, with as much seeming ease as if the action were agreeable."

You should resolve to secure such a grade of will by doing disagreeable things, or things of apparent insignificance which ordinarily you shirk doing. Every lifting of a weight by the biceps is adding muscular power to your arms; every little act of will deliberately carried to completion is adding to your power of will.

"The powers of the human intellect," says Professor E. S. Creasy in "Fifteen Decisive Battles," "are rarely more strongly displayed than they are in the commander who regulates, arrays, and wields at his Will these masses of armed disputants (in battle); who, cool, yet daring in the midst of peril, reflects on all and provides for all, ever ready with fresh resources and designs, as the vicissitudes of the storm of slaughter require." But these qualities, however high they may appear, are to be found in the basest as well as the noblest of mankind. Catiline was as brave a soldier as Leonidas, and a much better officer. Alva surpassed the Prince of Orange in the field; and Suwarrow was the military superior of Kosciusco. To adopt the emphatic words of Byron:

> "'T is the cause makes all,
> Degrades or hallows courage in its fall."

The law of the right Will is the law of the all-round symmetrical character.

HEED NOT THY MOODS

When tyrant moods their meshes gossamer,
  Belied as steely bonds no slave may rend,
  Fling o'er thy spirit, oh, my friend,
And ill portend where dreams all goods aver,
Call thou Lord Will: confess, and yet demur;
  Moods fickle from the phantom world ascend,
  And ever to that Master-Servant bend.
Shall Will on films a cable's strength confer?

The clamorous flesh breeds fantasies unreal;
  E'en psychic states deceive th' abiding soul.
The things which seem, th' eternal things conceal.
  And life is this: to find the deeper whole,
Thy changeless self, the heart of being's wheel,
And in God's silence make all woe thy weal.
—The Author.

CHAPTER VI

TRAINING OF THE WILL, CONTINUED: A STUDY OF MOODS

"THE man who is perpetually hesitating which of two things he will do first will do neither. The man who resolves, but suffers his resolution to be changed by the first countersuggestion of a friend — who fluctuates from opinion to opinion, from plan to plan, and veers like a weathercock to every point of the compass, with every breath of caprice that blows — can never accomplish anything real or useful. It is only the man who carries into his pursuits that great quality which Lucan ascribes to Cæsar, *nescia virtus stare loco;* — who first consults wisely, then resolves firmly, and then executes his purpose with inflexible perseverance, undismayed by those petty difficulties which daunt a weaker spirit — that can advance to eminence in any line."— *William Wirt.*

Man's conscious life is largely a matter of mood: — of mind, heart, soul, spirit — a temporary *muse* inspiring the individual to be or to do in certain ways. A mood is a disposition or humor, a morbid condition of mind, a heat of anger, a kind of zeal, a capricious state of feeling.

"The weaker emotive states," says Titchener in "An Outline of Psychology," "which persist for some time together, are termed *moods;* the stronger, which exhaust the organism in a comparatively short time, are called *passions*. Thus the mood of cheerfulness represents the emotion of joy; the mood of depression that of sorrow. Like and dislike have the moods of content and discontent; sympathy and antipathy, those of kindliness and sulkiness; attraction and repulsion, those of 'charm' and tedium. The mood of care is anxiety; the mood of melancholy, gloom. The mood of hatred is 'not getting on with' a person; the mood of exasperation is chagrin."

The above are merely examples of a very familiar subject. Many of our moods are good and indispensable to our best work, as, the mood of labor, the mood for creation, the mood of hopefulness, the mood of mastery, and so on. Every evil mood may be banished from mind and life. The method is simply that of persistent determination to conquer and build up only such moods as stand for personal welfare. Your undesirable moods will vanish if you multiply yourself faithfully into the pages of this book. The end requires work, to be sure, but, as Orison Swett Marden remarks in "Every Man a King," "Training under pressure is the finest discipline in the world. You know what is right and what you ought to do, even when you do not feel like doing it. This is the time to get a firm grip on yourself, to hold yourself steadily to your task, no matter how hard or disagreeable it may be. Keep up this rigid discipline day after day and week after week, and you will soon learn the art of arts — perfect self-mastery."

Summary of Moods

Moods are, therefore — *First*, special states of mental person in general; *secondly*, states of reference to the action of the Will. Their influence never ceases during consciousness. As the individual is servant or master of his moods, he is servant or master of himself. The sum-total of moods exhibits the conscious and the sub-conscious man. Moods manifest in the objective man, but they originate, in part at least, in that deeper self of which so little is directly known — the subconscious.

No error is greater than that theory which makes mind the product of matter. The theory is a "fad" and will soon pass away. An equal error is seen in the notion that the man's self is an entity absolutely separate as an existence from the body. The man is spirit bound up in body; both entities are real, but exist and manifest the one through the other. What the connection is between body and spirit is a fathomless mystery; but that connection stands for the mutual dependence of the physical and the immaterial in man. There is as much evidence of the reality of the immaterial inner ego as of the existence of an objective universe. And the demonstration of the physical man as an actual entity is just as sure as the demonstration of the inner ego. All evidences go to show mutual dependence, both for existence and for manifestation, of body and spirit.

These evidences cover — the influence of mind over body; the influence of body over mind (over mind directly and over mind through bodily states) — the mind affecting itself intermediately by means of its influence upon the body. It is with the power of mind on the body and itself that the present chapter deals.

Let it be understood, this book has nothing to do directly with any so-called "science of healing," whether "Christian" or "Mental," except as immediately following.

All genuine cases of healing by these so-called methods are results of "suggestion," either by self or by others, by means of a great law as yet little understood.

"There are but two really distinct fundamental phases which the doctrine of metaphysical healing has assumed, and to one or the other of these the varying special claims belong. The first is the pure metaphysical idealism upon which the original 'Christian Science' is based — the non-reality of the material world and sense-experience, and so of disease. The second is the doctrine of what is properly called 'Mental Science,' which does not ignore the reality of the physical world nor of the body and its sensations in their normal relations to that world, but is based upon the recognition of the absolute supremacy of the mind over them."

Supposing it denies the material world, sense-experience, disease, and evil or sin. Herein are its errors manifest. To deny, yet seek to cure, disease, to deny, yet seek to eliminate sin, disorganizes a normal dealing with life. To will that that which one believes or strives to believe does not exist shall be one thing or another as to its states, is to dethrone the normal Will. The Will volitionates only toward that which is believed to exist, never toward that which is believed to be non-existent. The fact that body yields to suggestion in genuine cases of healing, may not show that body exists, but it does show that one believes it exists. The belief that one believes it does not exist is pure delusion. It is impossible to will to change any physical condition which is really believed to be non-existent. It is equally impossible to will to eliminate sin — which is believed to be non-existent — and to take on holiness — the absence, for one thing, of that which is believed to have no existence, and the possession of those moral qualities, for a second thing, which signify the shunning of that which is believed to have no existence. In all this we have the willed influence of mental states over body which is denied and over mental states that are believed to be without actuality. In other words, the Will, a power given to man to guide him through realities, not fictitious imaginations fully understood to be non-existent as facts, is here dethroned as a normal faculty.

What is called " Mental Science " asserts the reality of matter, body, spirit, disease and sin, but bases its theories upon the power of "mind over matter." Its error consists in constructing a " science " on partial data and on laws which are but imperfectly understood, and in asserting the " absolute supremacy " of " mind over body." The Will is here set toward a claim which cannot be substantiated — the "absolute supremacy" of "mind over body"; which, indeed, is disproved, unless a multitude of facts in life are to be willed out of the field of belief. It is no province of Will to will a disbelief in plain facts. There are innumerable instances which show that the " supremacy of mind over body" is not absolute. Moreover, the Will here sets itself to the task of ignoring what are at least intermediate agencies for assisting person to control bodily conditions. It may be that the supposed necessity for food is a delusion, but the normal person at least employs the eating of food as an intermediate means for exerting its influence over the physical organism. Medical Science may be no true science — as yet — all and all — but its treatments certainly assist, if in no other way, in establishing right mental conditions for the action of self over the body. Of course the necessity for foods is real. A genuine medicine is, in a large sense, a food — " whatever sustains, augments, or supplies nourishment to organic bodies." Some foods and some medicines are false, in themselves, or in particular applications. It remains for the normal person to select right foods and to use right medicines *as parts of the present system of things,* with the influence of mental states sought and cultivated as being originated and maintained intermediately through the employment of that which is real in itself and real in its power over belief. Medical Science needs to become less empirical and materialistic, and " Mental Science " needs to enlarge its field by recognition of facts and the medicinal utility of nature. We now return to the discussion of moods.

DIVISION OF MOODS

I

First General Division of Moods. Special mental states of mind in general which exert various influences over the *body.*

" A process set up anywhere in the centres reverberates everywhere, and in some way or other affects the organism throughout, making its activities either greater or lesser."

Sorrow increases the flow of tears. Anxiety may induce perspiration or the opposite. Intense nervous anxiety or fear in a public speaker sometimes almost totally stops the flow of saliva. It is now disclosed that great anger poisons the blood. Any great emotion may increase or retard the circulation. Exaltation of feeling or thought frequently brings about insensibility to pain. Great mental depression makes latent disorders patent. A surgical operation causes some spectators to faint, and a noisome object may bring on vomiting. By fixing the attention upon certain parts of the body the blood may be directed to those parts. Muscular energy is increased by violent emotions, and is sometimes vastly diminished, and is always made greater by an exertion of the Will. The fury of the madman is accompanied by superhuman strength. Ideas frequently induce actual physical sensations, as nausea at the thought of disgusting food, or the setting of the teeth "on edge" at the thought of saw-filing. Worry cultivates dyspepsia. Incessant mental activity robs the body of assimilated nourishment. Disease may be incurred through conditions of mind, and is often warded off by the same agency. Cheerfulness and hope tend to tone up the entire system.

Similarly with the *influence of states of person over mental activities.* Fear quickens some intellects, but dulls others. Many persons can accomplish large things only under great excitement, while with others excitement paralyzes the powers. Hate blinds all mental faculties not immediately engaged in its gratification, but quickens the latter. Musicians, public speakers and exhibitors are greatly influenced by the psychic atmosphere about them. Interest always increases the perceptive powers. The mind's ability to recall past scenes, events and knowledge is increased by a clear brain and a healthy tone acted upon by some pleasing emotion. The imagination is sometimes obscured or confused by disease, sometimes made more powerful by the same, and is always rendered vigorous and facile by exalted trains of thought. The logical faculties are swayed by the passions, and dulled or sharpened as the mind seems sluggish or keen in other respects. Consciousness of right or wrong often depends upon the mental tone of the individual.

Such illustrations disclose the value to life in general of an intelligent understanding of psychic states. And among the mind's powers the Will is no exception to the sway of its various moods. These considerations make clear the

II

Second Division of Moods. Mental states having direct reference to the act of willing.

The Will has its own moods, by which its functions may be analyzed, and by which it may and ought to be cultivated and made to regulate itself in the highest manner. These volitional moods are of importance because they are creative states and may be maintained, thus exercising the Will and becoming permanent factors in the conduct of life. They indicate person's attitude toward the act of willing, and so reveal, now the individual nature, now the individual character. Brought into definite and abiding thought, they will always assist in cultivating both the Will's power and its stability. It is the function of Will to regulate them. Hence, no better means of cultivating and training the Will itself can be devised than the deliberate and intelligent control of volitional moods. For if the will can control such peculiar mental states, a determination to do so must increase power of Will and direct it into its legitimate activities.

Resolve to acquire that permanent mood of mind which views yourself at your best. Constantly flood your arena of action with new interests and freshness of spirit which enables you to "live life to the limit."

Moods of Will

The Moods of Will may now be enumerated as follows:

I

The Mood of Feeling, or Interest. Feeling may be defined as any pleasurable or painful condition of the person in mind or body. The steps from such condition to Volition are four: a mental impression or object of attention brought to mind; a feeling with regard to the same; a mode of mental action, or attention; and the Volition. The degree of attention sometimes depends upon the Will, but more frequently upon interest in the object or impression. Interest is of two sorts, spontaneous and willed. Spontaneous interest is indifferent to the quality of the feeling involved — whether pleasurable or painful; a toothache receives spontaneous interest as truly as a good dinner. But willed interest, or acquired attention, always involves the idea of personal pleasure, at least the gratification of some desire.

The Mood of Feeling or Interest may be cultivated. One ultimate purpose for doing so, providing constant gratification, will be the intelligent increase of the Mood itself, and through that increase, of the mind's steadfast power of Will. In all large living this Mood of Interest is ever present and powerful. If it is suffered to collapse here and there, a loss of Will is sure to follow. The sum-total of the Will's activities depends upon the sum-total of its acquired interests. Hence spontaneous interest should be utilized for the maintenance of acquired, and above all should be made over into good habits of living.

As a guiding rule for the acquirement of such artificial interest and the keeping alive of feeling with " go " in it, a principle of Prof. William James may be followed:

"Any object not interesting in itself may become interesting through becoming associated with an object in which interest already exists. The two associated objects grow, as it were, together; the interesting portion sheds its quality over the whole; and thus things not interesting in their own right borrow an interest which becomes as real and as strong as that of any natively interesting thing."

If such a principle is practically and persistently carried out, the effort will invariably cultivate great volitional power.

II

The Mood of Energy. This is a general forceful and determined state of mind. It is the Mood which carries things on. It may act swiftly or slowly, depending upon other characteristics. The energetic man may be swift in action as compared to the bulk of his mind, while slow as compared to men of lighter calibre. Energy may exhibit on the surface of action, or it may hide behind an unmoved exterior; it may be violent in its manifestations, or as calm as a resistless iceberg. Whatever its characteristics, it is of vastest importance. To maintain it may draw heavily on the Will, but its continued possession and control furnish among the surest means of cultivating and training the Will's power and stability. For further study of this subject reference may be had to the author's work, *Power for Success.* Learn to summons, on occasion, the feeling of being alive, alert, energy-charged.

III

The Mood of Permission. The Will, in this Mood, having originated certain actions of the body or in the mind, simply permits the movements involved to "go on of themselves," as it were, without interference, except to modify or prohibit, at intervals, and as occasion may require. Examples of such permissive action of the Will may be seen in walking, carried on automatically so far as conscious effort is concerned, while the mind is engaged in thought; in reading while conversation is in progress in the vicinity; in musical performance while the player converses with others.

In all such cases it is probable that the "underground mind" involves consciousness of the various activities, but that the objective mind remains a sort of passive spectator or ruler who does not interpose his power.

The Mood of Permission is also seen when the conscious Will refrains from interfering with a state, an action, or a line of conduct. Thus the Will permits various mental or bodily conditions, as reverie or rest, or an act or series of acts to continue, or a habit to remain undisturbed, or a course in life to proceed — the mind in all cases being conscious of its own or bodily activities, and that it may at any moment exert the Will in a contrary direction.

This mood should be cultivated, yet always with reference to the formation of good habits and the growth of Will. It is especially valuable in permitting rest both of body and of mind for the sake of psychic tone. But it must be wisely exercised, for otherwise it will drop to the line of indolence, and thus destroy rather than build up power of Will.

IV

The Mood of Decision. This Mood involves the Mood of Energy. It signifies promptness with more or less of force. It is instant in its action, having thus fulfilled its function. Nevertheless, it is a Mood to be cultivated and continually possessed, as the emergencies of life make incessant demands upon its exercise in the Will.

"The irresolute man is lifted from one place to another; so hatcheth nothing, but addles all his actions."

> "For indecision brings its own delays,
> And days are lost lamenting o'er lost days.
> Are you in earnest? Seize this very minute.
> What you can do, or dream you can, begin it.
> Boldness has genius, power, and magic in it.
> Only engage, and then the mind grows heated—
> Begin, and then the work will be completed."

Every effort to maintain the decisive state of mind acts directly on the Will. A determined resolution to decide intelligently and forcefully all questions of life as they may present themselves — rather than suffer them to hang for something "to turn up" — will be found to be a perfect Will-tonic.

V

The Mood of Continuity. This Mood involves energy and decision. It is, as it were, a chain of decisions — the Mood of Decision perpetuated. In evil, it is a man's ruin; in right conduct, one of the methods of success. It is a creator of interest, and a prime source of voluntary habits.

"Habit is a second nature as regards its importance in adult life; for the acquired habits of our training have by that time inhibited or strangled most of the natural impulsive tendencies which were originally there. Ninety-nine hundredths or, possibly, nine hundred and ninety-nine thousandths, of our activity is purely automatic and habitual, from our rising in the morning to our lying down each night." Hence the supreme importance of forming habits of action which are rational and make for the mind's education.

"A capricious man is not one man merely; he is several at once; he multiplies himself as often as he has new tastes and different behavior."

"Success prompts to exertion, and habit facilitates success."

"Habit also gives promptness; and the soul of despatch is decision."

VI

The Mood of Understanding. In this Mood the person wills to attend intelligently to the thing in hand. He concentrates in order to know. He insists upon knowing that to which he attends. This Mood usually results in decision and continuity — but not always, for Reason may dictate inactivity, and the man may refuse to follow his moral convictions. But the Mood of Understanding is imperative in an intelligent exercise of power of Will. It often prohibits action. It provides the ground for rational endeavors. It is the check of rashness. It is the inspiration of some of the most resistless exhibitions of Will-energy known. When Grant was ready, he swept on to victory. Great commercial enterprises are all born of this Mood. It is the very genius of Science. Faraday, about to witness an experiment, said, "Wait; what am I to expect?" That was the mood of understanding. A determination to cultivate this mood, and to have it present in all deliberations, will obviate innumerable mistakes in life, and infallibly develop great power and wisdom in the exercise of the Will.

"Nine men out of every ten," says Professor William Matthews, "lay out their plans on too vast a scale; and they who are competent to do almost anything, do nothing, because they never make up their minds distinctly as to what they want, or what they intend to be."

VII

The Mood of Reason. In this Mood the person employs the preceding, but goes on to ascertain definite reasons for one action in preference to another. One may understand a subject, a motive, or the alternatives of conduct, yet be at a loss for the right decision. The Mood of Reason asks, Why this action or that? It holds the Will back until satisfactory answers are given. Undoubtedly it is a Mood which may be over-cultivated, and there are occasions when the inability to discover determining reasons for action or cessation of action must furnish the sole reason for decision, as wrong action may be better than a perpetual deadlock of the Will. Nevertheless, the Mood of Reason stands with that of Righteousness in its importance to the conduct of life. Its development and perennial judgment in the court of mind are scientific guaranties of a strong and intelligent Will.

"Count Von Moltke," writes Orison Swett Marden, "the great German strategist and general, chose for his motto, *Erst wägen, dann wagen,* 'First weigh, then

"*Know Thyself*" 93

venture,' and it is to this he owed his great victories. He was slow, cautious, careful in planning, but bold, daring, even seemingly reckless in execution the moment his resolve was made."

VIII

The Mood of Righteousness. In this Mood person is bent on ascertaining the moral quality of actions. It is the loftiest of Moods having reference to Will. It has developed some of the greatest Wills of the ages. It clears the mind, uncovers all motives, illumines the judgment, inspires resolution, induces perseverance, arouses the understanding and guides the reason. By nothing is the Will so easily disorganized as by the opposite Mood — that of Evil. The Mood of Righteousness governs the universe — that is its superiority — and exhibits the strength of an Almighty Will. He who nourishes and holds to the fore this Mood is infallibly sure of a good Will; — which may err in directions really unimportant, but cannot err in the direction of an ultimate power of Will that guarantees success against all the assaults of evil forever.

Let us now observe: Many people exhibit the Moods of Feeling, Energy, and Decision.

A less number possess adequately the Moods of Understanding and Reason.

Few there are, seemingly, who show the Mood of intelligent Continuity in life.

Fewer still manifest the Mood of Righteousness as a permanent factor of conduct.

The Will, then, may be graded according as it discloses these Moods. *The perfect Will exhibits them in symmetrical combination: the Mood of Right Feeling merging into the Mood of Energy, prompt to act, but* pausing for Understanding, guided by Reason and controlled by Righteousness. When all these Moods obtain, there is the perfect static Will capable of enormous dynamic energy for any length of time and working towards the noblest ends in life.

At this point appears a

BASIC PRINCIPLE IN WILL-CULTURE

Intelligent cultivation of the Will involves exercises dealing with every department of human nature:

First. Will-bent practice of the *perceptive powers* — exercise of feeling and knowing for growth of Will.

Second. Exercise calling the *imagination* into play with the idea of strengthening and training the Will by deliberate activity and by clean consideration of motives and consequences.

Third. Practice in *memory,* as a mind-improver and as a Will-grower; and also for the purpose of rendering experience more vivid, and, hence, a more forceful teacher.

Fourth. Practice in *reasoning,* for the cultivation of the whole mind, and in order to develop the habit of acting according to definite reasons, together with the elimination of impulse and thoughtless decisions.

Fifth. Exercise in *self-perception* and *self-control,* in the eradication of injurious tendencies and habits and immoral acts and conduct, in order that all Moods of the Will may be brought to the fore in a life mastered by righteousness. For here only is the perfect Will.

Sixth. The *persistent state of resolution for Will.* This means the preservation always, and under all circumstances of the attitude — I WILL TO WILL.

He who would acquire the perfect Will must carry into all his thoughts and actions the resolute assertion: I RESOLVE TO WILL! This resolution, borne out in persistent practice, has never been known to fail.

THE GREAT PSYCHIC FLOWER

See I in fields our dandelions yellow,
And lights in forest vistas warm and mellow,
Flowers of sun on leafage tapestry?
See I the heavenly ships sail lazily
Above, huge shadow-flowers blessed with motion,
And the white lilies of the restless ocean?
See I in poet's words the efflorescence
Beautiful of spirit, thought's quintessence?
See I illumination in the human face,
Eternal Truth's fair flower in time and space?

See I all this and count my soul a clod,
Less than the blooms of sky or sea or sod?
Behold yon cloud-bank drifting toward the West.
Its form is but material force compressed,
Symbol of that vast Cloud, the Universe,
Through which, in which, th' Eternal streams and stirs
And I, the dust, am also Shape of Him,
But more, a psychic Star-Self on the rim
Of Being Deathless. Count I soul-form least
Among near suns or worlds beyond the East?
The mighty Cosmos is one Psychic Flower,
Bloom of the Infinite's exhaustless power.
One Life expands in atom or in mind;
I see, I know, I feel the Undefined,
And thrilled as willed, life, power, unfoldment, health,
Inherit, seize, fr——

CHAPTER VII

Some General Rules

"THE exercise of the Will, or the lesson of power, is taught in every event. From the child's possession of his several senses up to the hour when he saith, 'Thy will be done!' he is learning the secret, that he can reduce under his Will, not only particular events, but great classes, nay the whole series of events, and so conform all facts to his character."—*Emerson.*

Part I may be closed with some general rules.

The purpose in suggesting a number of practical rules at this point is two-fold: in the first place, the rules furnish examples of what is conceived to be the right use of the Will; and, in the second place, the effort to employ them and fix them in mind will bring into play that fundamentally important factor of our nature, the sub-conscious self. A sea captain wrote the author in regard to these rules: "I found myself during a stormy passage without effort calling the rules to mind and bringing them into action, and I never got through bad weather so easily."

"There exists in all intellectual endeavor," says Jastrow in "The Subconscious," "a period of incubation, a process in great part sub-conscious, a slow, concealed maturing through absorption of suitable pabulum. Schopenhauer calls it 'unconscious rumination,' a chewing over and over again of the cud of thought preparatory to its assimilation with our mental tissue; another speaks of it as the red glow that precedes the white heat. * * * We develop by living in an atmosphere congenial to the occupation that we seek to make our own; by steeping ourselves in the details of the business that is to be our specialty, until the judgment is trained, the assimilation sensitized, the perspective of importance for the special purpose well established, the keenness for useful improvisation brought to an edge. When asked how he came to discover the law of gravitation, Newton is reported to have answered, ' By always thinking about it.' "

First Set

Rules pertinent to the exercise of Will in the conduct of life.

These paragraphs should be studied and thoroughly fixed in mind. They are born of experience, and should be practised daily until they become automatic in the working outfit of character.

1. Be master of your own Will.
2. When in doubt, do nothing; wait for light.
3. Cultivate perfect calmness.
4. Never become confusingly excited.
5. Never yield to temper, nor entertain irritation.
6. Make no decision when out of temper.
7. If inclined to rashness, cultivate conservatism.
8. If inclined to excessive — injurious — conservatism (experience must decide this), cultivate the prompt and progressive spirit.
9. Decide nothing without deliberation where deliberation is possible.

All Problems Close in Adjustment 99

10. When deliberation is not possible, keep cool. Confusion is mental anarchy; it dethrones the "King."

11. After a decision under such circumstances, entertain no regrets. The regretful mind is an enemy to a good Will. If the mind has held itself with an iron grip and decided on the spur of dire necessity, the gods could do no more.

12. Make no decision without an adequate purpose. Rely upon your own intelligent idea of adequacy.

13. Permit no difficulties to turn you aside from an adequate purpose. Mirabeau called the word "impossible" "that blockhead word."

14. Never try to make a decision the carrying out of which involves a real impossibility.

15. In the pursuit of an adequate purpose, sift means according to ends, then shift them intelligently. It is folly to tunnel a mountain if you can get a better and cheaper road by going around it. A man in Ohio spent thousands of dollars in laying a roadbed, and abandoned it to purchase another railroad. He should have made sure about the operating road first. But if it is necessary to sink money in a new road in order to compel sale of an old one, that is the thing to do.

16. The best Will is not that which pounds through all circumstances, whether or no, merely for the sake of persistence, but that which "gets there" by taking advantage of shifting conditions. Ends, not means, are the goal of a wise Will.

17. Never lose sight of the main thing in hand.

18. Admit no motive into court which you do not clearly see. A motive is like a would-be soldier; it should undergo medical examination in the nude.

19. Never permit a motive for a decision to tangle up with a motive against. Example: This city is a

good business centre; but then, you have to earn your money a second time in collecting it. Such a marriage of motives breeds confusion. Compel every motive to stand alone.

20. Remember, that a decision of Will involves judge and lawyer. You are merely and always the judge. When desire takes the bench and the judge pleads, it is time to adjourn court. You can get a correct "judgment" only by sticking to the bench. In other words, never permit yourself to plead, either with, for or against a motive.

21. In making an important decision, summons the whole mind to this one act. I RESOLVE TO WILL! ATTENTION!!

22. Make no decision while the mind is partly occupied with other matters. It is impossible to angle for fish and shoot buffaloes at the same time.

23. Never work at cross-purposes. Set the Will either for one thing or for the other. The man who tries to kill two birds with one stone usually misses both. Where the two birds are taken a second stone has stolen into the case.

24. Take all the advice that is offered; — *then act upon your own judgment.*

25. Never discount your own experience. This is "dollars"— except to the fool. *The chief value of the fool's experience is its worth to others.*

26. Never act upon merely passive resolution. This is weakness. It may be phrased in these words: "I guess I will do so and so." One may say thereto, with Shakespeare, "What a lack-brain is this!" Nothing comes of the lackadaisical Will.

27. If this is the general tone of your Will, stimulate it by imitation of fierce resolution.

28. The first secret of persistence is a good start; the second is a *constant review of motives.*

29. When tempted to discouragement, defer action to a time of sounder mood.

30. Never embark in an enterprise in which you do not thoroughly believe. To do otherwise is to introduce confusion among the judicial powers. If it turns out that your want of faith has been wrong, you have nevertheless kept those *judicial powers on the bench.* That is worth more than the success which you have missed.

31. If you have any settled fears in life, consort with them, resolutely and persistently, *until you know them for liars.*

32. Don't worry! To worry about the past is to dig up a grave; let the corpse lie. To worry about the future is to dig your own grave; let the undertaker attend to that. The present is the servant of your Will.

33. Never decide an important matter when the mind is confused by sickness. Store this rule in your soul during health; it will stand by you in disease.

34. Never yield a resolution after three o'clock in the afternoon. The morning may bring a better thought.

35. Never make an important decision after three o'clock in the afternoon, nor before ten o'clock in the forenoon. Before ten you have not "limbered up." After three you are "unlimbered."

The two preceding rules are merely for suggestion.

36. Never ignore in deliberation a possible consequence.

37. Insist upon seeing clearly all possible consequences.

38. In *deliberation, consequences* should always be separated from *motives;* in *judgment, motives* should always be considered with reference to *consequences.*

39. Before making a decision, magnify all possible difficulties.

40. After decision, minify every actual difficulty, and throw out of mind every difficulty which seems to be imaginary. Here are some things that are hard to decide; but then, all life is a taking of chances.

41. If you must take chances, *take those that lean your way.*

42. Learn to emphasize in thought, and to see clearly, remote motives, contingencies and consequences. Be sure that they are not overshadowed by those which are near. Example: I wish to economize in order to secure a home; but at present, I desire a vacation. The home is very remote, while the period of rest is very near and clamorous.

43. In weighing motives, have a care that desire does not tip the scale. "In making an effort to fix our mind on a distant good or a remote evil we know that we are acting in the direction of our true happiness. Even when the representation of the immediate result is exerting all its force, and the representation of the distant one is faint and indistinct, we are vaguely aware that the strongest desire lies in this direction. And the resolute direction of attention in this quarter has for its object to secure the greatest good by an adequate process of representation."

44. Never lie to yourself in the consideration of motives and consequences. *If you must lie, practise on other people; they will find you out; but if you continue to lie to yourself, you are a lost fool.*

All Problems Close in Adjustment

45. Remember always that the *lie is the dry rot of Will*.

46. Be absolutely genuine and sincere. Yet, withal, this gives you no right to ride rough-shod over neighboring humanity.

47. Never perform an act, nor make a decision, in opposition to what Socrates called his "Daimonion," — the inner voice that whispers, "Better not!"

48. When you write to an enemy a letter in which you scorch his soul, be happy — but do not mail it until to-morrow. You will then see that you have written too much. Condense it by half — but do not mail it until to-morrow. It will keep. Do not destroy it. It is a good letter. To-morrow you will again condense it. When you can write a brief, plain, but courteous letter, in which you reveal good breeding and disclose reticence, do so, and instantly mail it, grateful for common sense.

49. Never resolve upon an act which will, or may — injure other people, or injure yourself.

50. *Measure motives by your noblest selfhood.*

51. Dismiss without consideration motives or actions which you clearly recognize to be contrary to your best instincts.

52. In all conflicts between duty and pleasure, give duty the benefit of the doubt.

53. Never act contrary to your clearest judgment. Others may be right; but, in the long run, better is mistake in your own judgment than right on the judgment of others. *Do not abdicate the throne.*

54. Cultivate as a permanent habit of mind the positive Mood of willing.

55. Never will to be an imitator or a follower.

You can so will unconsciously; therefore resolve to lead and to invent and move out on new lines.

It is impossible to deliberate over every detail of conduct. Hence life must become habituated to right general principles. "A force endowed with intelligence, capable of forming purposes and pursuing self-chosen ends, may neglect those rules of action which alone can guide it safely, and thus at last wholly miss the natural ends of its being. To such a being, eternal vigilance would be the price of liberty."

SECOND SET

Rules having reference to the Moods of mind.

I.— *The Mood of Feeling:*

1. Never yield to the Mood of Feeling without scrutinizing it closely.

2. In cultivating this Mood, be sure that it is wholly free from wrong desire, fear, hate, prejudice, jealousy, anger, revenge, nervous disorders, mental depression, misconceptions and partial views.

3. At no time permit this Mood to explode in impulse.

4. Keep the Mood constantly at a high, but rational and controlled, pitch or tone.

II.— *The Mood of Energy:*

1. Seek every opportunity to intensify consciousness of the determined Will.

2. Maintain the resolute sense of the emphatic personality.

3. Keep the Mood under firm control.

4. Permit no explosion without deliberate decision and adequate cause.

5. Bring this Mood to all activities.
6. Hold the eye of energy upon life's ultimate goal.

III.— *The Mood of Decision:*
1. Precede all decision by deliberation.
2. Cultivate decision in so-called unimportants.
3. Endeavor constantly to reduce the time expended in arriving at decision. Do everything as swiftly as possible.
4. Never defer decided action. Go immediately into the business determined upon.
5. Always conjoin with this Mood that of energy.

IV.— *The Mood of Continuity:*
1. Count the cost.
2. Repeat constantly the resolution involved.
3. Do not brood over difficulties.
4. Keep the goal in sight.
5. In all continuous effort hold to the fore the Mood of utmost energy, and cause decision to act like a triphammer incessantly on the purposed business.
6. Regard each step or stage as a goal in itself. Act by act — the thing is done!

V.— *The Moods of Understanding and Reason:*
1. Know, first, what the matter proposed involves.
2. Know, secondly, what defeat means.
3. Know, thirdly, what success signifies.
4. Understand your own weakness.
5. Understand your own powers.
6. Thoroughly understand *how* to proceed.
7. Become acquainted with all details connected with an undertaking, and with the reasons for one method of procedure or another.

VI.— *The Mood of Righteousness:*
1. Have perfect faith in yourself.
2. Have faith in men.
3. Be honest — absolutely honest — with yourself.
4. Permit nothing in self to hoodwink judgment.
5. Put yourself always in the other man's shoes.
6. Examine all moral traditions.
7. Reject nothing because it is old.
8. Approve nothing because it is new.
9. Settle no question by expediency.
10. Seek all possible light.
11. Live up to all light possessed.
12. Follow your best instincts.
13. Try your ideas by the opinions of others.
14. Surrender to all good and *wise* impulses.
15. *Love truth supremely.*
16. Be as anxious to discover duty as you ought to be to perform it when discovered.

The following remarkable paragraph, by John Stuart Mill, almost epitomizes the right use of Will-power:

"He who chooses his plan for himself, employs all his faculties. He must use *observation* to see, *reasoning* and *judgment* to foresee, *activity* to gather materials for *decision, discrimination* to decide, and when he has decided, *firmness* and *self-control* to hold to his deliberate decision. And these qualities he requires and exercises exactly in proportion as the part of his conduct which he determines according to his own judgment and feeling is a large one. It is possible that he might be guided in some good path, and kept out of harm's way, without any of these things. But what will be his comparative worth as a human

All Problems Close in Adjustment 107

being? It really is of importance not only what men do, but also what manner of men they are that do it. Among the works of man, which human life is rightly employed in perfecting and beautifying, the first in importance surely is man himself."

But the work of this chapter will not be finished so long as dependence is placed on the objective self alone. There is a deeper self which must be trained to accept and act on the rules above suggested. It is a mistake to expect self-development from external activities exclusively. If you go over the rules until they are thoroughly imbedded in the sub-conscious phases of your mind, they will then "germinate," so to speak, and in time become "second nature." In the meantime, it will be advisable to affirm mentally somewhat as follows: "I am absorbing these principles of conduct, and in so doing am affirming that the moods indicated are surely becoming mine, actual factors in my every-day life."

For remember, you cannot find reality, truth, life, a universe, by going forever outside of self nor by gazing into some imaginary sky. So far as you are concerned, none of these things exist save as each is given existence within your selfhood. The Universe passes solemnly through every growing soul from the region of the ungrasped and below the ordinary consciousness. No knowledge comes from upper airs — though half the reality of any knowledge lies there because every individual centers Infinite Existence — but all emerges from the under realm of the unknown in consciousness. No possession is yours until it has swept up from the lower inner fields of life.

Stand, therefore, for the objective life, of course, but always as well for the inner existence which allies you with all worlds. If, taking the outer life as it comes, you will for long affirm that your deeper self is also in relation with all right things and growing because of that relation, you will in this way realize the remarkable quotation from Mill. Otherwise, it is nothing better than commonplace school instruction.

Now the object of these many rules is to bring out the greatness within you. Pertinent thoughts on the subject can be given from Sigurd Ibsen (son of the great dramatist): "People can be more or less great; some oftener than others. . . . In certain people the genius appears only as an isolated flash. . . . Most well-equipped creatures probably have a great idea, at some moment or other of their lives, but such an inspiration appearing by fits and starts, is not genius. . . . The great tragedy of the incomplete man is that his vision is sublime, *while the means of expressing it escapes him* (power of will). . . .

"All greatness, that of the intellect, the feeling or of the will, can finally be comprehended in the concept personality. Great is the man who is equipped with a personality of unusual intensity. And so, what is personality? It is potentiated humanity, humanity in quintessence. The patternable great man would be he who united all purely human qualities in perfect harmony and in the mightiest phase of development.

"Consciousness of any kind whatever is the aim and content of all life. The highest form of life consists in the most intense consciousness, connected with the freest expansion of feeling, thought, and action, and the most supreme beings are those who are capable of securing for themselves such an invigorated existence."

So, practice the foregoing exercises; use the different sets of rules. They will gradually establish in your conscious mind the feeling that you are living and acting according to infallible law. You will soon realize that you are directing your own course — that you can deliberately proceed this way or that, as you choose. And with the unfolding of this higher consciousness there will come forward the deep inner confidence that you are your own master — that you are unswayed by external forces of men and nature which drive most people with ruthless jocularity.

It is this supreme consciousness — this expanding arena of expression — which Ibsen refers to as the measure of great men — the gauge of a man's independence — his qualifications to come and go upon the earth, a super-man.

And always does such a career demonstrate the outworking of the power we are all along seeking to develop — the Will.

THE KING

*Silent the great audience-room. Yet stirs
In all the place a premonition vague
Of imminent events. A breath proclaims
Through swaying curtains Majesty's approach.
Guards stand alert. Low murmuring sounds arise
Of retinues attendant. Then, the pause
Of homage . . . and the Sovereign enters in.*

*The chamber of the kingly life is nought
Save place expectant till the Lord of all,
Assumptive ever of his rightful throne
Though absent for siesta or the chase,
Stride in and speak his omnipresent power.
'Tis vacancy whose meaning sole is this:
His coming to await, his presence guard.
And thus, forsooth, all eminent domain,
From chamber to frontier, whose value lies
In his great self. As king is, so the land!*

*As Will is, so the man! The vacant mind,
Eventless years, breath signifying nought,
Senses as idle as the summer clouds,
Attendants loosed and chattering — all breed
Dread anarchy, or worse, a bankrupt soul.
Lo, if the Will fails, kingdoms baubles are!
But if he reigns, the desert's boundless waste
Bursts into splendor and proclaims his power!*

*As Will is, so the man! The brain alert,
The household true, the message bearers swift,
The five great overlords leal servants, friends,
The five good gates co-ordinate and sure,
A song of action in the sun-charged air,
And those three ministers of glorious life —
Faith tireless, unboisterous Confidence,
And courage, soft of speech whose word is hope,
Beside the royal Presence alway. Thus
The realm be when his Majesty, the Will,
Rules, potent. Thus comes Power invisible
From Heaven to company the Sovereign,
To bless the kingdom of the human soul,
To make its Lord imperial, throned on law:
One to outlook the worlds, and conquer them!*

— The Author.

PART II—THE WILL AND SENSE-CULTURE

RESOLUTION

Realizing the necessity of a strong and well-trained Will for the largest success in secular affairs and in morals, and recognizing various defects in my own Will-power, I hereby RESOLVE to give the present work a thorough trial in all its exercises and suggestions, and to embody these, with others that may occur to me during such trial, so far as any of them are evidently designed to be so embodied in conduct, for the remainder of my life.
[Signed.]
....

CHAPTER VIII

SUGGESTIONS FOR PRACTICE

"NATURE is often hidden, sometimes overcome, seldom extinguished. He that seeketh victory over his nature, let him not set himself too great nor too small tasks; for the first will make him dejected by often failings, and the second will make him a small proceeder, though by often prevailings. Let not a man force a habit upon himself with a perpetual continuance, but with some intermission. For both the pause reinforceth the new onset; and if a man that is not perfect be ever in practice, he shall as well practice his errors as his abilities, and induce one habit of both. And there is no means to help this but by seasonable intermissions."—*Lord Bacon.*

Should the exercises given in this division of our work, Part II, seem unessential or tedious, you are invited to remember that, as Royce has said ("Outlines of Psychology"):—

"The development and support of mental activities of every grade is dependent upon the constant and proper use of the sense organs. Every cultivation of even the highest inner life involves a cultivation of the sense organs."

But observe: "The life of the senses does not constitute a sort of lower life, over against which the higher intellectual, emotional and voluntary life stands, as a markedly contrasted region relatively independent of the other, and ideally capable of a certain divorce from it. On the contrary, sensory experience plays its part, and its essential part, in the very highest of our spiritual existence. When we wish to cultivate processes of abstract thinking, our devices must therefore include a fitting plan for the cultivation of the senses, and must not plan to exclude sense experience as such, but only to select among sensory experiences those that will prove useful for a purpose.

We are now prepared for the actual work of Will-culture in Physical Régime. The present chapter is preliminary yet eminently practical, and it should not only be carefully read but thoroughly studied until its suggestions are deeply grounded in daily life.

At this point *certain principles* appear which form the basis of all Physical Régime.

First Principle

Continuous and intelligent thought on the growth of any mental power, with exercises carried on to that end, exerts a developing influence upon the function itself. In the case of the Will this would follow without systematic practice, but regulated exercise tends to hold attention to the desired goal and to increase the power of the idea of Will-culture. The value of the abiding thought, "I resolve to acquire a strong and well-trained Will!" can scarcely be overstated.

Second Principle

Exercises involving one department of body or mind will exert various beneficial influences:

Of the body, on other parts of body;
Of the body, on various powers of mind;
Of the mind, on other powers of mind;
Of the mind, on various functions and organs of the body.

An illustration of the general law may be seen in the increased grip-power of one hand caused by daily practice with the other. Thus, Professor E. W. Scripture, in "Thinking, Willing, Doing," remarks:

"It is incredible to me how in the face of our general experience of gymnasium work some writers can assert that practice makes no change in the greatest possible effort. At any rate, in experiments made under my direction the change could be traced day by day.

"Curiously enough, this increase of force is not confined to the particular act. In the experiments referred to, the greatest possible effort in gripping was made on the first day with the left hand singly and then with the right hand, ten times each. The records were: for the left, fifteen pounds, for the right, fifteen pounds. Thereafter, the right hand alone was practised nearly every day for eleven days, while the left hand was not used. The right hand gained steadily day by day; on the twelfth day it recorded a grip of twenty-five pounds. The left hand recorded on the same day a grip of twenty-one pounds. Thus the left hand had gained six pounds, or more than one-third, by practice of the other hand."

In practice seeking development of Will, what is true of hands will be true of mental powers. Indeed, *steadfast, purposeful exercise of physical powers in general will develop power of Will.* The same writer goes on to say on this point:

"A great deal has been said of the relation of physical exercise to Will-power. I think that what I have said sufficiently explains how we can use the force of an act as an index of Will-power. It is unquestionable that gymnastic exercises increase the force of act. The conclusion seems clear; the force of Will for those particular acts must be increased. It has often been noticed that an act will grow steadily stronger although not the slightest change can be seen in the muscle.

"Of course I do not say that the developed muscle does not give a greater result for the same impulse than the undeveloped one; but I do claim that much of the increase or decrease of strength is due to a change in Will-power. For example, no one would say that Sandow, the strong man, has a more powerful Will than anybody else. But Sandow's strength varies continually, and, although part of this variation may be due to changes in the muscles, a large portion is due to a change in force of Will. When Sandow is weak, make him angry, and note the result."

Third Principle

Lower forms of exercise in bodily movement prepare the way for higher exercises. "All the higher actions of life depend on the attainment of a general control of the bodily organs." This is true even when such control is left to hap-hazard methods. It is immeasurably truer when control is intelligently sought. "Consequently," in the highest sense, "the exercising of these capabilities involves a rudimentary," and a very complete "training of the Will, for a definite reaction on the Will itself is absolutely certain."

Fourth Principle

Intelligent work in Will-culture must begin with perception. Perception precedes mental growth. The senses are our common miners for raw material of mental life. Yet how few people adequately attend to sensation or intelligently employ their own senses! Strange as it may seem, here is a large *terra incognita*. One of the chief differences among men is the matter of vision. By vision is meant the ability to see, hear and feel reality. Some people perceive a great deal on the surface of things; others catch but little even here. Some perceive not only the superficial aspects of reality, but also its inner contents; others, again, discover neither the surface of things nor their hidden meaning. Eyes, ears, nerves they have; but they see not, hear not, feel not. To such people a strong Will-power is a stranger. They are governed largely by caprice.

The *first requisite,* then, *of Will-growth,* is *observation.* The mind must learn to see things as they are, to hear things as they are, to feel things as they are.

"Eyes and No-eyes journeyed together," says the author just quoted. "No-eyes saw only what thrust itself upon him; Eyes was on the watch for everything. Eyes used the *fundamental method of all knowledge — observation, or watching.*

"This is the first lesson to be learned — the art of watching. Most of us went to school before this art was cultivated, and, alas! most of the children still go to schools of the same kind. There are proper ways of learning to watch, but the usual object lessons in school result in just the opposite. We, however, cannot go a step further till we have learned how to watch."

Hence, the watchword all along must be ATTENTION! The Will must begin its work by resolving upon persistent ATTENTION. To the various operations of the senses Will must mightily attend! In all exercises the watchword must never be forgotten: ATTENTION! But attention for what purpose? For one sole purpose — *Will-power!* The commanding formula, then, is:—"I RESOLVE TO WILL! ATTENTION!!"

FIFTH PRINCIPLE

Systematic exercise, with power of Will constantly kept in mind as a goal never to be yielded, *develops the Will-habit.* Hence the value of persistence. Practice develops persistence; persistence perfects practice. Emerson said truly:

"The second substitute for temperament is drill, the power of use and routine. The hack is a better roadster than the Arab barb. . . . At West Point, Colonel Buford, the Chief Engineer, pounding with a hammer on the trunnions of a cannon, until he broke them off. He fired a piece of ordnance some hundred times in swift succession, until it burst. Now, which stroke broke the trunnion? Every stroke. Which blast burst the piece? Every blast. '*Diligence passe sens,*' Henry VIII. was wont to say, or, 'Great is drill.' . . . Practice is nine-tenths. . . . Six hours every day at the piano, only to give facility of touch; six hours a day at painting, only to give command of the odious materials, oil, ochres, and brushes. The masters say that they know a master in music, only by seeing the pose of the hands on the keys; — so difficult and vital an act is the command of the instrument. To have learned the use of the tools, by thousands of manipulations; to have learned the arts of reckoning, by endless adding and dividing, is the power of the mechanic and the clerk."

"Not only men," says Thomas Reid, the English Philosopher, "but children, idiots, and brutes, acquire by habit many perceptions which they had not originally. Almost every employment in life hath perceptions of this kind that are peculiar to it. The shepherd knows every sheep of his flock, as we do our acquaintance, and can pick them out of another flock one by one. The butcher knows by sight the weight and quality of his beeves and sheep before they are killed. The farmer perceives by his eye very nearly the quantity of hay in a rick or corn in a heap. The sailor sees the burden, the build, and the distance of a ship at sea, while she is a great way off. Every man accustomed to writing, distinguishes acquaintances by their handwriting, as he does by their faces. In a word, acquired perception is very different in different persons, according to the diversity of objects about which they are employed, *and the application they bestow in observing them.*"

All such acquired powers are the results of long-continued practice. And back of them lies the persistent Will. In the most of such and similar instances no great amount of Will is required at any one time; they are rather outcomes of steady application to the thing in hand.

Thus, unfailing attention to the exercises here to follow, with the idea of power of Will constantly in mind, will impart facility as regards the directions given, and in turn will develop the controlling faculty of mind to an astonishing degree.

But this work, to be successful, must be conducted with labor and patience. Think not to acquire a great Will without toil. Nor imagine that such a boon can come of a month's training or of spasmodic effort. There is but one way to get a good Will; to will to will, and to carry out that will with unflinching perseverance.

The insane are sometimes able, *for a purpose,* to "wind themselves up," and act like the sanest, by a supreme effort of Will. If the present book costs you many months of endeavor, it will "wind up" the Will to great power and persistence, and will justify all time and toil.

SIXTH PRINCIPLE

The value of drill depends largely upon system. This requires not only regular labor, but regular rest-periods as well.

In the ten-day exercises continue five days, then rest — preferably Saturday and Sunday.

From first to last, cultivate and sustain the Mood of Will. Put the Will at the fore. Here alone is our *ne plus ultra!*

Finally, in order that the principles involved may become an intelligent part of the system carried out, the following suggestions applicable to the Physical and Mental Régimes should be thoroughly worked into the student's mind as to:

First.— *In Regard to Perception.*

1. Keep the perceptive powers always at their best: eyes, ears, smell, taste, touch, nerves.

2. Attend to the *consciousness* of each sense.

3. *Observe frequent and regular periods of rest.* The law that "voluntary attention comes only in beats," requires this rule.

4. With attainment of facility, invent new methods of practice.

5. Carry the idea involved in practice into all your life.

6. While habituated actions that are not *naturally* automatic are certainly voluntary, the presence of *conscious* Will should be maintained as much as possible in all such activities. Example: piano playing; hold the mind consciously to every movement.

7. Continue the practice of the perceptive powers until the greatest willing power has been acquired.

Secondly.—*In Regard to Memory.*

1. If the memory is weak all round, resolve to strengthen it.

2. Seek to discover the peculiarities of your own memory. Then make the most of it.

3. If the memory is weak in some particulars, but strong in others, cultivate it especially where weak, and compel it where strong to assist in this effort.

4. Subordinate the verbal memory to that of principles.

5. Give memory for principles a good foundation in memorized facts, dates, etc.

6. Rely resolutely upon the ability of your memory to do your bidding.

7. Frequently review all work of the memory with great Will-power.

8. Make use, as often as possible, in conversation

and writing, and in public speaking, of all the acquirements of memory.

9. Always put the Will into the effort to remember.
10. Arrange materials by association. Then systematize and associate memory's possessions.
11. Resolve to acquire a perfect memory.
12. Abstain from all use of tobacco and alcohol.
13. Put no reliance in mnemonics, or any arbitrary "helps," but employ natural laws of association, such as

"Contiguity . . . . Horse and rider.
Contrast . . . . . Light and dark.
Resemblance . . . Grant and Sherman.
Cause and effect . . Vice and misery.
Whole and parts . . United States and New York.
Genus and species . . Dog and greyhound.
Sign and thing signified . Cross and Catholic faith."

Thirdly.—*In Regard to Imagination.*

1. Do not indulge in revery.
2. Abstain from all evil imaginations.
3. Deal, in the imagination, with facts and essential reality alone.
4. Fill mind with wholly admirable material.
5. Put the Will-sense into the imagination.
6. Make the imagination a *conscious* and *intelligent* instrument. Use it for practical purposes.
7. Beware of the "squint" brain. Look at things squarely and without prejudice.
8. Do not fall in love with the wonderful for its own sake.
9. Do not permit the imagination to dwell upon any one thing, nor upon any one quarter of thought or life, for long at one time.

10. Provide for the imagination the greatest variety of material.

11. Rigidly exclude from the realm of fancy all imaginary ills, and especially misconceptions about men or reality. Guard against deception here.

Fourthly.—*In Regard to Self-perception.*

1. Do not suffer mind to become morbid.
2. Subject the testimony of the senses and of mind to the closest scrutiny of reason.
3. Maintain in all seasons the healthy mood. Keep up your supply of ozone.
4. Live among wholesome people.
5. Companion only with large and vigorous truths.
6. Thrust the Will into all perception of self. Banish the dream-mood. Turn a hurricane in on hallucinations.
7. Become familiar with self-perception in every phase: seeing, hearing, smelling, tasting, touch, muscular consciousness, nerve-testimony; feeling, memory, imagination, reason, Will, moral states. Be absolute master here.

Fifthly.—*In Regard to Self-control.*

1. Habituate normal and right actions.
2. Eliminate eccentricities.
3. Study and overcome your personal faults.
4. Destroy immoral, injurious and obnoxious habits.
5. Expend no unnecessary amount of force in legitimate effort, and none at all in illegitimate.
6. Welcome criticism; but sift it thoroughly, and then act upon results.
7. Never gratify impulse or desire if either offers a

single chance of permanent injury to the *highest tone of mind*.

8. When about to lose self-control, anticipate consequences, and foresee especially what you may be required to do in order to regain position.

9. Make discipline an ally, not an enemy.

10. Believe mightily in yourself.

11. Unite belief in self with faith in man.

12. Keep the loftiest ideals fresh in thought.

13. Never, for an instant, lose consciousness of self as a willing centre of power.

Seventh Principle

"*There is nothing which tends so much to the success of a volitional effort as a confident expectation of its success.*"

Cultivate, therefore, the Mood of Expectancy.

There are underlying, scientifically demonstrated truths of tremendous import in this connection. Space does not allow going into a lengthy explanation. But the idea is: The positive mind that DEMANDS, mentally, the things it wants, is far more likely to get them than the cringing, shrinking, negative state of mind. Some rules in this connection follow:

1. Be sure the intended effort is one within the possibility of your powers to carry through.

2. If it is possible to choose the time of applying the final effort, select a period when you are at your best physically and mentally.

3. Impress upon your mind, over and over again, the demand that you simply MUST win. Scout and ridicule the little flickering thoughts that pipe up: "*There's a big possibility that you won't get it.*"

4. Mentally demand, over and over, and with in-

Great Is Drill

tensest vigor of thought, that you shall and will get what you seek. Say: " I DEMAND health. I DEMAND luxuries. I DEMAND better things in life. I simply MUST have them. I DEMAND the universal forces to bring into my career the values I seek. I DEMAND THEM!

If this seems far-fetched — just bear in mind that you are using that positive state of mind which is exactly the opposite of the cringing, timid condition which you know is the sort that gets "kicked aside." If the negative phases of mind gets what it expects (kicks, drudgery, slights, life's dregs) then beyond any question the POSITIVE mind can get the big things it demands.

THE RIDDLE

What ho! Sir Watchman of the eye
  Aloft amid the brain,
Denote to me the mighty sky
  All round the tumbling main;
Report the vision far and by—
  Nought from the truth refrain.
    "'Tis as the captain saith," quoth eye;
    "All round the mighty sky—
      No more nor less see I."

Now, tell me, empty hole of life,
  Mere socket of the mind,
What is thy office, echo's wife,
  If thou thyself art blind?
Is't thine to see, or bandy strife,
  An't please you to be kind?
    "'Tis as the captain saith," quoth eye;
    "All round the mighty sky—
      No more nor less see I."

Now, Captain, pray the riddle clear;
  Is this great eye a knave?
"'Tis as he holds," quoth captain dear,
  "All round the tumbling wave;
And that's the secret full, I fear,
  Of many a good ship's grave."
    "I am the captain's self," quoth eye;
    "Who scans the mighty sky.
      No more nor less am I."

CHAPTER IX

Exercises for the Eye

"IT IS estimated that the human eye is capable of distinguishing 100,000 different colors, or hues, and twenty shades or tints of each hue, making a total of 2,000,000 color sensations which may be discriminated. If we considered the infinite variations in the color of earth, of plants and their blossoms, of clouds, in fact of all natural objects, such an estimate as this hardly seems excessive."—*Dr. Harold Wilson.*

Theory of this Chapter

The whole mind in the eye;
The eye an index of white honesty;
The straight line the path of power.

Epictetus said: "Did God give the eyes for nothing? And was it for nothing that He mingled in them a spirit of such *might and cunning* as to reach a long way off and receive the impression of visible forms — a messenger so swift and faithful? Was it for nothing that He gave the intervening air such efficacy, and made it elastic, so that being, in a manner *strained*, our vision should traverse it? Was it for nothing that He made Light, without which there were no benefit of any other thing?"

Preliminary

The eye exists for the supreme power of Will.

Eye, ether, light, are ministers to the soul. The eye may be brightened in its gaze by energetic summonsing of consciousness. Emotions of joy, fear, hate, love, desire, aversion, illustrate this deepening influence of energy within. These emotions may be simulated, as on the stage, at the imperious call of Will. If so, one may acquire a keen eye, without the assistance of these feelings, by sheer and persistent resolution.

The present chapter is to deal with the eye. It may, nevertheless, be here said that it partakes of a law which obtains with all the organs of sense: "*A process set up anywhere in the centres reverberates everywhere, and in some way or other affects the organism throughout.*"

Effort at Will-growth by means of exercise of the senses will bring this law into action. Each particular variety of practice will more or less affect the whole man — that is, the central Will.

Vision, hearing, taste, smell and touch depend upon certain stimulations from without — as mechanical (touch), molecular (taste and smell), physical (sight, hearing), muscular (muscle sense), vital (sense of life).

But at times the required stimulation may arise within the nervous system. Examples: In referring to certain hallucinations, a Boston physician said, "The cerebral processes by which vision is produced may not only be started in the brain itself, but when so started, they are identical with those set going by an objective stimulus in the ordinary way."

The Eye and the World Are One

Professor Sully says: "A man who has lost his sight may be able to picture visible objects. The brain is now able to act *independently* of external stimulation, having acquired a disposition so to act through previous exercises *under* external stimulation." But it could not picture objects it had never seen.

Two remarks may now be made:

The Will has power to concentrate energy upon a given point in the organism. "By fixing the attention upon certain parts of the body the blood may be directed to these parts." A strong attention directed to the eye enriches its various elements. "In looking attentively at anything, the various ganglia in which the optic nerve is rooted are richly supplied with blood, and the end organs of vision and the eye muscles are vigorously innervated."

Similarly attention increases the supply of nervous force at the point where Will is focused.

Vision is intensified by attention, which induces a degree of muscular effort: — physical energy from within directed to appropriate muscles. "In all close attention there is a feeling of *tension or strain* which appears to indicate muscular effort. As Fechner says, in looking steadfastly this feeling is referred to the eye; in listening closely, to the ear; in trying to 'think' or recollect, to the head or brain."

"Thus it is presumable that when we attend to a visible object a stream of (nerve-) energy flows downward from the motor centres, partly in the direction of the muscles, and more particularly the ocular muscles which move the eye, and partly in that of the sensory centre which is concerned in the reception of nervous impressions."

If a person tries to grip the hand of a paralyzed arm,

he cannot, but muscular effort will manifest in some part of his body. Energy has been expended.

In other words, "the stimuli that excite the nervous force or irritability are of two kinds, physical and mental. Physical stimuli embrace all external excitants of whatever nature — light, heat, sound, odor, and every variety of chemical, mechanical, and galvanic irritant. *Mental stimuli result from the exercise of the Will and thought.*"

The Will is thus the power back of vision.

Professor James cites the case of a girl, born without arms or legs, who "came as quickly to a right judgment of the size and distance of visible objects as her brothers and sisters, although she had no use of hands."

Many children have the power of calling up "queer" forms in the darkness.

Cases like the following are not altogether rare: "A man in the Greek island of Hydra was accustomed to take his post every day for thirty years on the summit of the island, and look out for the approach of vessels; and although there were over three hundred sail belonging to the island, he would tell the name of each one as she approached with unerring certainty, while she was still at such a distance as to present to a common eye only a confused white blur upon the clear horizon." The long practice which resulted in this ability involved volitional acts.

The greater the Will (with a good eye), the greater our capacity for correct vision.

As exercise with vision improves the eye, so such exercise augments the flow of energy to the appropriate muscles and nerve-centres connected with sight.

Hence, conversely, all right exercises with the eyes

The Eye and the World Are One

tend to growth of that power which controls the eyes — the Will — provided they are carried on with that end held intensely in view.

In the following practice, therefore, the mind must take on energy, and it must energetically, *attend* to the thing in hand by the whole of itself, excluding all other elements of perception. This will at first be difficult; as in the case of any muscular or nervous exertion. But to him who constantly declares, "I RESOLVE TO WILL! ATTENTION!!" perfect power of continued and exclusive concentration comes at last to be second nature.

"*The culminating point in education is the power to attend to things that are in themselves indifferent, by arousing an artificial feeling of interest.*"

Hence, in the exercises that follow, the Mood or feeling of Will should be kept strongly in mind.

RÉGIMES

Exercise No. 1. Select an object for attention, in the room, or out of doors, say, a chair or a tree. Gaze at this object attentively, persistently, steadily. Do not strain the eyes; use them naturally. Now note the object's size. Estimate this. Observe its distance from yourself, and from other objects around it. Note its shape. Determine how it differs in shape from other things near it. Clearly note its color. Does it in this harmonize with its surroundings? If so, how? If not, in what respect. Make out its material. How was it made? What is its true purpose? Is it serving that purpose? Could it in any way be improved? How might this improvement be brought about?

In seeking the above information, *hold mind rigidly to its task.* It will be hard at first; but persistence in the exercise will ultimately secure ease and swiftness.

Now, without looking further at the object, write out all results as nearly as you can remember.

Repeat this exercise for ten days, resting two days, one of which should be Sunday, with the same object, and on the tenth day look at the object and observe improvement.

Always keep the Will-idea in mind.

Exercise No. 2. At a moderate gait pass once through or around a room, observing, quickly and attentively, as many objects as possible. Now, closing the door so as to shut out the room, write down the names of all articles which you remember at that time to have seen. Depend upon your memory, not your knowledge.

Repeat this exercise for ten days with rest, as above, and on the tenth observe improvement.

Finally, go into the room and note carefully every object which you have not discovered. Estimate the percentage of your failures.

Exercise No. 3. Procure twenty-five or thirty marbles, of medium size. Let eight or ten be red, eight or ten yellow, eight or ten white. Place in an open box and thoroughly mingle the colors. Now, seize one handful, with right and left hand at once, and let the marbles roll out together onto a covered surface, of a table or the floor. When they are at rest, glance once at the lot, and, turning away, write the number, as you recall (do not guess) for each color.

Repeat this exercise for ten days, with rest, and on the tenth day, estimate your improvement.

Exercise No. 4. Procure fifty pieces of cardboard,

The Eye and the World Are One 133

two inches square, each having one letter printed upon it in plain, good-sized type. Place them all, scattered, letters down, upon a table. Take in one hand ten of these squares, face down, and throw, face up, all at once, but so as to separate them, upon the table. Now, look at them sharply one instant. Then turn away, and write down the letters recalled. Immediately repeat this exercise with ten other cards. Immediately repeat with ten other cards. Repeat these three exercises for ten days, with rest, and on the tenth day note improvement for each successive corresponding throw over first.

The above exercises should all be practised each day, for ten days, at least. They may be continued indefinitely with profit, both to attention and to the Will. But the rest periods must be observed.

Exercise No. 5. Let the eyes be wide open, but not disagreeably distended. The gaze should now be directed straight in front, with every power of attention alert. Try to observe, without turning the eyes a hair's breadth, all objects in the field of vision, while gazing ten seconds, determined by slow counting. Write out the names of all objects recalled. Depend upon memory, not knowledge.

Repeat the exercise ten days, with rest, as above, always from the same position, looking in the same direction, to preserve the same exercise, and on the tenth day note improvement.

Exercise No. 6. Repeat the above exercise in all respects except that the position and field of vision of each day is to be different from those preceding, and on the tenth day note improvement.

Observe: Counting off the seconds is a slower process than is ordinarily supposed. The speed with which one must count in order to pronounce "sixty" at the end of a minute may be easily noted by counting while following with the eyes the second-hand of a watch as it moves once around the minute-circle.

Exercise No. 7. Gaze steadily, winking naturally, at some object not very far away, say, ten or sixty feet. Keep the mind intently upon the object. Count sixty to a minute while so gazing intently and observingly. Now, shut the eyes, and strive to call up a mental image of the object.

With some people the image may be as vividly defined as the real object. With most, probably, it will not be so vivid. Look up that word "vivid." Write a description of the image, whether clear or indistinct, with all parts mentally seen. Do not help the writing by looking a second time at the object; trust the image. Repeat this exercise on ten different objects on the same day. Repeat these exercises for ten days, with rest, as above, making and marking records each day, and on the tenth day note improvement.

Although the time set for practice is ten days, the exercises may be profitably continued for any length of time.

Remember: the purpose here is to learn to see things as they are, and to impress them upon mind. Great improvement, both in distinctness of vision and in details of single mental objects may thus be made as practice goes on. The essential thing, now, is patience and persistence. Whether the mental image may be cultivated so that the mental objects shall assume the electric or sunlit tone, seems doubtful.

The Eye and the World Are One 135

But, within certain limits, the eye of the soul will come to see more and more clearly as persistent endeavor continues. Especially will this be the case if the soul steadfastly wills that it be so.

The value of the end sought — clear perception — connects ultimately with the consideration of motives. This requires that things shall be seen as they actually are, that outcomes or consequences shall be vividly noted, in themselves individually and as comprehended in groups, in order that their full effect upon mind may be felt, and that adequate comparison among motives may be instituted. These exercises cultivate eye-perception, memory, mental vision and self-control. The end of all is the developed Will.

Exercise No. 8. Lastly, the eye may be trained to directness of gaze. Some eyes never look into other eyes steadily, but glance and shift from eye to object, here and there, without purpose or gain. Some public speakers never look squarely into the faces of their auditors, but gaze either up at the ceiling or down to the floor, or roam over all their hearers, seeing none. One of the subtlest elements of inspiration is thus missed — the face, mouth, eyes, attitude of eager humanity. As a rule, a large element in successful personal address lies in the eye. Directness of gaze is psychological winner. The straightforward, frank eye is a power wherever it is seen — on the street, in the store, at the social gathering, on the rostrum.

The might of a good eye can be cultivated. In order to this, mind must be put into the " windows of the soul." What men get out of life and nature depends upon the amount of mind that can be put into the look. If reality is to be possessed, mind must come forward and take it "by force." The soul in the eye means power with men. Cultivate, therefore, with every person met, the habit of the direct and steady look. Do not stare. Look people full in the eyes. The soul must always be in the eye for this exercise. Let the gaze be open, frank, friendly. And remember, that the vacant stare is a sign of idiocy, and in the domain of Will is ruled out.

Exercise No. 9. Gaze steadily, but winking naturally, at a small spot on the wall of a room, eight or ten feet away. *Do not strain the eyes.* Count fifty while so gazing. Keep mind wholly on the thought: *The Direct Eye.* Put back of that thought the Mood of a strong Will: "I WILL! I AM FORCING WILL INTO THE EYE."

Repeat this exercise ten times for ten days, with rest, as above, adding each day to the count fifty, twenty counts; thus, first day, fifty; second day, seventy; third day, ninety; etc.

Exercise No. 10. A dull gaze is akin to the vacant stare. The steady, direct look ought to be bright and full of energy. The energy of the eye's regard may be developed, and with profit, if the soul behind it is honest.

Gaze at any object in the room near by, steadily, but naturally, that is permitting the eyes to wink as they will. Put the whole soul into the eyes. Observe, *the soul is to be put into the eyes,* not into or upon the object. And do not look at the nose; look at the object, but bring consciousness forward to its windows. Summon your entire energy to the act of looking. Do this repeatedly, resting properly, and

The Eye and the World Are One 137

never permitting the eyes to grow weary or to be strained.

Now, think of, and simulate, some emotion, and try to look that feeling with great power. Examples: Intense interest — Throw delighted attention into the eyes. Deep joy — Assume a genuine joyful feeling and expression. Avoid the grinning mimicry of the clown. Fierce hate — Blaze a look at the ink-stand sufficient to annihilate its black shape. Thus with all emotions of the soul.

Repeat these exercises daily for months. It is really worth while. After a time you will discover that you are the possessor of a good eye, and that your power of Will has grown correspondingly.

Meanwhile, having caught the knack of calling the mind's energy to the act of looking, persist in gazing with all possible forcefulness at all persons and objects met. Acquire the habit of throwing, not the eye upon the object, *but the soul into the eye as it regards the object,* and the idea of Will clear forward in the consciousness. In other words, cultivate the habit of the direct and penetrating regard, avoiding the stare and all violations of good taste.

The eye of the average interested child is bright, full of soul-power, "magnetic;"— unless it happen to be an infant still in the thraldom of arms, when the human gaze frequently becomes something uncanny, preternaturally capable of disconcerting sinners, and altogether above the plane of practical illustration. The four-year-old, the saintly mother, and the righteous police judge, have all straightforward and powerful eyes. The eye of Saint Michael is surely like his sword. The regard of the man Jesus must have been equal to His word — naked verity. Hence the two secrets of masterful eyes are, *directness* and *honesty*. Here, after all, lies the foundation of Will-culture: *straightforward means — honest purposes.*

Exercise No. 11. Having acquired the art of putting soul into the act of vision, straightforward and honest, now resolve on seeing, naming and knowing the various objects that exist in your neighborhood, and on any street or road over which you may pass. Cultivate the habit of intelligent and accurate observation. It is said that " in Siberia a traveler found men who could see the satellites of Jupiter with the naked eye." Multitudes fail to see a thousand things which they pass daily during life. A Will-fed eye is a rich minister to the values of life. Browning's lines are symbolic of the outcome:

"German Bœhme never cared for plants
Until it happed, a-walking in the fields,
He noticed all at once that plants could speak,
Nay, turned with loosened tongue to talk with him.
That day the daisy had an eye indeed!"

In personal interviews the power of the eye is well known. It plays a very important rôle. The following suggestions are of value: "One of the most important things about the beginning of an interview, is that you should look the other person squarely in the eye, with a firm, steady, attracting gaze. . . . During the conversation you may change the direction of your gaze, but whenever you make a proposition, statement or request, or whenever you wish to impress him strongly, you must direct a firm, steady, magnetic gaze towards him, looking him straight in the eye."

Remember: *Directness of gaze is psychological winner.*

A great law now emerges: *The value of the use of any sense depends upon the amount and quality of person thrown into its exercise.*

The person who unceasingly asserts to his eyes: " I RESOLVE TO WILL! ATTENTION!! " cannot fail to develop a look or gaze which is perennially direct and full of energy.

THE SOUL AND THE EAR

How marvelous the " great within "
Of mind! From life's incessant din
It chooses as it will,
With a weaver's skill,
Sounds for its need, and builds a scheme
Of use or thought, or, in the dream
Begotten by sweet reverie,
A flower of heavenly harmony.

Simple motion
Of the vast ocean
Unseen around us breaks on the strand
Of soul — and we understand!

We understand, for we are
Soul's hearing, or love or war.
All knowing's self-made. What self hears
Self is, in concentric spheres
Outrunning on the larger tide;
Nay, giving this its being wide.
The ear but adds ethereal beats,
The self reality completes:
Building a hut of jarring sound,
A prison set with discord round,
A palace royal fit for kings,
A temple meet for worshippings,
Aye, God's great Universe of Truth,
Of beauty, life and deathless youth,
Wherein huge organs thunder,
Filling with wonder
Soul for that it surely is
One with, master of, this.

— THE AUTHOR.

CHAPTER X

Exercises for the Ear

"I HAD an opportunity of repeatedly observing the peculiar manner in which he (Dr. Saunderson) arranged his ideas and acquired his information. Whenever he was introduced into company, I remarked that he continued some time silent. The sound directed him to judge of the dimensions of the room, and the different voices of the number of persons that were present. His distinction in these respects was very accurate, and his memory so retentive that he was seldom mistaken. I have known him instantly to recognize a person on first hearing him, though more than two years had elapsed since the time of their meeting."—*Manchester Philosophical Memoirs.*

Theory of this Chapter

The discriminating mind in the ear;
The mind master of hearing;
Direct improvement of Will through willed employment of this sense.

"Well, early in autumn, a first winter-warning,
When the stag had to break with his foot, of a morning,
A drinking-hole out of the fresh, tender ice,
That covered the pond till the sun, in a trice,
Loosening it, let out a ripple of gold,
And another and another, and faster,
Till, dimpling to blindness, the wide water rolled."

PRELIMINARY

If you can see that picture from Browning, you probably can hear the sounds that go with it.

Natural defects aside, one good sense-power assists all the senses. When attention of the eye begins, the ear often follows. Here is the first communion. Hence three questions arise:

Do you *hear?* Do you hear *correctly?* Do you hear *what you wish to hear?*

Sounds are produced by vibrations in the atmosphere. The human ear is limited in its ability to respond to these vibrations. Within such natural limits, the more sounds one can make out the better one's hearing. Loss of sounds is due to defects of ear and abstraction of mind.

If one hears all noises does one necessarily hear correctly? That is, is the soul always in the ear? To distinguish tone, quality, direction, etc., of sounds? Is any difference obtaining in this respect due to endowment or education? Or both? Probably the latter is true. The value of exercises, therefore, to train the ear — to unfold latent powers — is evident.

Hearing what one wishes to hear may involve exclusion: one desires to shut out a noise. Or inclusion: one wishes to enjoy, truly, deeply, certain sounds, harmonies, music. All depends, now, on the soul. The nervous person hears everything. The dull person hears little.

Hearing may be shut out by Will. The door is closed to a certain sound. Hearing may be rendered more acute by Will. "Listen! A far-off bird is singing!" "Sh! A burglar is in the house!" Education in correctness of ear is preëminently a matter of Will;

— but of the persistent Will. The control of the ear exhibits some of the highest phases of self-direction. The educated soul now mounts up on wings through the realm of harmony.

But feeling, thought, imagination, are here the masters. To hear in the best sense involves the soul. Other things being equal, the largest soul hears most, most correctly, and with greatest powers of appreciation and appropriation.

The purpose of the exercises that follow is, as with those for the eye, development of ability to consider motives through discipline of attention, and thus the growth of intelligent Will-power.

Régimes

Exercise No. 1. How many sounds are now demanding your attention? Count them. Listen! Try to distinguish: — Their different *directions;* their different *causes;* their different *tones;* their difference in *strength;* their different *qualities;* their different *groupings.*

Repeat this exercise for ten days, with rest of two days, and on the tenth day estimate the improvement made.

Exercise No. 2. Single out some one prominent sound, and note everything which you can possibly say about it.

Repeat this exercise ten times on the first day with a different sound. Repeat these exercises every day for ten days, with rest of two days, and on the tenth day note improvement.

Exercise No. 3. Select the faintest sound that continues coming to you. In doing this try to distinguish some regular sound which you have not hitherto noticed. Note everything that can be said concerning it.

Repeat this exercise ten times on the first day, with a different sound. Repeat these exercises every day for ten days, with rest, and on the tenth day note improvement.

Exercise No. 4. Single out some one of the sounds that come regularly to you. Attend to this sound alone. Shut out all other sounds. Be filled with it. Become absorbed in it. Note everything which can be said of it.

Repeat this exercise ten times on the first day, with a different sound. Repeat these exercises every day for ten days, with rest, and on the tenth day note improvement.

Exercise No. 5. Select the most pleasant sound that continues to come to you. Note all possible reasons for its pleasantness. Do not fall into revery.

Repeat this exercise ten times on the first day with a different sound. Repeat these exercises every day for ten days, with rest, and on the tenth day note improvement.

Exercise No. 6. Listen carefully once to some simple melody played upon an organ or a piano. Try now to build up in your soul that melody entirely from memory. You may remember a note or two, but will forget the most of it. If, however, you are persistent, you can gradually reconstruct the lost tune. The author has often accomplished this building up of music. Make the exercise a frequent task.

"A Harp of 8,700 Strings" 145

Exercise No. 7. While one is striking the keys of a piano, first one, then another, endeavor, without looking at the player, to distinguish the notes, whether sharp or flat, position on the board, and name of each note.

Repeat with two keys, one hand striking.
Repeat with four keys, both hands striking.
Repeat with full chord, one hand striking.
Repeat with full chords, both hands striking.

Practice in the above exercises should be continued until you can detect improvement in compass of hearing, correctness of hearing, control over hearing. Do not become discouraged. The purpose is Will. Resolve to go on to the end. That end is *Will-power.*

Do nothing without thought. Put the soul into the ear in all these exercises, willing, with great energy, attention to all sounds, or to one, or to none, as the case may be.

Carry the Mood of Will through every exercise.

Exclusion of sound is often an exhibition of Will, both in the act of shutting sounds out, and in controlling the nerves in regard to sounds which refuse to vanish. Why, then, should not a more regulated and conscious mastery of ear be acquired?

Perhaps your hearing is defective and you are not aware of the fact. Or the defect may be due to a want of acute attention. In order to ascertain the real difficulty, the following exercise is suggested:

Exercise No. 8. When all is quiet, hold a watch at arm's length from the right ear. Do you hear it ticking? No? Move the watch gradually nearer the ear until you hear. Note the distance at which the ticking first becomes audible. Write the result and mark,

"Ear No. 8," and date. Repeat this exercise ten times on its first day. Repeat these exercises every day for ten days, with rest, and on the tenth day note improvement.

Meanwhile induce several other persons to practise the same exercise so far as to ascertain the distance at which they can hear the ticking of the same watch.

During the ten days repeat all the exercises with the left ear, correctly marking results.

If you make no improvement in hearing, this may still be due to a constitutional limit. Continue the practice until you are satisfied that your hearing cannot be improved. Then consult a physician.

If you do not hear as well as others, this also may be due to constitutional limit. It will, nevertheless, be wise to consult a physician.

Perhaps certain sounds which you hear incessantly are destroying you with the threat of nervous prostration or insanity. Your dear neighbor's piano played through everlasting hours, or his dog barking all night long, or street hawkers, become evidences of civilization's chaos. Procure the cessation of these sounds, if possible. If not, resolve to shut them out of mind. Hence:

Exercise No. 9. Never fight disagreeable noises by attending to them. Select some particularly hateful sound which comes to you regularly. Make this a practice for the day. Now, by an enormous effort of Will attend so powerfully to some other sound or many sounds as to shut out the one you wish to banish. Continue this effort five minutes. Do not become discouraged. You can do this act of exclusion if you will do it. After five minutes, rest, by turning the

"A Harp of 8,700 Strings" 147

attention away from sounds in general. Then repeat the exercise by shutting out the sound ten minutes. Give the matter a half-hour, increasing the time of exclusion of sound with each exercise a few minutes, and resting between efforts by diverting attention to other things.

Vary the effort to exclude sound by attending with great energy to some agreeable thought.

Do not will directly to shut a sound out of the ear. Will to become directly absorbed in other sounds or in other matters of thought. Repeat these exercises until you are master.

Exercise No. 10. At night, when you are disturbed by hideous noises, stop thinking about them.

Insist that you do not care, anyway.

Think of a particularly pleasant tune; or thought; or experience. Do not work: take the matter easily.

Call up, mentally, a sound which is totally different from the one that disturbs you. Cause it to run in the mind, taking care that it has a certain regularity and rhythm. Imagine the loud ticking of a large clock, or the droning of an old-fashioned water-wheel, or the steady booming of the sea.

Remember, that all thought about the hateful sound only intensifies its power over you. To rage at a barking dog signifies one of two consequences: the death of the dog (possibly of its owner), or more nervousness on the part of the man who has no Will. Similarly with other disturbing noises. The Will that masters them is a growing Will. The growing Will comes of intelligent exercise, with the Will-idea always present, "I RESOLVE TO WILL! ATTENTION!!"

Exercises for the Ear

Everybody knows how acute the hearing of the blind becomes, probably as Dr. M. P. Hatfield has observed, "not because they have any better hearing than the rest of us, but because their misfortune makes them continually cultivate their hearing, for like all of our faculties it is susceptible of very great improvement under cultivation."

The power of the soul to become so absorbed in itself as to lose consciousness of all around it, is illustrated by an incident in the life of Thomas Aquinas. "Upon one of the many occasions when he sat at the table of the king, by invitation, he forgot everything going on about him, sunk in reflection upon some difficult question in theology, with which he had been engrossed; suddenly he cried out, striking the table with his fist 'I have got it.'" He had heard and observed nothing but the important thing in hand.

So, also, the soul may become so habituated to the routine of duty that accustomed calls to duty are recognized while all other appeals are made in vain. Thus a telegraphic operator, overpowered by sleep, could not be awakened by any ordinary knocking at his door, but when his station, "Springfield," was rapped out he immediately aroused. A fire-department chief was said when asleep to be deaf to his baby's cry, while instantly alert to the alarm of his gong. Sleeping sentinels sometimes walk their beats, soldiers march when buried in slumber, and riders guide their horses though the body rests. These and similar incidents reveal the Will still dominant. If so, the ear and all senses may be brought under its perfect control.

Remember: *The value of any sense depends upon the amount and quality of soul thrown into its exercise.*

"Not only awaking from sleep do we immediately recognize what the objects around us are, because, in fact, we have the memories or images of them already in our minds," says Edward Carpenter in "The Art of Creation"; but the simplest observation of things involves a similar antecedent condition — *the knowing what to look for*. How hard to 'find the cat' in the picture, or the wood-cock in the autumn leaves, till the precise image of what one wants to see is already in the mind, and then, how easy! The townsman walking along the high-road perceives not the hare that is quietly watching him from the farther field. Even when the countryman points it out with all circumstance, he fails; because the kind of thing he is to see is not already in his mind. Why is it so difficult to point the constellations to one who has never considered them before? The sky is simply a mass of stars; it is the mind that breaks it into forms. Or why, looking down from a cliff upon the sea, do we isolate a wave and call it *one?* It is not isolated; no mortal could tell where it begins or leaves off; it is just a part of the sea. It is not one; it is millions and millions of drops; and even these millions are from moment to moment changing, moving. Why do we isolate it and call it one? There is some *way of looking at things,* some preconception already at work, in all cases, which determines, or helps to determine, what we see, and how we see it. All nature thus is broken and sorted by the mind; and as far as we can see this is true of the simplest act of discrimination or sensation — the knower selects, supplies, ignores, compares, contributes something without which the discrimination or sensation would not be."

Since this statement is law, your sound-world—

that which you construct by your choices and thought-feeling — depends upon yourself. And the deeper and richer is your consciousness *in a state of harmony*, the larger and richer will be your life in all the products of sensation. This means that you should cultivate the mental life in as great and harmonious a variety as possible, and that the senses should be so trained that through them you may get the most out of living and put the most of self into life and Nature. If you will carry the assertion and the feeling: *I am now conscious of myself in relation to the world — now of sounds, now of vision, etc. — I am attending to these worlds* (one or another), *putting myself into them, drawing from them constant values,* you will find your life-consciousness, your world-consciousness, your soul-consciousness, growing broader, deeper, more satisfying and more potent for your own good from month to month and year to year.

AWAKENING OF THE WILL

There is a practice which can well be introduced here, though it is not alone confined to interpretation of sounds. It is Leland's method as follows: "Resolve before going to sleep that if there be anything whatever for you to do which requires Will or Resolution, be it to undertake repulsive or hard work or duty, to face a disagreeable person, to fast, or make a speech, to say "No" to anything; in short, to keep up to the mark or make *any* kind of effort that *you* WILL *do it* — as calmly and unthinkingly as may be. Do not desire to do it sternly or forcibly, or in spite of obstacles — but simply and coolly make up your mind to *do it* — and it will more likely be done. And it is absolutely true that if persevered in, this willing yourself to will by easy impulse unto impulse given, will lead to marvelous and most satisfactory results."

The application of this in the art of sense culture is this: frequently, before going to sleep, impress upon the subconscious mind that you want more values and richer mind-life from the impressions coming in from the outside world. Confidently expect that your sense of hearing, of tasting, of touching, of sight, etc., are to store broader knowledge, experience and thought material in your mind. Demand of your servants — the senses — that they shall unite to the limit of their ability in giving to you, their master, the values which they create.

TASTE

I pluck an apple from its tree
  And taste its perfect meat;
Lo, in the act, Reality
Crosses the gulf of mystery
  My self to greet.

The budding nerves upon the tongue
  Link brain with realms unseen:
Mind leaps the void around it flung
And stands a king all kings among,
  Equal, serene.

The fruit of life is self matured;
  The world is but my thought;
And self comes great as self is lured
From self in lower self immured:
  All's mine as sought.

— The Author.

CHAPTER XI

Exercises in Taste

THE German Physiologist, Valentin, could detect bitter at 100,000th of a solution of quinine.

" Taste can be educated, as the nice discriminations of the professional tea-tasters show. In subconscious conditions it is also abnormally acute."—*Text Book.*

Theory of this Chapter

A discriminating mind in taste;
A cultivated mind in taste;
Willed attention habituating the Mood of Will.

Preliminary

" The ordinary individual," remarks Mary Whiton Calkins in " An Introduction to Psychology," " asked to name what he had tasted at dinner, might respond with some such list as the following: beef-bouillon, roast duck, potato, onion, dressed celery, peach ice and coffee. But the psychologist would conclude at once that some of the tastes enumerated were complex experiences, made up of simpler elements. He would take means to isolate, so far as he could, the conditions of tastes, so that other sense-elements should be shut out from consciousness. He would select, as subject of the experiments, a person without smell-sensations, or else he would close the subject's nostrils, so as to eliminate most of these smell-sensations; and he would certainly blindfold the subject, to prevent his seeing the articles which he tasted. These substances would be presented to him at an even temperature, and the solids would be finely minced so as to be indistinguishable in form. Judging by the results of actual experiments, the results of such a test as applied to our suggested *ménu,* would be the following: the blindfolded and anosmic (without smell-sensations) subject would as likely as not suppose that he had tasted chicken broth, beef, potato, an unknown sweetish substance, another unknown material mixed with a thick tasteless oil, a sweet unflavored substance and a slightly bitter liquid — perhaps a dilute solution of quinine. A normal person, also blindfolded, but without closed nostrils, would recognize the onion, the peach, the coffee and often the olive oil; but would be as likely to confuse the beef and the duck; whereas, if these were unsalted, the anosmic subject would fail to recognize them even as meats.

"What we know of the different tastes are complex experiences, made up of odors, motor experiences, pressure and pain sensations, visual elements and a far more limited number of taste-elements than we ordinarily suppose. The odor is the significant element in such 'tastes' as egg, milk, fruit, wine, onion, chocolate, coffee and tea. Tea and coffee are, indeed, undistinguished from quinine, when the odor elements are excluded, and are differentiated from each other only by the slight astringency of the tea, that is by the peculiar pressure-experience, the 'puckering,' which it excites.

"The number of tastes seems to be four: sweet, salt, sour and bitter. But of the physical stimuli of taste-sensations we know even less than of the indefinitely localized physiological organ. Chemically distinct substances may even arouse the same sensational quality, for example, both sugar and acetate of lead give a 'sweet' taste. Only one general statement may be hazarded: the taste-stimulus is always in liquid form. If the tip of the tongue be carefully dried, a crystal of sugar placed upon it will seem tasteless, until the tongue again becomes moist enough to dissolve it."

The experiments and investigations which have given us the meagre knowledge we have on the subject of taste-sensations and their brain-area (little known), have all involved attention, discrimination, judgment, and so on. The object of the exercises in the present chapter has exactly similar ends in view — but above all, such work under direction as may make you the better acquainted with yourself and give to you a greater scope of consciousness and self-control.

The tongue tastes; it also feels.

The sensation of touch is often confounded with that of taste. During a heavy cold in one's head the tongue feels much, but tastes little. Aërated water gives the tongue a lively sensation of touch or feeling. Alum "draws" it. Pepper irritates it to burning. Some strong sweets are slippery. Some strong bitters are smooth. Cold food is lacking in the taste of warmer. The sensation produced by very cold water is largely that of feeling. Luke-warm coffee is not enjoyable because the aroma of its steam and the cold of ice are absent. The facts suggest some experiments.

Remember that the greatest mind is one which has, through the five senses, grasped the most of the outside world.

RÉGIMES

Exercise No. 1. Procure a piece of alum. Merely touch it with the tongue. Now try to perceive its taste in distinction from its feeling. Repeat this exercise with other " puckery " substances. Repeat these experiments every day for ten days, with rest of two days, and on the tenth day observe improvement.

Exercise No. 2. Close the nostrils between the thumb and forefinger, and, touching the tongue with some " puckery " substance, try to perceive the taste. Is the idea of taste real or imaginary? Repeat with various similar articles. Repeat these exercises every day for ten days, with rest of two days, and on the tenth day note improvement.

Exercise No. 3. Place a little pepper on the tongue. Try to distinguish the taste from the irritation. Is there any difference? Repeat with other substances which " burn " the tongue. Repeat these exercises every day for ten days, with rest of two days, and on the tenth day note improvement.

Exercise No. 4. With white sugar or syrup placed on the tongue, try to distinguish whether the slippery feeling or the sweet taste is first perceived. Repeat these exercises every day for ten days, with rest, and on the tenth day note improvement.

Exercise No. 5. Sweeten equally two glasses of water. Let a friend, while you are not observing, place in one glass a minute quantity of quinine or other bitter substance. Now taste and note which glass contains the drug by observing the greater sweetness of the water in which it has been placed. The quantity of "bitter" may be increased until additional sweetness can be perceived. If the water begins to taste bitter before increased sweetness is perceived, the experiment has failed. But do not be discouraged. Repeat until success is reached. Repeat these exercises every day for ten days, with rest, and on the tenth day note improvement.

Exercise No. 6. Try to recall, with great vividness — with the vividness of reality — from memory, the taste of various articles — sugar, lemon, quinine, onions, cheese, etc. Note whether one taste is recalled more vividly than another. Is such recalled taste always associated with a mental picture of its object, or is it abstract? Does the memory seem to be located in the brain or on the tongue? Whether in the brain or on the tongue, is it associated with some past experience? Now think of the tongue, and try to place the remembered sensation, abstracted from all past experience, there alone. That is difficult, but it can be done. Repeat these exercises every day for ten days, with rest, and on the tenth day note improvement.

Exercise No. 7. Procure six articles that are fragrant and six articles that have a pleasant taste. Arrange in pairs — one article of smell with one of taste, and so on until all are thus paired. Take one pair, and compare the sensation of smell with that of taste. Note similarity and difference between the sensations. Repeat with each pair. Repeat these experiments with articles that are odoriferous but not fragrant, and articles that have not an agreeable taste.

Now note whether, in all tests with pairs of articles, the effect upon the "mind" is greater when the sensation is that of smelling than when it is that of tasting. Then note whether the difference or similarity of sensation is greater in the case of the first six articles (fragrant and pleasant) or in the case of the second six articles (odoriferous and unpleasant). What is the reason for the facts? Repeat these exercises every day for ten days, with rest, and on the tenth day note improvement.

Why is a meal of the same kind which is eaten in solitude with the same degree of hunger vastly less agreeable in itself than when eaten among pleasant companions? If this is not true, you evidently need lessons in sociability. With most people it is true. Eye, nose, tongue have changed not. Yet the meal looks better, smells better, tastes better. Is this due to imagination? Is there not, rather, a mutuality of ministration among the senses which requires the inspiration of friends to bring it fully out? A good eye, a good nose and a good tongue make a trinity of dining felicity. Add, then, a good heart and a pleasantly active soul, and the function of Will-power in the realm of vision, hearing and taste is discovered.

Exercise No. 8. While dining with friends, make the exercises of this chapter the subject of conversation and experiment so far as consistent with the business in hand, namely, dining in the most agreeable manner.

Exercise No. 9. It is a human privilege to put the soul into bodily sensations, or to withdraw it therefrom. In the one case the word is *attention,* in the other case it is *abstraction*. The following exercise deals with abstraction.

Secure the sensation of any taste or any smell. Now resolutely try to recall from memory some other different sensation so vividly as to banish the first from mind. For example: smell of a rose, and then think strongly of the odor of onions. You must entirely forget the flower while thinking of the vegetable. Or, taste a little sugar, and then put the sensation out of mind by recalling the memory of wormwood. Or the senses may, as it were, be crossed. Smell of a pink and banish the sensation by strong thought of the taste of pepper. Or taste alum and think about the smell of ammonia so keenly as to banish the first sensation. Repeat these exercises every day for ten days, with rest, and on the tenth day note improvement.

After all, *abstraction* is only another name for *attention* — withdrawn from one quarter by being massed upon another. Whoever *attends* intelligently and masterfully to eye, nose, tongue, has either new worlds of pleasure or new guards against displeasure. Above all, has this person Will. Attention cultivated involves Will always present.

THE FRAGRANCE

Across the fields of time and space
  Old flowery perfumes drift and beat
Upon my spirit's eager face
With waves of subtle, sensuous grace,
  Heavily sweet.

A farmhouse dooryard all aglow
  In colors loved by simple eyes,
Restores dear memory's passing show,
Which life a-now can never know,
  Of fields and skies.

So near to sense is life divine,
  So quick the soul to pierce the veil:
A lilac's fragrance is like wine,
And, as I quaff, the joys are mine
  Of youth's lost trail.

The Nature-World, a mighty rose
  Borne on the tree of Chaos vast,
Into my soul its nerve-life throws,
Till I am all that round me grows —
  Made one at last.
                              —The Author.

CHAPTER XII

Exercises in Smell

"It is stated in Mr. Stewart's account of James Mitchell, who was deaf, sightless and speechless, and, of course, strongly induced by his unfortunate situation to make much use of the sense we are considering, that his smell would immediately and invariably inform him of the presence of a stranger, and direct to the place where he might be; and it is repeatedly asserted that this sense had become in him extremely acute.—'It is related,' says Dr. Abercrombie, ' of the late Dr. Moyse, the well-known blind philosopher, that he could distinguish a black dress on his friends by its smell.'"—*Professor Thomas C. Upham.*

Theory of this Chapter

Keenness of attention through discrimination in the sense of smell;
Persistently willed attention a feeder of Will;
A neglected sense cultivated and fullness and power of mind increased.

"In all ages of the world," Dr. William Matthews has said, "a liberal allowance of proboscis has been admired, while a niggardly one has been held in contempt. The Romans liked a large nose, like Julius Cæsar's; and it is a significant fact that the same word in Latin, *Nasutus,* means *having a large nose,* and *acute* or *sagacious.* All their distinguished men had snuff-taking organs not to be sneezed at." " In modern days, large noses have been not less coveted and esteemed than in the ancient. 'Give me,' said Napoleon, 'a man with a large allowance of nose. In my observations of men I have almost invariably found a long nose and a long head go together.'"

PRELIMINARY

"The faculty of scent may be cultivated like all other faculties, as is proven by blood-hounds and breeds of dogs which have been specially trained in this direction until it becomes an hereditary faculty. Those who deal in teas, coffees, perfumes, wine and butter, often cultivate their powers to a wonderful degree in their especial lines, but with the majority of people it is the least cultivated of the senses, although Dr. O. W. Holmes thinks it the one which most powerfully appeals to memory."

The sense of smell, it would seem, then, has been greatly neglected, as is seen in the fact that the names of odors are almost entirely artificial or derived from association. That it may be trained may be proved by any druggist or manufacturer of perfumes. The druggist does not recognize the "smell" of his own shop, but he perceives by the nose when he enters that of another. Always must he discriminate among odors in his business. The perfumist lives on the acuteness of his olfactory nerves. The glue-maker and soap-refiner exist in spite of their pursuits.

"We have little scientific knowledge of odors," says Calkins. "Even our names for them are borrowed, usually from the objects to which we chance to refer them, and occasionally even from their affective accompaniments. Thus we know some odors only vaguely as good or bad, that is, pleasant or unpleasant, and at the best we can say nothing more definite than 'heliotrope fragrance' or 'kerosene odor.' This chaotic state of affairs is largely due to the limited significance of odors in our intellectual and our artistic life.

"Many smells are, of course, like tastes, obviously complex experiences containing elements of taste, touch and vision, as well as of smell. The pungency of such smells as that of ammonia is thus a touch quality; and such experiences as smelling sour milk are perhaps due to the entrance of particles through the nose into the throat.

"The most satisfactory classification of smells, as we meet them in nature, is that adapted by the Dutch physiologist, Zwaardemaker, from the classification of Linnæus. It recognizes the following classes:

"Ethereal smells, including all fruit odors.

"Aromatic smells, for example, those of camphor, spices, lemon, rose.

"Fragrant smells, for example, those of flowers.

"Ambrosiac smells, for example, all musk odors.

"Alliaceous smells, for example, those of garlic, assafœtida, fish.

"Empyreumatic smells, for example, those of tobacco and toast.

"Hircine smells, for example, those of cheese and rancid fat.

"Virulent smells, for example, that of opium.

"Nauseating smells, for example, that of decaying animal matter.

"We have sensational experiences, known as smells

or odors, distinguished from each other, but not designated by special names; they are probably analyzable into a few distinct elements, but this analysis has never been satisfactorily made; and they are often compounded, and sometimes confused with tastes and touches.

"The structure of the physiological end-organs of smell is not very clearly made out. Two phenomena indicate, however, that these organs are so distinct that they correspond both with different physical stimuli and with different smell-experiences. One of these phenomena is that of exhaustion. Experimental investigations show, for example, that a subject 'whose organ is fatigued by the continuous smelling of tincture of iodine can sense ethereal oils almost or quite as well as ever, oils of lemon, turpentine and cloves but faintly, and common alcohol not at all.' Evidently, therefore, different parts of the end-organs are affected by these distinct smell-stimuli, else the nostrils would be exhausted for all smells at the same time.

"We know little of the physical conditions of smell. Two statements only can be made with any degree of assurance. It is highly probable, in the first place, that the smell-stimulus is always gaseous, not liquid; and it is almost certain that the property of stimulating the end-organs of smell is a function of the physical molecule, not of the atom, since most of the chemical elements are odorless. Summing up both physiological and physical conditions, we may say, therefore, that certain gaseous particles are carried by inspiration into the nostrils, where they stimulate cells found in the mucous membrane, and that these nerve-impulses are conveyed by the olfactory nerves to the temporal lobes of the brain."

An Odor or a Perfume — Which? 165

The action of the olfactory nerves may be controlled by thought — that is by power of Will. Arranging paper tubes in such a way as to convey separate perfumes to each nostril, as suggested by Professor Scripture, "we can smell either one in preference to the other by simply thinking about it." An experiment may be made of this fact.

Régimes

Exercise No. 1. Take some fragrant flower. Inhale its odor. Walk about the room, away from the flower. Now recall the quality and intensity of the smell. Repeat this exercise with various extracts and perfumes taken separately. Care must be had to give the nostrils sufficient rest between whiles, otherwise the sense of smell will become confused.

Repeat these exercises every day for at least ten days, with rest of two days. It will be better to go on until improvement is certainly noted in keenness of scent and mental power to describe smells or odors. On the tenth day note improvement.

During all the above and following practice the feeling of strong Will must be kept constantly at the fore. *Put your soul into your nose.*

Exercise No. 2. Procure two different kinds of extracts. Inhale the odor of one. Do the same with the other. Think strongly of the first odor; then of the second. Now try to compare them, noting the difference. Repeat this exercise every day for ten days, and on the tenth day note improvement.

Exercise No. 3. While sitting erect, gently inhale the air, and try to name any odor perceived. Is it real? Where does it originate? Let friends secrete some odoriferous substance in a room — a number of pinks or an open bottle of perfumery, not known to you, and while you are in another room. Enter and endeavor by smell alone to find the article. All other pronounced odors must be excluded from the place. Repeat these exercises every day for ten days, and on the tenth day note improvement.

Exercise No. 4. Ask some friend to hold in the hand an object which is not known to you and is fragrant or odoriferous. He is to hold the article some distance from you, and then gradually to move it, held unseen in his two hands placed together, nearer and nearer, until you perceive the odor. Note the distance at which you perceive the object by smell. Can you name the smell? Can you name the object? Repeat the experiment with intervals of rest, with various different " smellable " articles.

Do you perceive some at a less distance than others? Why is this? Is it due to strength of odor or the quality? Repeat the exercise every day for ten days with rest of two days, and on the tenth day note improvement.

Humboldt declared that Peruvian Indians can, in the darkest night, determine whether a stranger, while yet far distant, is an Indian, European or Negro. The Arabs of the Sahara can detect by smell the presence of a fire forty miles away.

Exercise No. 5. Each of the five senses has the power of continually new discoveries in the world of reality. Impressions appropriate to each may be related to the huge things of life. High living puts great significance into even the sense of smell. The

An Odor or a Perfume — Which?

present exercise may be made perpetual. Build up in your life the habit of associating the agreeable odors perceived in garden, field or wood, with true and great thoughts. Examples: new-mown hay — Whittier's poem, "Maud Muller"; sea-flats — Sidney Lanier's "Marshes of Glynn"; fresh-turned soil — the teeming life of the world; flowers — beauty regnant in the earth. Such a habit will open new worlds, and it will develop energetic attention, and so tend to build up a strong Will in your life.

This work may be so conducted as to make improvement possible. Its value always depends upon the amount of soul put into it — that is, into the nose. The exercises will cultivate a neglected sense, but more, will develop a power of attention that will surprise you, and through this a power of Will, which is the end sought. The idea of Will must always be present. In every act preserve the willing attitude.

SELF AND WORLDS

If you could touch the outer rim
  Of life's huge wheel of being,
Lo, knowledge still would seem but dim,
  As now, forever fleeing.
And if your thought could penetrate
  Below the last existence,
Still, ignorance would be your fate,—
  In vain all such insistence.

The primrose by the river's brim,
This is the wheel of being's rim;
Love it: all life you penetrate;
Love's boundless knowledge then your fate.

You touch in self the farthest bound
  Of matter and of spirit:
When the last glory here you've found,
  Self only shall insphere it.
For Mind's below the self, you see,
  And Mind's below the flower;
And in Love's touch of harmony
  All knowing finds its power.

Great Nature is the outer rim,
But self the deepest centre dim;
If you will farther penetrate,
Knowledge your goal, but love your fate.
— The Author.

CHAPTER XIII

EXERCISES IN TOUCH

"THE sense of touch is the most positive of all the senses in the character of its sensations. In many respects it is worthy to be called the leading sense."— *Noah Porter.*

"All the senses are modifications of the sense of touch."— *Demosthenes.*

THEORY OF THIS CHAPTER

Mind thrown into or abstracted from physical feeling at Will;

Will-attention making Will-action deliberative and second-nature;

Will prohibitions rendering mind supreme at least cost.

PRELIMINARY

"The sensations of contact and temperature," says Royce, "are due to the excitation of points on the skin which differ for the various special sorts of experiences in question. Experiment shows that certain points of the skin are especially sensitive to stimulations given by cold objects, while other points are sensitive to disturbances due to hot objects. Our ordinary sensory experience of warmth or of cold is due to a complex excitement of many points of both these types. Still other points on the skin very wealthily interspersed among the others, give us, if excited in isolation, sensations of contact or of pressure. Complex sensory excitations, due to the disturbances of the skin, sometimes with and sometimes without, notable accompanying organic disturbances, give us our experiences of hard and soft, of rough and smooth, of dry and moist objects."

There are many very curious facts to be observed in connection with touch. The degree of feeling arising from touch is usually dependent to a great extent upon attention. We do not, for example, ordinarily feel our clothing, but when thought turns to the matter it becomes very apparent. If garments do not fit well, the nerves are likely to take on some habit of twitching or other unnatural movement. Such habits in children are often due to this fact. For the same reason tickling sensations plague sleep away at night. That wise fool who calls himself a "business man" bolts his dinner in eight minutes, and tastes and feels nothing until dyspepsia makes taste and feeling perennial dominators of an unhappy existence. Another fool consumes alcohol in winter for warmth and in summer for coolness; the secret of its "beneficent" ministry is its paralyzing power over physical consciousness. In latter days this man feels heat and cold with the keenness of a skeleton veiled in the rotten gauze of ruined nerves. The orator who is absorbed in his flights regards not the busy fly upon his nose nor the physical pain which was insistent before his soul afire took mastery of sense. The epicure, every sense to the fore, lingers while he dines, and nourishes delighted boon fellowship with kindred spirits. When the orator has it before him to listen to another man's lucubrations, his fly becomes a Dante for torture, and

The Soul's "Open Sesame" is Purpose

his pains possess the power of a Spanish Inquisition. So, too, when Xantippe appears at the philosophers' board, the world must lose in Socratic wisdom.

To attend or not to attend is always with feeling an important question. The end nerves may be brought under large control of the Will. The soldier frequently fails to note that his arm has been shot off in the onslaught of a charge. Your tooth will cease aching if your house is afire or your horse is running away with you. If feeling may be thus dissipated, it may, as well, be called in and controlled by the exercise of Will. Exercises in touch are therefore suggested for development of Will.

RÉGIMES

Exercise No. 1. Pass the ends of each finger of the right hand in turn very lightly over any flat uncovered surface. Try first a surface which is rough; then one which is smooth. Note the difference in "feel" between a rough surface and a smooth. This will require a good deal of attention, for the difference is manifold. Repeat these exercises with several rough and smooth surfaces. Repeat as above with the fingers of the left hand. Note whether the feeling is greater with one hand than with the other. Now repeat the experiments with cloth — of linen, cotton, woolen, silk. The "feel" of each material is peculiar. Compare, by act, the sense of touch as given by one piece of cloth with that given by another. Continue these exercises with several pieces of cloth in pairs. Repeat with one hand, then with the other. What is the main "feel" of silk? Of cotton? Of woolen? Of linen? Have you any sensation other than touch with any of these kinds of cloth? If so, is it disagreeable? Then resolve to handle that variety of cloth until the aversion has been mastered. This can be done, as clerks in great department stores will testify. Repeat all the exercises here given every day for ten days, and on the tenth day note improvement in touch — delicacy, kinds of sensations produced, etc.

Exercise No. 2. Practise touching lightly the surface of an uncovered table, with the separate fingers, one after the other, of each hand. Note the degree of steadiness with which this is done. Now repeat the experiment with strong pressure upon each finger of the hands separately applied. What is the difference in sensation between the light touch and the strong pressure? Repeat the exercise every day for ten days, with rest, and on the tenth day note improvement in discrimination.

Exercise No. 3. Grasp a small object, say, a paperweight or a rubber ball, very lightly, just an instant, dropping it immediately. Then grasp it firmly, and instantly drop. Did you feel the object with each finger in the first instance? In the second? Make no mistake. What, if any, difference in sensation did you observe? This requires that the Will command great attention. Hence it cannot be done carelessly. Repeat every day for ten days, with rest, and on the tenth day note improvement in touch and power of discrimination and attention.

Exercise No. 4. Look at the back of either hand. Now twist the second finger toward you and cross the first finger behind it. While the fingers are so crossed, press the unsharpened end of a lead-pencil between

The Soul's "Open Sesame" is Purpose 173

the finger ends. Look sharp! Do you seem to feel one pencil or two? Shut the eyes and repeat the experiment. Again, is the sensation of one pencil or two? Is the deception stronger with eyes closed or open? When the pressure of the pencil between the crossed fingers is light, or when it is strong? Explain the fact that there are apparently two pencils. Repeat the experiment with three pairs of fingers. Repeat every day for ten days, with rest, and on the tenth day note improvements in the various respects suggested.

The eyes being closed in the first experiment, you will probably thrust the pencil against the side of the third finger, which is now on the outside of the hand. Explain this little mistake.

Exercise No. 5. With eyes closed, place several objects, promiscuously and separated, upon a table. The eyes still being closed, move the right hand lightly over the objects and endeavor to estimate the several distances which separate them. Do not measure by length of hand or finger. Repeat the exercise with the left hand. Keep the question in mind: which hand is more nearly correct in judgment. Repeat every day for ten days, with rest, and on the tenth day note improvement.

Exercise No. 6. While your eyes are closed, ask a friend to present to you, so that you can examine by touch alone, but not by taking in your hand, several small objects, one after another. Now try to determine what the articles are. Examples: small onion, small potato, flower bulb, piece of dry putty, piece of amber, piece of wax; or some sugar, sand, ground pepper, salt, etc. Repeat every day for ten days, with rest, and on the tenth day note improvement.

Exercise No. 7. Procure small blocks of any material — wood, iron — round in shape, and of exactly the same size, but differing slightly in weight. Say two blocks weigh each 1 ounce, two 1½ ounces each, two 2 ounces each, and so on to a dozen, always having two blocks of the same weight. Let the weights be stamped or written on one side of the blocks only.

Place them promiscuously on a table, blank side up. Close the eyes and at random pick up one block and then a second, using the same hand. Determine by "feel" whether the weights so picked up are equal or not. Estimate the weights in each experiment. Repeat with the left hand. Repeat with both hands, used alternately. Repeat the experiment in all cases many times. Continue every day for ten days, with rest, and on the tenth day note improvement in judgment.

Exercise No. 8. Procure twenty-four small wooden models of crystals, cut from blocks about three inches square. Throw them promiscuously all at once upon a table. With eyes closed, take one in the hand and observe the mental picture that arises by the sense of touch. Count the faces, lines, angles. Now open the eyes and note the difference between this mental picture and the reality. This experiment will be difficult because you are not familiar with the forms of crystals, and judgment is left to touch alone. To assist, therefore, look at the crystal models until you are able to shut the eyes and perceive with the eye of the mind the form just examined. Repeat every day for ten

The Soul's "Open Sesame" is Purpose 175

days, with rest, and on the tenth day note improvement in judgment.

Exercise No. 9. When you shake hands with people, note in their grasp any index of their character that may be suggested. Cultivate the gently-firm grasp. Instantly rebuke the bone-crusher; he has a vice which needs destruction. Is the touch of some hands disagreeable to you? Note in what particulars. Be not ruled by that aversion, but seek such hands, and resolve to throw off the feeling. This may be useful to you in the "control of others." The effort to overcome an aversion always develops Will. Determine that nothing which you must touch more or less habitually shall control the sensation which it produces. Let this aversion be a type of all tyrannous aversions. Such an aversion means the inability of a small mind to divert its attention. The really large soul masters irritations and dislikes. But the guide and controller here is Will. Every aversion conquered signifies power of Will increased.

"I RESOLVE TO WILL! ATTENTION!!"

HARMONY

The mighty whirl of suns and stars
  With infinite complexity
  Goes ever on. Inflexibly
Law crushes discord's evil wars.

Inflexibly (no less) law links
  The vaster movements and the small
  Together in harmonic thrall:
Thus evil into welfare shrinks.

Obey! Not as the slave who hates,
  But as the son who loves the sire;
  So shall the Cosmos life inspire
Worthy high toil — and higher fates!
— The Author.

CHAPTER XIV

EXERCISES FOR THE NERVES

"STANDING at the centre of the universe, a thousand forces come rushing in to report themselves to the sensitive soul-centre. There is a nerve in man that runs out to every room and realm in the universe.

"Man's mechanism stands at the centre of the universe with telegraph-lines extending in every direction. It is a marvelous pilgrimage he is making through life while myriad influences stream in upon him.

"Some Faraday shows us that each drop of water is a sheath for electric forces sufficient to charge 800,000 Leyden jars, or drive an engine from Liverpool to London. Some Sir William Thomson tells us how hydrogen gas will chew up a large iron spike as a child's molars will chew off the end of a stick of candy."— *Newell Dwight Hillis.*

THEORY OF THIS CHAPTER

Cessation of unnecessary motion conserves force;
Control of nerves tones up body and mind, and increases the sum total of personal power;
Habituated control of nervous energy exercises and therefore strengthens and regulates the Will.

PRELIMINARY

Sir Michael Foster once said: "When physiology is dealing with those parts of the body which we call muscular, vascular, glandular tissues, and the like, rightly handled, she points out the way, not only to mend that which is hurt, to repair the damages of bad usage and disease, but so to train the growing tissues and to guide the grown ones as that the best use may be made of them for the purposes of life. She not only heals; she governs and educates. Nor does she do otherwise when she comes to deal with the nervous tissues. Nay, it is the very prerogative of these nervous tissues that their life is, above that of all the other tissues, contingent on the environment and susceptibility to education."

We are conscious of sensations apprehended through the various sense-organs. But we are possessed of what is called "general consciousness." One may discover this by sitting a little time in a room that is perfectly still. The general testimony of the nervous system will then be perceived. The movement of the heart may be felt; the breathing may become audible; a murmur may perhaps be noticed in the ears; a general feeling of warmth or coolness will be observable. You are alive! You are aware of yourself in a physical sense. You are conscious in particular spots, to be sure, but in a general way also over almost the entire body. With this "general consciousness" we begin the exercises of the present chapter. They are important. Do not slight them.

Régimes

Exercise No. 1. Attend to this "general consciousness" a few moments. Sit quietly, exclude from the mind all external matters, and take cognizance of the whole body. Put your entire thought upon this one thing; it will be difficult, for you will desire to think

Ethereal Force Awaits Control 179

of a thousand foreign things; but it can be done by persistence and patient willing. Now write out every fact that makes itself known to you by the testimony of the body. Repeat every day for ten days, with rest of two days. On the tenth day compare the records. Observe the sum total of facts made known. Note also any improvement in power of attending to "general consciousness" and reports of facts or sensations.

Exercise No. 2. Sitting quietly in a room which is undisturbed, attend as before a few moments to "general consciousness." Now throw consciousness to some particular part of the body. Let it be the arm from hand to elbow. Put the whole mind there. Exclude all sensations except those that arise there. What are the reports? Write these facts for reference.

Repeat this exercise with the hand. With the shoulder. With the back. With the foot. And so on, with different parts of the body. Always get at the facts testified by consciousness.

Repeat this exercise with the head. Now attend wholly to hearing — not to sounds, but to the sensation of hearing — in the ears. Again, give undivided attention to sight: let the whole mind be at the eyes, not on the objects of vision.

Now press upon some spot in the body, say, the back of a hand, or on one cheek, and, while doing so, locate attention at some other spot so resolutely as to forget the sensation of pressure. Write the results in each case. Repeat every day for ten days with rest. On the tenth day compare the records and note the sum total of facts reported, together with any improvement in number of facts observed and power of attention gained.

Exercise No. 3. Walk about the room slowly and quietly, keeping the mind wholly upon "general consciousness." Now rest a moment. Repeat — always retaining your hold on consciousness, never allowing it to wander — ten times. Make a record of the most prominent facts reported. Repeat every day for ten days, with rest. On the tenth day compare the records and note results as before.

Exercise No. 4. Stand erect in a quiet room, and pass through a regular series of exercises *without weights.*

(*a*) Move the right arm, slowly and evenly, directly up from the shoulder, six times. Keep your mind on the work.

(*b*) From the shoulder, directly out in front, six times.

(*c*) From the shoulder, directly out to the right, six times.

(*d*) With the right hand at arm's length above the shoulder, swing the whole arm in a semi-circle, arm straight, directly down in front, bringing hand to leg, without bending the body, six times.

(*e*) From the original position down to the right side of leg, six times.

(*f*) With the right arm extended at the right side straight out from the shoulder, swing it around in front until the hand is directly before the face, six times.

(*g*) With the right hand and arm, reverse all the above movements.

Ethereal Force Awaits Control

(*h*) Repeat the same movements with the left hand, six times.

(*i*) With the left hand and arm, reverse all the movements.

Remember: these movements must be made deliberately and slowly. Attend to each exercise with the whole mind. Do not permit wandering thoughts. Put the entire thought of yourself into every act. Be wholly conscious of what you are doing. Above all, keep the sense of willing present during each movement. Thrust the Will out into the very muscles.

Repeat every day for ten days, with rest. Or indefinitely.

(1) *Exercise No. 5.* Stand erect in a quiet room. Without supporting yourself with the hands, swing the right foot directly out in front as far as possible while retaining the balance of the body. Return it to the floor in former position. Make these movements deliberately and slowly, six times.

(2) Swing right foot out to right, sidewise. Return to former position, six times.

(3) Swing right foot out in front, around to right, back to position, six times.

(4) Swing right foot back and out and up as far as possible, preserving balance. Return to position, six times.

(5) Swing right foot back as before, around in a semi-circle past right side, back to position, six times.

(6) Reverse each movement with right foot, six times.

(7) Repeat all movements with left foot, six times.

(8) Repeat these exercises every day for ten days, with rest.

The work here suggested must be performed with great vigor, yet slowly and deliberately, with intense thoughtfulness.

(*a*) *Exercise No. 6.* Stand erect in a quiet room. Look straight ahead. Slowly turn the face far around to the right, and return, six times.

(*b*) Look ahead. Turn the face slowly to the left, and return, six times.

(*c*) Bend the head slowly back as far as possible, and return, six times.

(*d*) Bend the head slowly forward and down, as far as possible, and return, six times.

(*e*) Drop the head forward on the chest. Slowly swing it to the right, in a circle up to the right, to the left backward down and back to the left shoulder, to the right in a circle down to former position, six times.

(*f*) Drop the head back between the shoulders. Swing it, to the right up in a circle to the right shoulder, to the left down around in front and up to the left shoulder, to the right down and back to former position, six times.

(*g*) Repeat all exercises every day for ten days, with rest.

(1) *Exercise No. 7.* Stand erect in a quiet room. With the mind upon the act, slowly lift the right shoulder up as far as possible, and return in like manner to natural position, six times.

(2) Repeat with the left shoulder, six times.

Repeat the exercises ten times for ten days, with rest.

(*a*) *Exercise No. 8.* Stand erect in a quiet room. Without moving the feet, twist the body slowly around as far as possible, to the right, then to the left. Practice six times.

(*b*) Stand erect, hands hanging prone at the sides. Bend the body at the hips; straightforward and down in front; to the right; to the left. Practice six times.

(*c*) Repeat the exercises every day for ten days, with rest, as above.

These exercises are designed to be suggestive. They can be varied. Nevertheless, an order should be determined upon and rigidly followed. Perform all acts slowly, deliberately, with the mind intently fixed upon the movement. Keep the Will-idea present. Throw this thought into the limbs and muscles: " I RESOLVE TO WILL! ATTENTION!!"

(1) *Exercise No. 9.* Stand erect. Concentrate thought upon self. Now let the mind affirm, quietly, resolutely, without wandering: "I am receiving helpful forces! I am open to all good influences! Streams of power for body and mind are flowing in! All is well!!" Repeat these and similar assertions calmly yet forcibly many times. Do not be passive. Keep the sense of willing strongly at the fore. Will to be in the best possible moral condition. Rise to the mood of the three-fold health: — of body, of mind, of soul.

(2) Continue this exercise fifteen minutes, with brief intervals of rest, at least every morning of your life.

(3) Whenever worried or perplexed or weary, go into this assertive mood and welcome the forces of the

good. These directions if followed will prove of priceless value to you.

(*a*) *Exercise No. 10.* Stand erect. Summons a sense of resolution. Throw Will into the act of standing. Absorbed in self, think calmly but with power these words: "I am standing erect. All is well! I am conscious of nothing but good!" Attaining the Mood indicated, walk slowly and deliberately about the room. Do not strut. Be natural, yet encourage a sense of forcefulness. Rest in a chair. Repeat, with rests, fifteen minutes.

(*b*) Repeat every day indefinitely.

(1) *Exercise No. 11.* Stand erect. In the same Mood of Will, advance slowly to a table and take a book in the hand, or move a chair, or go to the window and look out. Every act must be a willed act, and full of Will.

(2) Repeat fifteen minutes with at least six different objects.

(3) Continue the exercises indefinitely.

(*a*) *Exercise No. 12.* After a moment's rest, deliberately walk to a chair and be seated. Force Will into the act. Do not lop down. Do not seat yourself awkwardly. Do not sit stiffly, but easily, yet erect. Now, with the whole mind on the act of getting up, slowly rise. Try to be graceful, try to be natural, for Will may add grace to nature. Cultivate the erect posture, whether sitting, standing or walking. Cultivate the vital sense in all movements. By the vital sense is meant the feeling, "I am alive! Splendidly alive!" If you are thin-blooded, dyspeptic and nervous, this may at first be difficult, but it will help you greatly.

(*b*) Repeat fifteen minutes.

(*c*) Continue indefinitely.

Exercise No. 13. The nervous system is very apt to become a tyrant. When it is shattered, or overtaxed, rest and a physician are imperative demands. But many people who regard themselves as well are subject to its tyranny. This may be due in part to a want of self-control. The following directions may appear to be absurd; nevertheless, they suggest a way out of some nervous difficulties:

Sometimes, when you are restive, you experience, on retiring, "creeping" sensations in the hair of your head; the back of your neck "tickles;" a needle is suddenly thrust into your arm, or a feather seems to be roaming here and there over your physiology. Distracted and robbed of sleep, one spot is slapped, another is pinched, another rubbed, while slumber merely "hangs around." How long is this torture to continue? So long as, and no longer than, you permit. Why should one be thus pestered? One needs not to be. It is simply a matter of Will and persistence. If you have practised the suggestions relating to attention and abstraction, you have already acquired power over your nerves by the dominance of mind. In regard to all such matters, therefore, cultivate the ability *to turn the mind elsewhere.* So long as one slaps and rubs and pinches, so long will sensations diabolic continue. Cultivate indifference to the fly by ignoring it. Do not think about it at all. Put the mind upon some important and absorbing subject of interest. Will that a particular "tickle" shall appear at some other place, making choice of the exact spot; it will obey, and meanwhile you will forget it. If it does not, will it from one place to another, and finally will that it shall vanish; it will certainly obey in the end. Similarly with regard to any other distracting "feeling."

As a matter of fact everyone exerts such self-control in a thousand instances daily. The clock's ticking is unnoticed; the railway train is not heard; the huckster's voice is not perceived; cattle low, and birds sing, and children shout, and a city roars, while the mind continues unmindful. Busy men who are surrounded by dense populations, and residents of Niagara, hear neither the "indistinguishable babble" of life nor the thunder of Nature. Shakespeare has said:

> "The crow doth sing as sweetly as the lark
> When neither is attended; and, I think,
> The nightingale, if she should sing by day,
> When every goose is cackling, would be thought
> No better a musician than the wren."

The accustomed ear is deaf to the world. But the Will hides behind the tympanum to make custom its beneficent muffler.

You should bear in mind that there is deep design in back of these exercises and tests offered for your use. You are pursuing this study for the sole reason that you wish increased power of Will. And precisely this will you secure if you earnestly follow the instructions given.

"There is one consolation, too, in the carrying out of these tasks. Not a jot or tittle of the effort expended will be lost or wasted. All is deposited in a very safe bank. What Professor Sedgwick has said of mind-culture is equally true of will-culture: 'It is impossible to estimate the ultimate good to be derived in indirect ways from any bit of mental cultivation one manages to give oneself.' Not only is nothing lost, but a profit which bears an analogy to compound interest, is derived. The will is not only laying by a supply of will-power, but by its various exercises it is increasing its own efficiency in winning will-power. The progression is geometrical. *It adds to itself its own newly-acquired will-power, and thus strengthened, it gains more and more."*

"I RESOLVE TO WILL! ATTENTION!!"

THE HAND

Wisdom designed it,
Struggle divined it,
Ages refined it.

Low life refused it,
Brute life abused it,
Spirit life used it.

Reason restrained it,
Discipline trained it,
Art, the king, gained it.

Put, then, thy Will in it,
Show the mind's skill in it,
Selfhood fulfil in it.

— The Author.

CHAPTER XV

EXERCISES FOR THE HANDS

"I AM, and have been, any time these thirty years, a man who works with his hands — a handicraftsman. If the most nimble-fingered watch-maker among you will come to my workshop, he may set me to put a watch together, and I will set him to dissect, say, a blackbeetle's nerves. I do not wish to vaunt, but I am inclined to think that I shall manage my job to his satisfaction sooner than he will do his piece of work to mine."— *Thos. H. Huxley.*

THEORY OF THIS CHAPTER

The hand, mind's executive organ;
The consequent need of a perfect executor;
Culture of mind through mastery of hands;
Enormous reaction upon Will-power of culture of mind resolutely determined in manual training.

The hands are said to indicate, in a general way, the nature of their owner. The so-called "science of palmistry" is based on the inner lines of the hand, and the delicate curving lines of the finger-ends are now observed in prison studies for the identification of criminals. Yet few people know their own hands. This is because few people really understand the one condition of all knowledge, *attention*.

Nevertheless, the hand is one of the most perfect

and obedient of servants. Industry, invention, science, art, reveal the range of its nobility, according to the soul behind it. To the ditch-digger it may be a claw only; to the painter and sculptor an instrument of creative power. A catapult or a wound-dresser, a sword-wielder or a swayer of the pen, a food producer or a mind-revealer, a tool or an instrument of the noblest humanity, the hand is servant and king among the senses, an index of spirit-values, a prophet of all the future.

PRELIMINARY

The hand is the executive organ of the body.

As the body is the instrument of mind, the hand, therefore, becomes mind's chief officer in life.

The savage wills to procure flesh for food: the outcome is the spear, the bow and arrow, the hook and net.

The hunter wills a permanent shelter: the outcome is the hammer, the axe, the saw, the trowel, nails and various building materials.

The house-dweller wills agriculture: the outcome is the spade, the pickaxe, the shovel, the hoe, the plow, the rake, the sickle, scythe, cradle, mower, reaper, thresher, mill.

The farmer wills education: the outcome is pen, ink and paper, the printing-press, the laboratory, the microscope and telescope, the library, the school and college.

The educated soul wills art: the outcome is the chisel and mallet, the brush and pallet, the canvas and the museum.

The artistic mind wills music: the outcome is the reed, string, horn — orchestral talent.

The King Must Also Serve

These all will government: the outcome is the throne and sceptre, the constitution, the court and council-rooms, the sword, gun, treaty.

Man wills religion: the outcome is the altar, the Book, the Church, the Rubric; the Concrete Philanthropy of Soul.

Every single step in this long journey, the hand has been omnipresent as the Executive of the Conquering Will.

Training of the hand always reacts upon the growing mind. It may become a medium by which to culture the soul and develop the Will. Like Will — like hand. But as well, like hand — like Will. Whoever puts his whole hand to the growth of Will-power, has power of will wholly in hand.

Régimes

The following should be practised:

(*a*) *Exercise No. 1.* Examine the hands carefully. Get acquainted with them. Note their peculiarities, so intently and thoughtfully that you can form a mental picture of them with closed eyes.

(*b*) Slowly move the limp fingers of the right hand toward the palm until they touch it, and return in the same manner, six times.

(*c*) Repeat while bringing the thumb in the same manner under to meet the fingers six times.

(*d*) Repeat with stiffened muscles, each exercise above, six times.

(*e*) With hand extended, open, slowly spread fingers and thumb from one another, and return to touch, six times.

(*f*) Repeat all exercises with the left hand, six times.

(*g*) Repeat every day for ten days, with rest of two days.

What is the value of these directions? None at all, unless you *think,* and above everything else, put Will into each movement.

(1) *Exercise No. 2.* Saw off six inches of an old broom-handle. Stand erect. Fill the lungs. With the right hand held straight out in front and at arm's length, grasp the piece of wood, and slowly and gradually grip the same, beginning with light pressure and increasing to the limit of strength. Repeat six times.

(2) Repeat with the arm straight out at the right side, six times.

(3) Repeat with the arm straight up from the right shoulder, six times.

(4) Repeat with the arm prone at the right side, six times.

(5) Repeat with the arm straight back from right side, and held up as far as possible, six times.

(6) Now exercise the left hand in the same manner, following the order above indicated. The exercises may be alternated between the right hand and the left. Example: Entire exercise with right hand; same with left, twelve times. Also, each part of exercise with right and left hands, twelve times.

Remember, the lungs should be inflated during each movement, and a slight rest should be indulged from time to time. Above all, a sense of Will must be kept strongly in mind.

(7) Repeat every day for ten days, with rest of two days.

(*a*) *Exercise No. 3.* Procure a spring-balance weighing scale, registering ten or twelve pounds. Insert the broomhandle in ring. Drive a nail into a table, the length of the balance from the edge, and enough more to permit the thumb of the hand grasping the wood to curve under the table edge and cling. Now throw the balance-hook over the nail, grasp the wood with fingers of right hand, thumb under table edge, and by finger movement only (do not pull with the arm) draw on the balance as hard as possible. The balance-hook must pull on nail far enough from the edge of the table to prevent the fingers while drawing as suggested from quite touching the palm of the hand.

(b) Repeat, with intervals of rest, six times.

(c) Make a dated record of pull indicated in pounds and fractions, mark right hand, and preserve.

(d) Repeat with the left hand, six times.

(e) Continue every day for ten days, with rest.

On the tenth day, compare records and note progress.

In this work, never fail an instant to put Will into each movement.

In particular, note, from time to time, whether or not you can increase pulling power of fingers by sheer exercise of Will. Observe which hand registers greater improvement in given time.

(1) *Exercise No. 4.* Rest two days from the tenth day. Repeat the above exercises with right and left hands alternately, six times in all, while some one is playing upon any good instrument a strong and rapid musical composition. Make record as before.

(2) Continue for ten days, with rest. Summons constantly a feeling of the greatest resolution possible, during all movements.

On the tenth day, compare records and note improvement in each hand. Observe which hand has now made the greatest improvement.

Observe especially whether music has seemed to increase Will-power. Explain that fact.

(*a*) *Exercise No. 5.* Imagine that you hold a revolver in the right hand. Now think of pulling the trigger. Throw a sense of great energy into the finger, but do not move it. Now hold the breath and repeat the imaginary act. Do you feel energy in the finger as before? Resolve to do so. Will mightily to that end.

(*b*) Repeat with all fingers in turn. Right hand. Left hand. Six times.

(*c*) Repeat for ten days. Observe final improvement.

Exercise No. 6. Set the hands to the learning of some useful mechanical trade — the skillful use of various tools, as carving, engraving, cabinet making. If already so employed, take up some musical instrument, or drawing, or painting. Resolve to master one thing! Persist until the goal is yours.

Exercise No. 7. Strive to cultivate and maintain a feeling of nice and confident skill while engaged in any manual work, as advised in "*Business Power*" under the caption, "Skilled Craftsmanship." "The idea is a sense in consciousness of *nicety, delicacy, perfection,* in every member of the body, used at any time. This gives harmony between the conscious and the deeper or subconscious self — a harmony always needful to the best work. One man is the 'bull in

The King Must Also Serve

the china closet;' another is deftness itself. As a matter of fact, the most skillful persons possess this consciousness without being particularly aware of it."

Exercise No. 8. "The best results demand a man's best conscious powers on the matter in hand. You are urged to multiply yourself into what you do. But in doing a thing skillfully, having the skilled *feeling* developed, you really depend on the acquired habits and ability which previous thought has 'bedded down' in the deeper self. You should, therefore, remember that the trained deeper self may be trusted. Oftentimes, when your ordinary thinking becomes over-anxious or 'flurried,' you confuse your own skill. Some things which we do perfectly without conscious effort, we immediately 'muss up' if we try carefully to attend to all details. Do not permit the hurried feeling to take possession of your nerves. When such feeling does occur, quiet yourself by an act of Will; turn, if necessary, to other work for a time, and thus prevent the habit of unsteadiness of spirit and body, so obviating 'hair-trigger' conditions and a thousand blunders."

Exercise No. 9. Above all, never permit yourself to be pushed in your work beyond a pace consistent with the best results. Remember, when the mind is steady the hand is almost sure to follow that condition.

These exercises may be continued with profit, provided the idea of Will is everlastingly borne in mind.

BUBBLES

Bubbles, filmy, evanescent,
Never a moment quite quiescent
Save when day's ethereal breath
Darks their rainbow hues in death.

Bubbles, surface ebulitions,
Born of alien attritions;
Rocks at bed and shores at side,
Jealous of the far-off tide.

Soul, thy many souls elusive
Sphere the outer life obtrusive:
Films diaphanous emerge
Where frets hinder, small things urge.

Seek the large life quintessential,
Holding self all reverential!
Seek thy sea, majestic, vast,
Where the steady stars are glassed.

Sea? Thou art the sea, ne'er river,
Power within is thy life's giver;
Peace be thine on stormless deeps!
Peace whose power thy selfhood keeps.
— THE AUTHOR.

CHAPTER XVI

EXERCISES IN STEADINESS

"THE most interesting fact about these experiments in steadiness is that the *Will* is to have a steady position, but the *execution* is defective. As the Will is exerted the steadiness of position is increased. This is sometimes so marked as to be visible to the eye directly. I have seen the scalpel tremble in a surgeon's hand so that a serious accident appeared inevitable; yet when the supreme moment came the hand guided the knife with admirable steadiness."—*Prof. E. W. Scripture.*

THEORY OF THIS CHAPTER

Physical quietness conducive to self-control;
Self-control the generator of energy;
Regulation of energy a dynamo of Will.

The importance of steady nerves is everywhere apparent. The unsteady duelist is doomed. The nervous surgeon acquires small practice. The trembling pen writes a crabbed "hand." The agitated speaker loses his audience. Great undertakings frequently require perfect mastery of the body — in games, in business, in national affairs. The ninth inning of an even game of ball will largely depend upon Will and self-control. When the engineer of a fast mail train cannot "hold himself up" to a mile a minute, he must give way to a better man. Diplomacy, in trade, politics and international councils, demands the impassive face. The movement of an eyelash often involves the destinies of life and of war.

Under fierce provocation men sometimes find the nerves giving way to pressure of anger or fear; the soul then commands itself: "Steady, now! Steady!" Body responds to conditions of mind. If mind is a-tremble, nerves reveal the fact. The panic of fear sets the nervous system on the edge of collapse, resulting, unless mastered, in the stampede of a western ranch or the tumultuous rout of a Bull Run battle. The controlling and fearless man is one who is "nerved" to the situation. The value of attention to steadiness is thus indicated. Such value has a physical relation through mind; but it may also affect mind through body.

PRELIMINARY

Of course "trembly" nerves which are the result of disease require medical treatment. But this trembling may frequently be overcome by intelligent practice and determined Will. In the end any such practice must tend to increase the power of Will itself. Dr. Scripture asks:

"Can steadiness be increased by practice? This problem can be answered in respect to the hand." And, after records of experiments, he says:

"The question of the possibility of gaining in steadiness by practice is thus definitely settled."

The chief object of the following suggestions is growth of Will. Hence, Will must always be present in the movements directed. Let the mind constantly affirm: "*Attention! I resolve to will! I am wholly engaged in willing this act!*"

Régimes

(*a*) *Exercise No. 1.* Stand erect. Breathe naturally. In the most resolute mood possible stand perfectly still while counting one hundred at a moderate rate. There should be no movements except those of breathing and winking. Do not stare. Do not permit the body to sway. Stand firmly, but naturally. Relax and rest one hundred counts. Repeat, with rests, six times.

(*b*) Be seated, erect, but in an easy posture. Remain perfectly quiet as above directed while you count one hundred. Rest as before. Repeat with rests, six times.

(*c*) Repeat above exercises every day for ten days, with rest of two days. The time suggested is merely an example; practice may well be continued indefinitely.

(1) *Exercise No. 2.* Stand erect. Breathe and wink naturally. Fix the eyes upon some small object on the wall of your room, say a nail-head or the corner of a picture, or a round spot made with a pencil, and large enough to be seen at a distance of eight feet. Place the tip of the forefinger of the right hand, palm toward face, directly on a line running from the right eye to such object or spot. Slowly move the hand, palm toward the face, from your body along such imaginary line, keeping the tip of finger rigidly thereon, until the arm is fully extended, and return to original position in the same manner — six times.

(2) Repeat with edge of hand toward face, six times.

(3) Repeat with back of hand toward face, six times.

(4) Repeat, shutting thumb and first finger, with second finger, six times.

(5) Repeat with each of the remaining fingers as above suggested, six times.

(6) Repeat with the fingers of the left hand.

(7) Continue these exercises every day for ten days, with rest.

(*a*) *Exercise No. 3.* Stand erect. Extend the right arm, limp, at full length, pointing with the forefinger. Move the whole limp arm, slowly and evenly, from left to right, so as to describe a perfect circle of several feet diameter, drawing it with the finger. Six times. Not too rapidly. Do not jerk. Control trembling and unevenness of movement.

(*b*) Reverse, six times.

(*c*) Repeat with arm stiffened, and reverse, six times.

(*d*) Move the limp left arm from left to right, running tip of finger along an imaginary line as diameter of the circle, six times.

(*e*) Reverse, six times.

(*f*) Repeat with stiffened arm, six times. Reverse, six times.

(*g*) Repeat with right arm limp, from right to left, on a straight line, six times; stiffened arm, six times.

(*h*) Reverse, six times.

(*i*) Repeat and reverse with left arm limp.

(*j*) Repeat and reverse with right arm stiffened, six times. Left arm, six times.

(*k*) Continue for ten days, with rest.

(1) *Exercise No. 4.* Assume any position with the entire body, or any part. Maintain it steadily while counting one hundred. Rest. Repeat six times.

(2) Repeat with various other positions, each six times, for ten days.

(3) During all this practice, the mind must not be permitted to wander in the least. You must think every act intently. Put the Will-sense into all movements. The eyes must follow the lines suggested. The head should not move with the arms. Throw the Will into the end of the finger. Maintain always the resolute mood. Remember the goal.

"He who is incapable of controlling his muscles," said Maudsley, "is incapable of attention."

Exercise No. 5. This exercise should be observed during life. Acquire the habit of physical quietness while the body is mainly at rest. Whether sitting or standing eliminate all unnecessary movements of hands, fingers, legs, feet, eyes, lips. A nervous youth who was subject to twitching of the hands and features, was cured by the threat of an old sea-captain, with whom he made a long voyage, that he would flog him unless the habit was mastered. Fear aroused the Will. Set your Will to the control of such movements. In order thereto, practise stated periods of sitting and standing while thinking of these motions but resolutely forbidding them. Set regular hours for this exercise, varied in position, in the morning, fifteen minutes. Always practise when weary or nervous. Put into the exercise great strength but calmness of Will.

A striking suggestion of your power in this direction may be seen in the following paragraph:

In the Life of Dr. Elisha Kane, the famous Arctic explorer, his biographer says: "I asked him for the best proved instance that he knew of the soul's power over the body. He paused a moment upon my question as if to feel how it was put, and then answered as with a spring: 'The soul can lift the body out of its boots, sir! When our captain was dying — I say dying; I have seen scurvy enough to know — every old scar in his body a running ulcer. I never saw a case so bad that either lived or died. Men die of it, usually, long before they are as ill as he was. There was trouble aboard. There might be mutiny so soon as the breath was out of his body. We might be at each others' throats. I felt that he owed the repose of dying to the service. I went down to his bunk, and shouted in his ear, "Mutiny! Captain! Mutiny!" He shook off the cadaverous stupor. "Set me up!" said he, "and order these fellows before me!" He heard the complaint, ordered punishment, and from that hour convalesced.'"

Exercise No. 6. The surest steadiness of nerves and muscles must come from poise of soul and tone of health. You can acquire the first if you will take a few minutes each day for absolute quietness of mind and body, shutting out all *ideas* of hurry, worry, business and activity of every kind, thinking intensely of, and asserting that you are now in, a state of perfect mental poise.

The tone of health is provided for in the following chapter and in *"Power For Success."* A self-controlled, vigorous person should possess steadiness of nerves, though occasions may arise in which the Will must be called on for assertion of existing power. Edward Carpenter tells a strong story in "The Art of Creation" which illustrates the value of great physical vigor on emergency, and suggests what general poise plus power of Will may achieve under *psychic* stress equal to that of the freezing conditions referred to in the incident.

"I knew a miner from Manitoba — and a good wholesome man he was — who told me that one night a stranger knocked at the door of his log-cabin on the edge of Lake Superior and begged help, saying that he and a companion had been crossing the lake on the ice, and that the companion had given out. He who had knocked at the door had come on alone for assistance. My friend picked up a lantern, and the two hurried down across the ice. The night was very cold and dark, but after some searching they found the man. He was lying stretched frozen and 'stiff as a log.' They picked him up and carried him back to the cabin, and sat up all night and into the next day continually rubbing and chafing his body. At last he came to and made a complete recovery, and in a few days — except for some marks of frost-bite on his skin — showed no sign of damage. Surely that was a holy man, in whom the frost, though it went right through his body, could find no sin."

A "holy" man is a whole man, and the latter possesses nerves and physical tone equal to all demands — as should be true of every human who is king (or queen) in the inner and the outer life. For when you are "holy," whole, sound, you *command* both body and mind.

HEALTH

The sea, the pine, the stars, the forest deep
  Bequeath to me their subtle wealth.
Or still days brood, or rough winds round me sweep.
  Mine is the earth-man's vibrant health:
All things for love of me their vigils keep —
  I have the health, the wealth.

  Run, sea, in my heart!
  Pine, sing in my heart!
  Stars, glow in my heart!
    For ye are mine, and my soul,
  Like ye, is a part
    Of the wonderful Whole.

There's no thing dear to me is not my wealth,
  No life that seeks me I would distant keep;
For swift possession is my earth-man's health
  Or still days brood, or rough winds round me sweep —
  I have the health, the wealth.
    —THE AUTHOR.

CHAPTER XVII

GENERAL HEALTH

"CARRYING any business or study in the mind all the time, day and night, morning and evening, does not really advance that business so much as forgetting it at intervals and letting the mind rest, as you allow your muscles to rest after any physical exertion. Mind allowed to rest gains new ideas and new force to carry out ideas.

"What is the remedy? More recreation. More variety of occupation. More selves in our one self. To attain the highest and happiest life we need to have two, and possibly three, if not four lives in one — to be merchant in the morning and artist or yachtman or something else in the afternoon, and in the second life forget for the time all about the first, and in such forgetfulness rest the first life or set of faculties, recuperate them, refresh them, and go back to business, or art, or science, or any occupation, next day, with more force, plan, idea, thought to put in it."— *Prentice Mulford.*

THEORY OF THIS CHAPTER

State of Will depends upon condition of physical health;

Physical health is a goal of science, and is reached through the resolute and persistent Will;

Every rule of health deliberately followed becomes a developer of Will-power.

The momentum of a well person thrown into Will-culture is enormous, and is certain of great attainments.

A condition of general health is of paramount importance to development of Will. In a sense, Will-power is emphatic personality, and the emphasis of personal resolution, which is the strong Will, depends largely upon physical conditions. There are great Wills in feeble bodies, but this is probably the exception. The influence of pain, discouragement, invalidism, upon our power of willing, is well known. Ordinarily a man's average power of Will is determined by his average of health. "Hence vigorous self-determination depends upon plentiful and wholesome blood supply, or ultimately upon good food well digested and good air well inhaled. The secret of energy, and even of ethics, in the last analysis, is largely in sound digestion and good ventilation. Lessen or vitiate the supply of blood, and you may produce any desired degree of inaction and helplessness. On the contrary, cerebral congestion in a vigorous person (as in the insane) may generate tremendous outbursts of muscular activity and stern resolution."

Undoubtedly the mind exercises a great influence over the body, and when sufficient Will-power can be mustered to banish fear and nervousness, and to summons a strong psychic condition, certain forms of ailing or disease may be benefited or even cured. "Will to be well! This, strictly speaking, is the 'mind cure'; is potent in nerve diseases, and is not useless in other maladies." Every intelligent physician understands this and seeks to cultivate in his patients the helpful, assertive and hopeful mood of mind. "A strong motive to live positively keeps some people alive," said a noted Scotch physician.

But mind is influenced by body. Frequently such influence masters the soul before Will can be summoned, and to such a degree that the necessary sense of Will can no more be put forth than a determination to perform a physical or religious miracle. Hence, the best advice of common sense in regard to health would attempt to combine these forces of nature — proper attention to physical conditions, a resolute state of Will, and tried and proved medical practice. But see Rule 14 below.

"Nevertheless, it is important fully to understand," as Dr. A. T. Schofield remarks in "The Unconscious Mind," "that when the brain is restored to health by good nerve tissue and healthy blood, it can be made by suggestion to exercise as healthy an influence over the body as previously it exercised a harmful one. If ideal centres can produce ideal diseases, surely the rational cure is to bring these ideal centres into a healthy condition, and then make them the means of curing the ideal disease. Mental disease requires, and can ultimately only be cured by, mental medicine."

In time of peace prepare for war. In time of health fortify against disease. Here notice

SOME IMPORTANT RULES

Rule 1. Food should be regulated according to peculiarities of body and general work performed. Water which is pure should be freely drunk. Plenty of sound sleep should be secured, and slumber should be enhanced by plenty of pure air. Most people drink too little water. The air of many sleeping rooms would kill a wild Indian. Regularity of habits should be cultivated. Sufficient exercise must be taken to keep the muscles from degeneration and to vitalize the blood by activity of lungs.

Rule 2. Rest is also important. For the laboring man absolute idleness is not always rest; interested activity which brings unused muscles into play is better. This general truth lies at the bottom of popular employment of the day called Sunday. But such employment is largely injurious rather than beneficial. It frequently involves wrong methods as well as various excesses. The most wholesome rest as yet discovered for that day is suggested by religion. If you sneer at this proposition, that shows that you do not know what real religion is — or that your Will is set in directions contrary to the deepest instincts of mankind. There are people who are always too tired to attend religious exercises on Sunday, who nevertheless waste health in other ways, or dawdle around with listless energies that exercise neither mind nor muscles. The normally and intelligently religious person never complains that his observance of the Day wearies or unfits him for the week following. To be sure, it is possible to "dissipate" in this matter, and some people shoulder the universe while church bells are ringing, leaving, apparently little for the Almighty to accomplish alone. Nevertheless, testimony agrees that a healthful religious use of Sunday tones the system in every department. This is not Puritanism; it is common sense. The laboring man would improve his condition if he would quit his enemies and ally himself with at least a little semblance of sound reason.

Rule 3. Above all, anger, irritation, jealousy, depression, sour feelings, morose thoughts, worry, should be forever banished from mind by the resolute, masterful Will. All these are physiological devils. They not only disturb the mind, but injure the body by developing poisons and distorting cells. They prevent an even circulation. The poisons which they generate are deadly in the extreme. They induce more or less permanent physiological states which are inimical to vigorous Will. They dispel hopefulness, and obscure high motives, and lower the mental tone. They should be cast out of life with the resolution that as aliens they shall always be treated.

Régimes

Rule 4. Resolve, then, upon the following perpetual régimes:

1. Determine to live in a regular manner. Nevertheless, be master of rules, not slave.
2. Shun rich pastries and foods and drink which stimulate but do not nourish.
3. Keep the body clean. Bathe frequently, always rinsing in fresh water, cooler than the first, unless you are convalescent, and dry thoroughly.

Rule 5. Attention! A bit of perfumery dropped into the bath, or applied thereafter, will cultivate physical pride — not vanity — which will prize the body and make clean flesh a delight.

Rule 6. After vigorous drying rub and knead and slap for a few minutes. If the bath has been taken during the day, keep up a gentle but resolute activity a short time before going out of the dressing-room.

Then assume a self-possessed and assertive mood of mind, with Will strongly at the fore.

If the bath is taken before retiring, get into a clean garment, and then sprawl over every foot of bed-linen, of a proper temperature, luxuriating, resting, conscious of being a clean and very good sort of person. Now note with shut eyes what you see of colors and shapes in the inky darkness before you, and sleep.

Rule 7. Drink at least four full glasses of *pure* water every day unless you are too fleshy, in which case consult a physician. For most people more would probably be better. In addition, drink whenever you want water, except when heated. If heated, refresh the mouth by rinsing, but do not swallow for a time. Of course it is here supposed that you have stopped exercise in a heated condition. Drink at your meals, before, after. Don't gulp ice-water. Don't boil your stomach with hissing hot water. A good drink is composed of rather hot water with milk to color well, and enough salt to taste. Drink water freely before retiring.

Rule 8. Make sure of pure air in your sleeping room. Don't sleep in a draft. If possible sleep with head away from open door or window. Place a light screen between yourself and the source of air. See to it, however, that the pure air can get to you. Don't sleep in a hot room. Don't sleep in a freezing atmosphere.

Rule 9. Keep your sleeping-room clean. Make it attractive. That room ought to be the best in the house. It is frequently the poorest. If it is a small hired room, sacrifice many things for furniture, pictures, ornaments, articles of toilet. Do not suppose that, because you are a male biped, you are above these suggestions. You are occupied with dirt all day; why not get away from dirt at night? Man is an animal with a soul, and therefore may not wisely "bunk down" like a dog, or "stall in" like a horse or an ox.

Rule 10. Keep body and clothing as clean as possible. Labor, in a clean shirt and blouse, can do better work than in garments grimy with dirt and grease. People who do not handle dirt have, of course, no excuse for being unclean. There is also unnoticed benefit in occasional change of the outer garments. It rejuvenates a suit of clothing or a dress to hang it in good air a day or two. The mind of the wearer in turn gets a fresh feeling by donning different clothing, or by varying the combination. Even a fresh necktie or polished shoes make a man feel new for an hour, and that is eminently worth the while. Few people are dandies or flirts; hence a flower on the person every day would minister to self-respect and a high-toned consciousness, having a direct bearing upon the soul's power of Will. A handkerchief touched with a bit of perfumery, though it be a red bandana in a mechanic's hands, would serve a similar purpose. Let fools laugh! A good Will has no care for asses' braying. A real man need be neither a prig nor a boor.

"It is related of Haydn, the musician, that, when he sat down to compose, he always dressed himself with the utmost care, had his hair nicely powdered, and put on his best suit. Frederick II. had given him a diamond ring; and Haydn declared that, if he happened to begin without it, he could not summon a single idea. He could write only on the finest paper; and was as particular in forming his notes, as if he had been engraving them on copper-plate."

Rule 11. Similarly as to good music. "Take a music-bath once or twice a week for a few seasons," said Dr. O. W. Holmes, "and you will find that is to the soul what the water-bath is to the body." This elevates and tends to maintain the tone of one's mind. Seek, therefore, every clean opportunity for hearing it. Purchase some kind of instrument for the home, and see that its beneficent harmonies are often heard. Let music be as much a part of the day's routine as eating or reading or working.

Rule 12. Discard, resolutely and forever everything thought to be injurious to health.

Rule 13. Always and everywhere cultivate high mindedness. Maintain the resolute Mood of Will. Assert yourself, for every good influence, against every evil thing. Carry with you in all activities the sense of nobility, of health, of success.

Rule 14. It should now be added that beyond dispute personal power for maintaining and securing health is not confined to mere Will as commonly understood. Below all moods of cheerfulness, hope, courage and Will — in ordinary thought — hides a dynamic psychic force which is capable even of "miracles," and which will ultimately rid the earth of disease and death. This psychic force is expressed partly in mental thought, but more perfectly and prophetically in a

A Temple for Emphatic Personality

psychic state which is a complex of assumption, assertion, Will or sovereign authority — an idea of command in action conquering illness and securing health — and confidence and profound realization — that is, thought-feeling of betterment.

The path leading to such state is that of expecting effort to feel the state within the inner centre of person. One should affirm that universal good is pouring in; one should assume and assert the fact; one should assume and assert that the ground of one's existence is the Infinite Reality, that one has deeply imbedded in the deeps of soul the idea of self as whole because the Infinite Ground does not and cannot wish otherwise, and that as the universal good enters from without and the Infinite Self emerges from below up into the subconscious personal self, all inharmonious conditions are necessarily passing away — being expelled.

The process above suggested cannot be acquired by brief and haphazard efforts. The soul must essay the process again and again until it discovers the process. Thereafter it must put the process into action incessantly until facility and power in its use are acquired.

But observe: In real illness *call your physician* AND at the same time *bring your psychic power into requisition.* The notion that the physician and psycho-auto treatment are inconsistent and antagonistic is utterly false. Do not omit either method. Rise to the highest level of a free use of anything under heaven which helps life to health.

Make all the above suggestions a perpetual régime of your life.

"ATTENTION! I RESOLVE TO WILL!!"

THY SELF

I asked of These revealment of my need:
 The Seas, the Hills, the Starry Vault, and Life.
The first cried, "Action! Thou art spirit freed;"
 The second, "Poise! Defeat is bred of strife;"
The third Galactic, "Power in the Deed!"

     To war I went with sounding drum and fife —
     To faith I turned, with moods receptive rife —
     At last stood awed where human empires breed.

But ne'er the thing I urged these Masters taught.
How act? How stand? What power — and how gain?
 Seas, Hills and Stars — War, Faith and World in vain!
Then up spoke Life: "Oh, simple soul destraught!
"Poise, Action, Powers for thy rule complain:
"Thou art the King, thyself the king's domain!"
                                     — THE AUTHOR.

Part III—Mental Régime

WHAT SEEST THOU?

The gracious light, in semi-sphere
  Created by the living soul,
  Encompasses the vision's whole
Of worlds afar and atoms near.

The vault of heaven, gemmed and deep,
  And earth and sea o'erwhelmed in light,
  Full complements of thought invite
That soul may all its empire keep.

And so the world within the flesh
  The larger gains, and grows apace
  To Truth's ideal and Beauty's grace
With understanding ever fresh.

Yet must the Wider Life emerge
  Within the lesser, welling up,
  If living spirit's wine-filled cup
Reflect the Drama's drift and urge.

What seest thou? Thy self alone:
  Thou art the world and all its parts.
  And this is being's Art of Arts:
To know the Vaster Life thine own.
— The Author.

CHAPTER XVIII

EXERCISES IN ATTENTION

"IT IS subject to the superior authority of the Ego. I yield it or I withhold it as I please; I direct it in turn to several points; I concentrate it upon each point as long as my Will can stand the effort."—*Dictionaire Philosophique.*

THEORY OF CHAPTER

Attention, become habituated, involves constant and strong action of Will;

The idea of Will-power, always present in the effort to habituate attention, will come to possess and dominate the mind;

Such domination, by a psychic law, develops the function which it concerns.

The preceding chapters have had in view the development of Will by means of physical exercises. If the suggestions hitherto given have been followed, self-culture has resulted with marked growth in this direction. While our work has been physical, the mind has nevertheless been directly involved, for always the Will has thrust itself forward, both as ruler and as object. We are now to enter more particularly the mental field, with the same end in view.

PRELIMINARY

The value to the Will of perseverance in this work would seem to be evident. A determined effort to develop the volitional power must certainly result in its growth. But mental activity having this end in view will generate unconscious processes making for the same goal. Doctor Holmes has said: "I was told, within a week, of a business man in Boston, who, having an important question under consideration, had given it up for the time as too much for him. But he was conscious of an action going on in his brain which was so unusual and painful as to excite his apprehensions that he was threatened with palsy, or something of that sort. After some hours of this uneasiness, his perplexity was all at once cleared up by the natural solution of his doubt coming to him — worked out, as he believed, in that obscure and troubled interval."

"We are constantly finding results of unperceived mental processes in our consciousness. Here is a striking instance, which I borrow from a recent number of an English journal. It relates to what is considered the most interesting period of incubation in Sir William Rowan Hamilton's discovery of quaternions. The time was the 15th of October, 1843. On that day, he says in a letter to a friend, he was walking from his observatory to Dublin with Lady Hamilton, when, on reaching Brougham Bridge, he 'felt the galvanic circle of thought close'; and the sparks that fell from it were the fundamental relations between $i, j, k,$ just as he used them ever afterwards."

If, then, the brain may unconsciously work out specific results of thought under the influence of a desired end, the idea of a mighty Will, kept constantly before the mind and directing given and continuous mental exercises, will undoubtedly generate a process always tending to build up the volitional powers. And

A Focused Soul Fears Nothing

as the Will is located throughout the entire mind, the latter must be wholly brought into action for the Will's training and development.

The secret of our future labor will be found in that which has been absolutely indispensable all along, to wit: ATTENTION. But attention is hereafter to be confined to the intellect. Its direction is not so much outward as inward; its subject is not so truly the senses as the mind and its extension, so to speak, by means of the senses.

"*The essential achievement of the Will,*" says Prof. William James, "*when it is most voluntary, is to attend to a difficult object and hold it fast before the mind.*" "*Effort of attention is the essential phenomenon of Will.*"

But what do we mean by the word Attention? Professor James Sully says: "Attention may be roughly defined as the active self-direction (this involves Will) of the mind to any object which presents itself to it at the moment." He refers to the make-up of the word: *ad tendere,* to stretch towards. "It is somewhat the same as the mind's 'consciousness' of what is present to it. The field of consciousness, however, is wider than that of attention. Consciousness admits of many degrees of distinctness. I may be very vaguely or indistinctly conscious of some bodily sensation, of some haunting recollection, and so on. To attend is to intensify consciousness by concentrating or narrowing it on some definite or restricted area. It is to force the mind or consciousness in a particular direction so as to make the objects as distinct as possible."

Now, Dr. Scripture remarks on the same subject: "The innumerable psychologies attempt to define it, but when they have defined it, you are sure to know just as much about it as before." Then, to show the difference between the "focus" (of the mind) and the "field" of the present experience (consciousness), he writes: "Ask your friend, the amateur photographer, to bring around his camera. He sets it up and lets you look at the picture on the ground glass. The glass is adjusted so that the picture of a person in the middle of the room is sharply seen; all the other objects are somewhat blurred, depending on their distance from him. Change the position of the glass a trifle. The person becomes blurred and some other object becomes sharp. Thus, for each position of the glass there is an object, or a group of objects, distinctly seen while all other objects are blurred. To make one of the blurred objects distinct, the position of the glass must be changed, and the formerly distinct object becomes blurred.

"In like manner, we fully attend to one object or group of objects at a time; all others are only dimly noticed. As we turn our attention from one object to another what was formerly distinct becomes dim.

"The illustration with the camera is not quite complete. You can keep the objects quiet in the room, but you cannot keep your thoughts still. The mental condition would be more nearly expressed by pointing the camera down a busy street. You focus first on one thing, then on another. The things in focus pass out of it, others come in. Only by special effort can you keep a moving person or wagon in focus for more than a moment." To "attend," therefore, is to keep the mind "focused" on the one thing, whether it lies among subjects of thought which correspond to the furniture of a room or to moving objects seen in a busy street.

A Focused Soul Fears Nothing

Attention is the "effort of the mind to detain the idea or perception, and to *exclude* the other objects that solicit its notice." This requires a strong action of the Will. Resolute exercise of attention, therefore, must strengthen the Will's power.

RÉGIMES

Exercise No. 1. Sit quietly at ease in a room where you will not be disturbed. By a supreme effort of Will, drive every thought and fancy out of mind. Hold the mind blank as long as possible. How long can you sustain this effort successfully? Be not discouraged. Persistence will win. After a genuine attempt, rest a few moments. Then try again. Practise the exercise daily for ten days, with rest of two days, making at least six attempts each day. Keep a record of results, and at the end of the period note improvement. The Will must be taught to be supreme.

Exercise No. 2. Sit quietly as before. When the mind is a blank, hold it so for a few seconds. Then instantly begin to think of some one thing, and now exclude every other thought. Keep the attention rigidly upon this particular subject as long as possible. The direction does not mean that you are to follow a train of ideas upon the subject, but that you are to fasten the mind keenly upon the one thing or idea and retain it in the field of attention, just as you may look at some object, focusing sight and observation there, and there alone. Rest. Repeat six times. Make record. Continue every day for ten days, with rest. Then note improvement in power.

Exercise No. 3. Permit the mind to wander whither it will one minute. Now write out all that you recall of these wandering thoughts. Then proceed to find and indicate in writing the connections that bind them into a chain. You will thus discover that mental activities may become aimless, but that the mind's roaming is not without explanation. Resolve to keep your thoughts well in hand. Repeat these exercises six times, and continue for ten days, with rest. On the tenth day compare records and note improvement in attention. Try, now, to discover any general laws that have governed the mind's uncontrolled action.

Exercise No. 4. Sit at ease for one minute while thinking of the mind as engaged in reasoning. Do not entertain fancies. Keep out wandering thoughts and sensations. Do not reason; think of the reasoning power of the mind. Now deliberately pursue some definite line of reasoning for, say, five minutes. Write results, from memory. Rest. Repeat six times. Continue for ten days, with rest. On the tenth day compare records and note improvement in concentration.

Repeat these exercises with the imagination, thinking a picture or plot of acting.

Repeat with the power of Will, imagined as to various acts.

Exercise No. 5. Summons a resolute state of mind. Now select some desired goal in life which you believe to be possible, and will, with all your might, that this shall be. Do not think of means. Fiercely resolve to overcome all difficulties. Do not dwell upon the enjoyment of success, for that will distract the mind. Attend wholly to the Mood of willing. Repeat six times. Continue at least ten days, with rest.

Bed the idea of the goal deeply in mind. Carry it with you into life's activities. Make the resolution a permanent matter, not only of Will, but of feeling as well.

Exercise No. 6. Sit at ease a few seconds. Now think of several acts, as, to walk across the room, or to take a book from a shelf, or to sit still. Continue about five minutes. Various impulses will arise to do one thing or another. Resist them all a little time. Now decide, quickly and resolutely, what you will do. Do not act lazily; do not decide impulsively. Force a real decision. Then act. Do exactly that one thing. Rest. Repeat six times, with different actions. During each act, put the Will into every part thereof. Keep to the fore a strong personal Mood. Continue for ten days, with rest. At the end of the period, note improvement in attention and power of Will.

Exercise No. 7. Set apart by themselves several small objects; books, coins, paper-knives, etc. Collect a miscellaneous lot. Now, after looking these articles over, decide to arrange them in some particular way according to a determined order of relations. The order may be that of similarity, or difference, and the like. Example: the objects are of many colors; arrange in a complementary way. Now note the general effect. It is probably bad. Why is this? How can the arrangement be improved? Has color anything to do with the arrangement of the furniture of your room? Can it be set into better order in this respect? Try that. Repeat with order according to other resemblances. Repeat with order according to differences.

Always keep the Mood of Will in the foreground during these exercises.

Arrange with a different order six times in each exercise. Continue for ten days, with rest. At the end of the period, observe improvement in attention, together with facility in making the arrangements.

Exercise No. 8. Select several like objects, say, books or articles of furniture. Now arrange the books according to titles. Is this the best possible arrangement? Try to improve it. Arrange the furniture for finest effect in the room, having color, shape, style, etc., in mind. Repeat with other similar articles. With each set of objects make six different arrangements. Continue for ten days, with rest. Then note improvement as before.

Exercise No. 9. Select several dissimilar objects. Lay them out conveniently before you. Take one of them in hand. What does it suggest? Connect that suggestion immediately, that is, without any intermediate idea, with another article. What does this suggest? Connect the suggestion with a third article. Continue in this way until all the objects have been connected. Place the articles, one after another, according to connecting suggestions, before you. Do everything slowly, deliberately and with a strong sense of willing. Rest after the first complete experiment a few seconds. Then repeat with different articles six times. Continue for ten days, with rest, and then note improvement in attention and facility of connections made.

Here is an example: Book — (suggesting) — Person — (suggesting) — Note — (suggesting) — Writer — (suggesting) — Pen — (suggesting) — Mightier —

A Focused Soul Fears Nothing

(suggesting) — Sword — (suggesting) — Sharp — (suggesting) — Knife — (suggesting) — Point — (suggesting) — Pin — (suggesting) — Bright — (suggesting) — Gold Watch.

The above exercises are somewhat difficult, and their practice will require patience and time. But the value of such work will appear when we remember "that the act of voluntary attention involves a conscious effort of the soul." It is the "*conscious effort*" that this book seeks to develop. And for two reasons: first, that the reader may acquire the habit of carrying with him everywhere the Will-pervaded Mood of the strong personality; secondly, that adequate power of attending to motives may become a permanent factor of his life.

Read, therefore, the following with greatest care:

"*Variations in the relative strength of motives mainly arise from the degree of attention that we give to them respectively.*" People often act wrongly or unwisely because they fail here. "*Thus, for example, a hungry man, seeing bread in a baker's window, is tempted to break the glass and steal a loaf of bread. The motive here is the prospect of satisfying his hunger. But the man is not a mere machine, impelled by a single force. He knows that if he is caught, he will be punished as a thief. He knows, too, that this is a wrong act which he is considering, and that his conscience will reprove him. Now he can fix his attention upon one of these restraining motives. The impulse to break the glass thus loses its power. The element of time is an important factor, for the longer he delays and deliberates, the more numerous will be the restraining motives which arise in his consciousness.*"

But avoidance of crime is a very small part of most people's lives. For the majority, "How to get on in all good ways," is a comprehensive, and the ruling, question. The value of attention obtains here in ways similar to those above suggested. A strong Will is demanded. Ability to hold the mind to one thing is imperative. Power of concentrating thought upon motives, and the best motives, is called for every day of our existence. The great symbol of all our exercises, therefore, is Attention! ATTENTION!

"From what has already been said, it can be inferred that tenacious attention is one of the strongest factors in a cultivated will. Some modern psychologists insist that attention is the only power of the will.

"The man who can hold uninteresting ideas before his mind until they gather interest, is the man who is going to succeed.

"The only way to cultivate attention is by a *continuous* effort of will. If the attention wanders from any subject for ninety-nine consecutive times, bring the attention back ninety-nine consecutive times. Make an effort to concentrate the mental powers each time. A habit of attention will surely grow in this way.

"It is hardly possible to over estimate the importance of tenacious attention. A man with half the natural ability of some geniuses often accomplishes far more, because he keeps his attention undivided on one thing until he has mastered it."

Here is an open secret of big, shrewd, notable men in the professional and financial marts of to-day — close, concentrated, calm-minded attention. It does not require a tight-fisted, muscle-tensed, set condition

A Focused Soul Fears Nothing

of body but rather a ONE AIM held closely in mind with distracting outside sensations excluded.

But the words which we have so often met in the preceding pages indicate the ultimate and priceless goal:

"I RESOLVE TO WILL! THE MOOD OF EMPHATIC PERSONALITY IS MINE!"

WHO READS?

Reads " Witless One"?
Behold him run
  The race of prose or rhyme!
Reading's an art
Of head and heart —
  Never a thief of time.

Love's "Thought" the pause
On trenchant clause;
  'Tis matter him engages.
The first has speed
And verbal greed,
  Devouring countless pages.

In Browning's book
Or Saturn's nook
  Hides God — the Question Mark.
Goes soul all in?
All, soul must win;
  Goes less? The thing is dark.

'Tis Truth's old fashion
To answer passion;
  'Tis soul's, to grow by giving.
Now if you read
As martyrs bleed,
  You know — then — glorious living.
                    — THE AUTHOR.

CHAPTER XIX

ATTENTION IN READING

"A DISTINGUISHED lawyer of an Eastern city relates that while engaged in an argument upon which vast issues depended he suddenly realized that he had forgotten to guard a most important point. In that hour of excitement his faculties became greatly stimulated. Decisions, authorities and precedents long since forgotten began to return to his mind. Dimly outlined at first, they slowly grew plain, until at length he read them with perfect distinctness. Mr. Beecher had a similar experience when he fronted the mob in Liverpool. He said that all events, arguments and appeals that he had ever heard or read or written passed before his mind as oratorical weapons, and standing there he had but to reach forth his hand and seize the weapons as they went smoking by."— *Newell Dwight Hillis.*

THEORY OF CHAPTER

Concentrated attention the price of understanding;
Exhaustive understanding the only true reading;
Review and discussion the storing methods of memory;
These exercises, deliberately and persistently followed, sure developers of the scholar's Will.

PRELIMINARY

There is at once too much reading and too little. The great modern dailies are harming the minds of metropolitan peoples. Multitudes read from sheer mental laziness. Journalism must therefore be sensational in an evil manner. Even magazine literature scours worlds for fresh chaff illustrated by "lightning artists." These influences, and the infinite flood of matter, make genuine reading among many impossible. For reading, in its real sense, is a deliberate process by which written thought is transferred to the mind, and there stored and assimilated. All this involves power of Will. But power of Will is a rare possession in these days of multitudinous distractions. Hence it is that true reading is almost a lost art. How shall this lost art be regained? By development of that reason-forged but magic gift, *Attention*.

"Read not to contradict nor to believe, but to weigh and consider," said the wise and "woodeny" Bacon. "To weigh and consider"—that is the *open sesame* of right reading. In order to acquire these abilities the following directions will serve:

Régimes

Exercise No. 1. Procure any well-written book on any subject worth knowing. Read the title with great care. State in your own language exactly what you suppose the title to mean. Look up the definitions of all words. Examples: "History of the United States." What is history? What is a written history? What is the difference between the two kinds of "history"? What is the main idea in "United States"? How did this name originate?

Now read the author's name. Before proceeding further, memorize an outline of his life. Ascertain his place in letters. What value are you to put upon his work?

The Will and the Eye Illumine 231

This done, read with some care the table of contents. You ought now to have the general drift of the book, together with its purpose. If these do not appear, take another book and repeat the above exercises. Continue this exercise during life.

Exercise No. 2. Presuming that, with such examination, you wish to go on, read the preface very carefully. Having finished it, ask yourself what the author has here said. Make sure that you know. Then ask, Why has he said this in the preface? Did he need a preface? Does this preface really pre-face, so far as you can now judge? Make this a permanent régime in reading.

Exercise No. 3. If the book has an introduction, read that with the greatest attention. An author is sometimes misunderstood in many pages because his introduction has not been read. At the end of its reading, outline from memory what it has brought before you. Now ask, again, Why should he have written that introduction, or what he has written here as an introduction? Very likely, you are at this time as ready to lay the book aside as you may become later. Make this exercise a permanent part of serious reading.

Exercise No. 4. To make sure about this, read attentively the first twenty-five pages of the book. In these pages do you see anything new, anything interesting, anything of value to you? If nothing new, interesting or valuable gets to the fore in twenty-five pages, you are probably ready to sell that book at a large discount. The rule, however, is not infallible.

Reading is frequently like gold-mining: the richest veins are not always readily discovered. Some of George Eliot's works require a yoke of oxen, so to speak, to drag the mind into them; but once in, it cannot escape her spell. Many books which are perennially acknowledged cannot be rigidly subjected to these tests. Something, too, depends upon the reader's mind. If the mind "adores" "awfully sweet" dresses and "perfectly elegant" parties, its judgments may be taken with a "lot" of "just the tiniest" allowance. These directions are not dealing with the "punk" order of intellect, nor the "green corn" era of criticism. They have in view the ordinary run of minds and the above-average grade of books. If twenty-five pages of a book do not get hold of a good mind, the author has done phenomenally fine work, or else he isn't worth reading. Make this exercise permanent.

Exercise No. 5. Supposing, now, that you resolve to go on with the volume in hand, it will be necessary, for our present purpose, to return to the first sentence. Read that sentence with exceeding care. What is its subject? — its predicate? — its object? What is the meaning of each word? If an abstract-thought, put this thought into your own language. Think it, resolutely and carefully and clearly. If it is an object-thought, stop now, and, closing the eyes, call up a mental picture of the object. If the word expresses action, ask what kind of action. Think the act so as to get a mental picture of it, if possible. If the sentence is involved, take as much of it as expresses a complete thought exhausted by ideas of "being," or "condition," or "action." Treat this as your first sen-

The Will and the Eye Illumine 233

tence according to the above directions. Then proceed with the next complete thought of the sentence, and so on until you have in this manner read the sentence as a whole. Then read the sentence again, put the thoughts together, and get into the mind a complete view of the entire statement. Always translate the author's thoughts into your own language. *Do not memorize, but* THINK.

Proceed in this way through the first paragraph. Then state in your own manner the connected chain of thought thus far presented.

The next day, write, without reading again, the substance of this first paragraph.

Continue such attentive and analytic reading until you have mastered the first chapter. Now put aside all writings hitherto made, and from memory write a connected statement of the substance of that chapter.

Proceed with the succeeding sentences, paragraphs and chapters. If these directions are pursued, few books will require a second reading. And one good book well read is better than a dozen read as books ordinarily are read.

Resolve permanently upon this kind of reading.

Such exercises will prove of immense value, because they are based on certain laws of mind. The eye acquires great facility in reading, and the reader is apt to content himself with whole but vague pictures of groups of ideas presented. In order that the thought contained in the printed page may be really obtained, it is necessary to break up these wholes and to put their parts into clear light. This requires attention to details, which in turn demands a distinct understanding of the meaning of words. We may catch the general thought of a sentence without knowing clearly what some of its words mean, and thus really miss, perhaps, the best part of our reading.

"Suppose I look out of my window," says Hill in "Elements of Psychology," "and see a black horse running swiftly. The whole picture, as presented by the sense of vision, constitutes one single image. It remains one and single until I have occasion to describe it in words. The moment I attempt to do so, an analytic process or process of resolution into parts is necessary. I must name the animal 'horse,' his color 'black,' his act 'running,' his speed 'swiftly,' and I must indicate whether it is a definite or an indefinite black horse that runs, and so must use an article, 'a' or 'the.' Putting all together, I say '*A black horse is running swiftly,*' a sentence in which my one visual image is broken up by five distinctions, each expressed in a separate word. There is truth in the proverb, 'No one knows a thing until he can tell it.'"

The object of putting thought into one's own words is also seen in the fact that the mere study of words, as the above writer indicates, is of little value. Hence in real reading it is always necessary to secure mental images, or mental conceptions clear-cut and pronounced, of "being," "condition" or "action" involved in each statement read.

Exercise No. 6. While reading any book worth the while, mark striking or useful passages, and, as you proceed, make an index on the rear fly leaf. No matter if the book has a printed index; your own will prove better for your purpose.

Exercise No. 7. Analyze chapters, about as you go on, and mark and number or letter the points made.

At the close of reading the chapter, review these points and fix in memory. This will facilitate Exercise No. 5.

Exercise No. 8. While some friend reads aloud, practise mental noting of the points made by the author, retaining them for a given number of pages. Then state them consecutively while the reader reviews to correct your errors. Continue this exercise indefinitely.

Exercise No. 9. Repeat the above exercise with conversations with the reader, making sure that both thoroughly understand the matter in hand. On the following day, review this work together from memory. Then continue as before. Practise these exercises indefinitely.

Exercise No. 10. If an author's name is not a sufficient guaranty for his statements, or if his book is written from an evident point of view or with a possible bias, and he is clearly bent on "making his case," bring to the reading of his work the interrogative attitude of mind. Do not accept him carelessly. Compel him to "make his case" fairly. Verify his alleged facts. See that his references are correct and rightly interpreted. Detect flaws in his arguments. Read him from his point of view as modified by your own. Make sure that your point of view is good. Therefore, be open to his convictions. Nevertheless, antagonize him in a fair field. Be not hasty to contradict, nor to surrender. To-morrow what you deny may be truth, what you accept may be false. Read resolutely to gather what he can contribute to your stock of facts, of realities, of sound reasoning, of sentiment, of life, of power.

In connection with the foregoing instructions on attention in reading, certain parts of Bacon's essay " On Studies " will be of interest:

"Studies serve for delight, for ornament, and for ability. Their chief use for delight is in privateness and retiring; for ornament, is in discourse; and for ability, is in the judgment and disposition of business. For expert men can execute, and perhaps judge of particulars, one by one; but the general counsels, and the plots and the marshalling of affairs, come best from those who are learned. . . . Crafty men condemn studies; simple men admire them; *and wise men use them.* . . . Read not to contradict and confuse; nor to believe and take for granted; nor to find talk and discourse, but to weigh and consider. Histories make men wise; poets witty; the mathematics subtile; natural philosophy deep; moral grave; logic and rhetoric able to contend.

"Reading maketh a full man; conference a ready man; and writing an exact man. And therefore, if a man write little he had need have a great memory; if he confer little, he had need have a present wit; and if he read little, he had need have much cunning, to seem to know that he doth not."

Beware what Ben Jonson called a " humor ":

"A Humour is the bias of the mind,
By which, with violence, 'tis one way inclined;
It makes our action lean on one side still;
And, in all changes, *that way bends the Will.*"

The work here suggested will be tedious at first, and it demands time and patience. As it proceeds, however, it will become more and more easy and delightful. Its justification is the double purpose in hand in all these pages: right reading and power of persistent Will. *A resolute sense of willing must therefore be preserved from first to last.* Learn to read in the Mood of the emphatic personality. Your Will shall then dissolve books, and mastered books shall culture the finest Will.

THOUGHT

When the self works the miracle, thought,
  In the laboratory of brain,
And the matter with meaning is fraught,
  Like the gift to the Widow of Nain,
  Or the war-cry of Marathon's Plain,
Tell me, who has the miracle wrought?

And of what is it fashioned, this thing
  That upsprings like a ghost of the night—
That evolves like a Saturnine Ring—
  This mysterious symbol of might,
  Born as well to a god or a wight,
Tell me, what is that sign of a king?

In the faith-haunted seasons of old,
  When the soul was diffusively great,
I was claimant, exuberant, bold,
  Of the power of thought and its fate;
  And I dreamed in the folly, elate,
That myself was its essence unrolled.

Gone the fancy! The power abides.
  Yet the mystery grows on apace:
For the thinker's the spirit that hides,
  And the thought is his unrevealed face.
  Can a man outrun self in the race?
Can the sea compass more than its tides?
—The Author.

CHAPTER XX

ATTENTION IN THINKING

"SOMETHING more reliable than a mere impulse is needed to make a strong mind. Back of all must stand a strong Will, with the ability and disposition to use it. M. Marcel well says, 'The great secret of education lies in exciting and directing the Will.' In later mental acquirements we recognize the omnipotence of Will. Nothing takes its place until we discover that *attention is under the control of the Will,* and until, by perseverance, we acquire the power of thus controlling it."—*Popular Science Monthly.*

THEORY OF CHAPTER

True thinking is a deliberative act of mind held fast to its task;
Such impelled action discovers the best use of mind, and develops and stores the whole man;
The mind thus improved throws itself into its operations with greater wisdom and increased energy;
This action unfolds the Will.

The best thinker is the best reader. This is true even of "reciters," so far as their work is concerned. To recite, one must interpret; to interpret one must think.

Thinking, in its noblest sense, is largely a lost art among the people. They indulge in a vast deal of mental jargon, but genuine thought seems a scarce article. A single "straw" is the fact that new matter presented in the simplest language is often declared to be "too deep for us." The difficulty is not depth, but unfamiliarity; the limits of popular thinking are narrow; outside these limits, even sunlight is opaque, and diamonds are mere quartz pebbles.

People "think," as they say, to be sure, concerning homes, business, politics, social and state affairs, together with a smattering of religion; but in an elevated way, this "thinking" is a good deal like the "thinking" of animals; vague, unconscious as thought, forced, disjointed, spasmodic, haphazard. Few seem to think out a great reality, build up a consistent theory, or elaborate a reasonable system. We have not here, altogether, it must be said, the pressure of dirt and moil. It is a case of mental laziness. One must work with muscles in order to exist; but one need not labor with the mind for assimilation of food and development of brawn. House-keepers and shop-tenders aver a great amount of thinking, "real and wearisome"; but we have here very largely the mechanics of mental routine. The world is flooded with "literature" every day, and the most of its readers relax in its enervating tide. Evidence: few "get on," few discover themselves and the universe about them — infinite globe of dynamic influences for the elevation of the human soul.

Preliminary

Nothing affords greater satisfaction than to mine into a fact or truth and ramify its various connections. Here is a process that is keenest tonic, a result of which is bank of deposit paying compound interest.

All Values Yield to Concentration

The ability to think clean through a subject puts a man apart as one of the victors of life. This power may be developed. Whenever it is taken in hand, resolutely and persistently, one of its hugest products is a giant Will.

But remember, true thinking depends upon, (1) Attention, (2) Knowledge, (3) Memory, (4) Correct Perception of Relations.

The swiftness and value of the process will depend upon the determined attitude brought into it by the soul. According to your Will, so be it unto you. In the last analysis, faith is Will shouting, "I will not let thee go!"

It is a mistake to suppose that one must be versed in all the rules of logic in order to become a good thinker. The mastery of logic is vastly helpful, to be sure; but after all, it is thinking that has produced logic, rather than logic thinking. A persistent effort to think correctly will in time develop a fair logical system, though its possessor may not be aware of the fact.

Be it remembered that good thinking may, and it may not, coincide with common sense. "Common sense is the exercise of the judgment unaided by art or system." Its only teacher is experience; but the lessons of experience seldom repeat themselves — the last has always some new element. The application of common sense is, therefore, a matter of inference, of reasoning. The best thinker ought to possess the greatest common sense.

Practiced thinking rather than common sense, governs the physician, the lawyer, the sailor, the engineer, the farmer, the business man, the statesman — though these must bring common sense to bear in thinking. When so done it is distinctly thinking.

The power to think, consecutively and deeply and clearly, is an avowed and deadly enemy to mistakes and blunders, superstitions, unscientific theories, irrational beliefs, unbridled enthusiasm, crankiness, fanaticism.

The lack of thought-power creates financial panics and ruins business, unsettles politics and government, keeps the masses down, makes the rich intolerant and unwise, and renders religion non-progressive.

He who cannot think cannot will, in the highest sense.

He who cannot will strongly, cannot think long or deeply.

All labor in thought involves a measuring capacity for willing.

All willed thinking develops Will.

RÉGIMES

Exercise No. 1. Take now, any simple and great truth. Concentrate attention upon this truth, absolutely excluding every other thought. Example: "Man is immortal." Think of man as immortal only. Think of man in every conceivable way as being immortal. Man is body; what is body? Is body immortal? Is *the* body immortal? If not, in either case, why not? If so, in either case, why? And in what sense? Man has mind; what is mind? Is it immortal? If so, what in mind is immortal? Why do you believe as you do? If mind is immortal, for what purpose? Man, again, has moral consciousness. What is this? Is this immortal? In what sense? What in moral consciousness is immortal? Why do you so believe? For what purpose is man, as moral consciousness, immortal?

Now think of immortality. What is it? Think of immortality in every conceivable way as connected with man. How does it concern him? Has it various supposable or believable states in relation to him? Where is he, as you suppose, in immortality? What is he, according to your idea, to become in immortality? What is he to take with him at death? With whom is he to exist hereafter? What is he to do? What relation have his present states to any believable states of his future life? How does he get his idea of immortality? What purpose does the idea serve in his life? In your life? Why should man be immortal?

When thinking of *man,* always keep in mind the idea " immortal," and when thinking of *immortality,* always keep in mind the idea " man."

The above is merely an example. These exercises should be repeated every day, with a different sentence or thought, indefinitely. It will be well also to preserve dated records, and to make frequent comparisons in order to discover improvement in analysis, attention and power of persistent thought upon a single subject. In six months, profit and pleasure will be apparent. You will surely find, as the main result of a faithful compliance with all suggestions, a tremendous power of straightforward Will-action. There can be no failure with resolute practice.

Exercise No. 2. Take any simple matter of observation or experience. You are riding, let us suppose, along a country road. Now look well at the landscape. You pronounce it beautiful. But what is the beautiful? Think that question to an answer. Now bury your mind in deepest thought concerning the landscape before you. The landscape —" what is *a* landscape?" Think that subject out carefully and distinctly. Proceeding, ask, "What is *this* landscape?" Observe the general outlines and salient features. What is there about the larger details which makes them beautiful? Observe the minor details. What is their beauty? How do they contribute to the beauty of the whole? How might this landscape be improved in beauty? How would this or that change add to the effect of the beautiful? Have you discovered all elements before you of a beautiful nature? When you next ride over the road, remember that question. Are you familiar with this country? Was it ever more beautiful than it is to-day? Do other people declare it to be beautiful? If not, why not, in your opinion? Ah! But are you certain that your ideas of the beautiful are correct? Do you think that the elements of this landscape appeal in the same way to others who pronounce it beautiful as they appeal to you? Do you suppose that they observe just the same colors, outlines, proportions, contrasts and blendings as yourself? Do you believe that the same feelings, thoughts, moods and desires are awakened in their minds by this landscape as in your own?

By such a process you may become absorbed in a deliberate and controlled train of thought. Have a care that your horse doesn't go over the ditch. If you have followed these directions, you have had experience in perfect concentration.

Concentration is the secret of great thinking.

This exercise should be varied at every attempt, with different subjects, as opportunity may present.

All Values Yield to Concentration

It must be continued six months at least, and practised in some suggested way every day.

Exercise No. 3. Take any simple sentence, say, " Success in life depends upon nobility of purpose and persistence of effort." Write the sentence out in full. Now strip the statement to a mere skeleton: " Success — depends — purpose — effort." Think clearly the meaning of each word. Then imagine the modifying words placed just above these. The sentence will read:

" Life — nobility — persistence."
" Success — depends — purpose — effort."

You have now two skeletons which may be filled out at your liking, almost, and yet give you the same idea in essentials. " The value of life consists in its nobility and its persistence." This sentence suggests the meaning of true success. That is not success which has no nobility or persistence. So, the lower skeleton may be filled out to read: " The quality of success depends upon the quality and abiding nature of its purpose and its effort." Low purpose and effort, low grade of success. Thus, the " value of life consists in its nobility of purpose and its persistence of effort."

Continue this exercise with different sentences for six months.

Exercise No. 4. Write the sentence used in the preceding exercise, as an example. " Success in life depends upon nobility of purpose and persistence of effort." Now ask the first part of this sentence closing with "purpose," a series of questions in which the words " how," " why," " which," " when," " where," " whose," are employed. " *How* does success depend upon nobility of purpose?" "*Why* does success in life depend upon nobility of purpose?" "*What* success depends upon nobility of purpose?" "*Where* does success depend upon nobility of purpose?" And so on until all the words are used. Write each answer in full. Then substitute "persistence of effort" for "nobility of purpose," and bombard the statement again with the same questions. Write each answer in the latter case in full. Then ask the entire sentence a question containing the word "whose." Finally, note carefully all that you have written upon the statement, arrange in logical form, and proceed to write a simple essay with the material thus gathered. You will find this to be an excellent way in which to bore into any subject. Continue six months, at least.

This is merely an example, and it is not a very full one. Every word and proposition of a sentence or subject thus may be compelled to give up its contents. In time, too, the mind will have acquired great facility and power in such analysis, so that whatever of value is read will come to offer its secrets to you almost as a free gift. This alone is worth all labor expended upon the exercise.

Exercise No. 5. The results of attention and concentration will very nearly approach composition. Every one who thinks can write, at least after a fashion. Writing is one of the best of aids to thinking. When you attempt to write, you discover, very likely, that what you supposed you knew has been apprehended in the vaguest manner.

Take, therefore, any object, fact, truth, law or proposition. Example: the law or force of gravitation. Now ask as many questions as possible concerning this

All Values Yield to Concentration 247

fact. Bombard it with "what," "whose," "why," "where," "when," "how," "with what conditions," "how long," and the like. Thus: what is it? whose is it? where is it? when is it? how is it? etc., until you have exhausted your power of thought upon it. Turn it about. Look at it from every side. Examine it under all conditions. Find its nature, its operation, its source, its purpose, its bearing upon other natural forces. Ravel it out. Tear it into pieces. Write all answers in full. Then proceed to arrange all answers in groups after some logical order. Now read the material thus arranged, and you will discover new thought springing up, which will necessitate a rearrangement. Write this in full. Then fill out your synopsis in the best manner possible. Continue this exercise frequently for six months.

Meanwhile, study the cleanest and clearest writers for details of expression and correctness of statement and form. Review your work occasionally, and note improvement, both in composition and ability to get into a subject. Keep the ideal of straightforward simplicity always in mind. Declare war upon superlatives, and reduce your adjectives two-thirds. In all cases use the fewest words consistent with clean statements and full expression.

Exercise No. 6. Proceed as in former exercise to completion of synopsis. Now think this out, fully and clearly, as written. Memorize the thoughts, but never the words, section by section, taking several days if necessary, until the entire subject lies in your mind ready to be spoken or written in full. In doing this, you must *think in words*. Let the purpose in mind be to speak the thoughts as if to an audience. When you are master of the subject, speak all your thoughts in order to an imaginary gathering of people. Have the audience before you. Be in earnest. Get excited. Over the law of gravity? Certainly. Over anything under the heavens! Make gestures. Fear nothing. Never mind mistakes. Be keenly alive to this piece of work. Forget every other reality in the world. You believe certain things in connection with the law; deliver your soul on that matter as if to an audience of people who never have heard of it or do not think as you do.

This exercise should be continued for many months. A few moments devoted to it each day will prove of incalculable value. Almost any real subject will answer for a topic. Business, Politics, Farming, Magazines. After some experience, it will be well to avoid general topics and to select those of a narrower range, as, The Tides, The Party, The Raising of Celery, The Liquefaction of Air, etc.

Exercise No. 7. Study unceasingly to detect errors in your own thinking. Are your main propositions correct? Do you employ right words in stating them? Are the conclusions really deducible from your propositions? Why do you believe certain things? Are they based on actual facts? Are the facts sufficiently numerous to form a basis for belief? Are you biased in examination of facts? Do you think as you do because of desire, or ignorance, or prejudice? Make sure of your facts! Make sure that the facts prove one thing, and none other!

Exercise No. 8. Follow the above suggestions as to the thinking of other people. They are swearing by a host of things which are not necessarily so. Do not

All Values Yield to Concentration

become a bore, nor a judge. But make sure that arguments actually prove matters as asserted.

This chapter may well close with a quotation, taken from the author's published work, "*The Culture of Courage*," concerning mental health.

"When the mental attitude concerns truth, the mind is sanely intelligent, and, in the long run, will exhibit reasonableness.

"Any illustration of the attitude will be more or less incomplete, because the process unfolded uncovers so much of life. It should, therefore, be remembered that the following are merely specimen leaves from the vast forest of experience.

"*Illustration No. 1.* A man sees a ghost in the highway. Our invitation requires that he see the fact as it is. It is *some* fact; what *is* that fact? It is a tall stump with two or three naked branches, various lights and shadows moving upon them. The fact-*thing* has now become a fact-*group*. It is an appearance — a fact suggesting a supposed truth. What was the *real* truth? The ghostly body was a stump, the arms were branches, the movements were due to flickering shadows and varying degrees of light. The supposed truth was a ghost. The real truth was a mental deception; back of that a stump under certain conditions.

"Ten thousand applications are possible. I take one only — cures of all sorts of disease attributed to all sorts of remedies. We need not deny the cures; there are millions of cures, blessed be Nature! But is the agency of cure in any given case precisely what it is said to be? Is this the ghost fact of Christian Science, Mental Healing, drugs, or prayer? All the things named contain values for us. I simply suggest that when you attribute your cure to one agency or another, you strip all claims down to naked fact. That is the one sane test of the question whether a thing is a ghost or a fact.

"*Illustration No. 2.* Witchcraft had its facts, its supposed truth, and — its real truth. When men insisted on seeing the real facts, many of the fictitious facts disappeared, the supposed truth vanished, and the real truth — awaited discovery. After science had adopted the above methods, instead of the old shout, 'superstition'— contentment in which has hurt science more than it has hurt any other department of our life — the backlying facts began to emerge, and the truths, clairvoyance, clairaudience, hypnotism, fear, imagination, etc., etc., came slowly into light. We are now trying to find out why science should say, 'all bosh' to 'mesmerism,' 'occultism,' spiritualism, religion, or any other thing under the heavens."

The conclusion is this: Make sure of the facts; get at the real truth; keep open house to every proposition claiming to be real, but accept nothing not clearly demonstrated to sane but inspired reason.

The purpose of these studies on attention in thinking is to train you to establish the habit of knowing all sides of any question that confronts you; to observe all possibilities and consequences attendant upon your decision to "do this" or "do that." "Those who have not early been trained to see all sides of a question are apt to be extremely narrow, and undesirable to live with."

However, the ferreting out and discovering all possible phases of any matter before you is but one part

All Values Yield to Concentration 251

of the complete circle. Having "attended in thinking," and seeing the proper course to pursue — then must be brought forward the great jewel of ACTION in the line of best interest. "The world demands for success not only plenty of thought, but quickness of thought. More than half the world thinks after it is too late."

Become accustomed to deep, attentive thinking.

Always try to "think all around a subject."

Try and do the required thinking before you go "into the game."

Once clear thinking is done, *swiftly carry it into ACTION*.

In every part of the work of this chapter, keep in mind the sentence: "I am conscious of the sense of Will." You will not be distracted, but rather helped by that recollection.

ONLY WILL! ALL THINGS ARE POSSIBLE TO HIM THAT WILLS.

REMEMBERED

In ancient days, when hearts were bold,
And courage burned to meet the foe,
The wandering bard his story told
To eager listeners, young and old,
Of deeds heroic, life sublime,
And gods and humans mighty all,
Till, swept by passion's fiery flow
His soul was lost to space or time
And theirs in valor's clarion call.

We wonder not the leaping words —
The syllables that lilted sweet —
Or the fierce breath that red blood curds —
Or the one Name dark awe engirds,
Should bind men to the singer's will,
Resounding through the windy hall,
Or answered from the wolf's retreat: —
The singer lost in passion's skill,
The listeners swept by valor's call.

The song was like to gold a-melt;
The voice a diamond pen to write;
And souls were wax: the story, felt,
It burned, and left, then, scar and welt
For love and altar, home and friend.
Oh, long the singer's woven thrall!
And high the story's growing might!
His heart in Iliad or in Zend,
And theirs alost in valor's call.

This is the Tale of Memory,
The living scroll of timeless earth,
Sung to the air; writ facilely
In spirits eager thrilled to be
By love and battle, home and Book; —
Responsive ever to the worth
Of Life, our Bard. All hail his thrall!
For in his passion's voice and look
We learn high valor's clarion call.

— The Author.

CHAPTER XXI

EXERCISES IN MEMORY

"I RETAIN a clear impression or image of everything at which I have looked, although the coloring of that impression is necessarily vivid in proportion to the degree of interest with which the object was regarded. I find this faculty of much use and solace to me. By its aid I can live again at will in the midst of any scene or circumstance by which I have been surrounded. By a voluntary act of mind I can in a moment conjure up the whole of any one out of the innumerable scenes in which the slightest interest has at any time been felt by me."—*Dr. John Kitto.*

THEORY OF CHAPTER

Review deepens mental impressions;
Storing of mind enlarges it, and gives it immense momentum;
The effort to secure mental force multiplies Will-energy.

It was John Ruskin who said, "There are but two strong conquerors of the forgetfulness of men, Poetry and Architecture." But Ruskin had the far outlook in mind. There is but one strong conqueror of the personal forgetfulness, and that is the determined Will. The poem and the cathedral preserve their age in the world's memory; the resolute Will preserves the individual's mind from becoming a sieve. The Rev. Dwight Hillis once remarked in a lecture, that he forgot with his memory. This was an old pleasantry. Men forget at times because of the rush of thought forbidding the quick grasp of mind necessary to the thing desired. But the real secret of forgetting lies in a vaporous condition of Will.

PRELIMINARY

There is therefore but one "golden rule" for improvement of the memory. The "golden rule" is the iron rule of *persistent and intelligent exercise*. The first requisite of memory-cultivation is attention; the second is found in the laws of memory. Memory depends upon mental impressions, and these upon attention, understanding, similarity and contrast, and Will. All elements of success here call primarily upon the latter.

Professor James has formulated the law: "*Whether or no there be anything else in the mind at the moment when we consciously will a certain act, a mental conception made up of memory-images of these sensations, defining which special act it is, must be there.*"

The secret of the Will is anticipation based on memory.

Not to refine unduly, it may be said that the power to remember is measured by the ability to attend. Joy, pain, and the like are easily recalled because they greatly impress the mind; to secure an equally adequate degree of attention in regard to other matters demands that the soul set itself about the task of deepening its own impressions. Hence we may say, speaking broadly, to attend is to will; to will is to attend.

"All determinate recollection," as remarked by Dr. Carpenter, "involves the exercise of volitional control over the direction of the thoughts."

RÉGIMES

Exercise No. 1. Select the best specimen of condensed and simple English that you can find. Read a paragraph carefully. Begin to read again, defining to yourself every word. If you are in the slightest doubt, consult a dictionary. Go hungry a month to possess a first-class dictionary. After satisfying yourself that you understand every word in the first sentence, make sure that you understand the sentence as a whole. Now proceed, attentively and with strong Will, to repeat the first few words, keeping words and *thought* in mind. Do not repeat like a parrot, but think, resolving to remember — *the words and what they say*. Continue until you have memorized this part of the sentence. Then go on in the same manner with the next few words. Fix these firmly in mind. Now recall all words and thought thus far committed, and repeat, again and again, thinking the thought as you do so with the utmost attention and energy. Proceed in this way until the entire sentence is mastered.

It will be better not to try too many words at a time; you will easily ascertain the number most convenient to your mind.

In this method, never for a moment forget to keep in mind the *ideas* presented by the language. As words often represent different shades of meaning, will attention to the shade here used. Let the work be done with the utmost concentrated energy.

If you will repeat that sentence frequently during the day, wherever you chance to be, *always thought-*

fully and determinedly, you will fasten it firmly in mind.

If you will repeat the same exercise with another sentence the following day, and frequently repeat both sentences, the first will become more deeply impressed upon memory, and the second will be acquired as fully as was the first.

The value of repetition is not new. But the point of this exercise lies not so much in repetition of words as in concentrated and continuous gripping of their thought. In all repetition, therefore, study and master the ideas which they present.

It may be supposed that you are memorizing some brief poem or bit of prose. When it has been acquired, you should frequently repeat it as a whole; say, once in several days, and later, once during several weeks. In a comparatively short time it will have become indelibly stamped upon the mind. Two or three times a year thereafter recall it, which will preserve it from " drifting out " again.

Read originals now and then for correction of unconscious errors.

If it is the thought that you are mainly concerned about, use it as often as possible in conversation or writing; work it over in your own material; you will thus work it thoroughly into your own mind. This done, words and source are of little importance. Here is plagiarism defensible before the gods. They, indeed, practise it more than their worshipers.

Some books are not worth much labor. There are others which will amply repay a resolve to master them. If you thoroughly master one small book during a year, as life and reading go, you will do well.

But there are few books that should be verbally

memorized. You wish the contents rather than the words. These may be acquired in the following manner, supposing the book is not largely technical, and to a degree, perhaps, if it is so:

Exercise No. 2. First, know what the book treats. Now read a paragraph very carefully, making sure that you understand every word and its thought as a whole. Then take the first complete statement of fact or theory, whether involving one sentence or many, and think it out aloud and in your own words. Read again, and restate the thought in different language from that employed by the author or by yourself in the effort just indicated. Imagine that you are speaking to some person; recite to him; compel him to listen; act as though trying to teach him. Seek opportunity to do the same with real people. Become, without ostentation, a walking instructor. Don't be a bore, but resolve to become the most interesting converser among your acquaintances. But remember, it is always the contents of that book which you are trying to make your own property.

In addition to the above, say to yourself frequently during the day: " This book affirms, at such and such a place, so and so "— stating where and what the matter is. Do this as often as it may be convenient. When you make this effort of memory, think backward and forward in the book from that point. At the close of the day, repeat all that you have thus far mastered. Then read the book for correction of errors.

On the following day, repeat the same process with the next complete statement.

Continue as above until you have passed through an entire chapter.

Now, without reading, try to make in your mind alone a mere skeleton of the main thoughts of the chapter. Then memorize the skeleton. The chapter may reduce to one or two general statements, or it may involve a number of general together with subordinate propositions. Make these in their order your own.

When the skeleton has been firmly fixed in mind, review from memory the series of statements already thought out and memorized, and of which the skeleton is a reduction. This will preserve the filling-in of the synopsis. Thereafter, at convenient intervals, proceed in a like manner, now to review the outline, now to recall the detailed propositions.

Now proceed in the same way to the next chapter. Always think the written thoughts in your own words. Repeat during each day all preceding thought-statements of the chapter in hand, as well as the one of that day. When the second chapter has been finished, think out from memory a skeleton of its contents. Meanwhile, during the exercises with the present chapter, occasionally recall the thought-statements, in outline and in detail, of the first chapter, looking well after their order. When the second chapter has been acquired, think out occasionally a consecutive statement of the contents of both chapters. Then construct a new skeleton of all thoughts thus far presented, and memorize as an everlasting possession.

Continue until you have mastered the book.

In all this work, ignore whatever is not strictly essential to any sentence-thought, or to any statement-paragraph.

Such labor will tax your patience, but it will surely make you master of your book, and will in time give you the greatest facility in reading. Ultimately the mind may be depended upon to supply all necessary filling-in, if the skeletons have been well understood and thoroughly memorized. You will have acquired the ability, if your author is worth reading, when you know his general propositions, to think the details without further reading, unless the matter is technical or historical, or the like.

Exercise No. 3. While passing slowly through a room, glance swiftly and attentively around. Then, in another room, recall as many objects noted as may be possible. Do nothing languidly. Put your entire energy into this exercise. Repeat every day for ten days, with rest of two days, making a record of results. On the tenth day, compare records and note improvement.

Exercise No. 4. When on the street, note, as you pass along, all objects around you. Having passed a block, recall as many objects as possible. Repeat frequently every day. Repeat during ten days, with rest, and on the tenth day, note improvement.

Exercise No. 5. Resolve with great Will-power, when you retire, to awaken at a certain hour, and instantly to arise. If you fail for a time, be not discouraged; persevere and your mind will surely remember. But you must instantly arise at the appointed time, or your self will discover that you do not really mean what you profess to will. Continue until you have acquired the ability to awaken at any desired hour.

Exercise No. 6. In the morning resolve to recall a certain thought at an exact hour. You must think mightily on this resolution and fix it firmly in mind. Then dismiss it from immediate thought and attend to other duties as usual. Do not try to keep it in mind. In time you will obey your own order. You will probably fail at first, but perseverance will make you master of appointments of this kind. The reflex influence in other matters will appear in due time. Continue at least six months.

Exercise No. 7. When you start for your school or place of business, intensely resolve to return by a certain different route from that followed in going. Put your whole mind into this determination. In time you will not fail to remember. Never by action contradict any of these resolutions. Continue at least six months.

Exercise No. 8. Walk or drive to your school or place of business, and return home, in as many different and previously planned ways as possible. Never deviate from the plan. At the end of each, arrange another for going and coming, and adhere to it as a matter of the utmost importance. Continue at least six months.

Exercise No. 9. At the beginning of each day make a plan for your general conduct until evening. Learn to have an order for action. Be master of yourself. Having decided upon such plan for the day, never, if possible to carry it out, vary its execution. Do not plan for more than one day at a time, unless the nature of your doings requires it, and in this event, leave particulars for each morning. Make your plans with care and strong Will, but do not burden the mind with them in a way to interfere with details that spring up. Command your mind to attend to the plan without forcing you to unnecessary strain of conscious thought. It is always better to arrange for results, leaving minute details to be decided according to demands of the moment. Continue six months.

Exercise No. 10. At the close of each day carefully review your thoughts and doings since morning. What have been your most valuable ideas? What your most emphatic sensations? What your most important actions? Have you carried out your plans? If not, why not? How might your thoughts, feelings and doings have been improved? What have been your motives? Have they been wise and worthy? Resolve upon betterment the next day, and incorporate this resolution into its plan. Continue this exercise indefinitely.

The preceding are suggestions only. They are based upon a law of the mind. If they appear to be unnecessary and tedious, that may be an evidence of the indeterminate and weak Will. It is a law, as remarked by Dr. James Sully, " that *increase in the power of foreseeing action tends to widen the area of resolution.* Thus, so far as our daily actions become ordered according to a plan, they all have a stage of resolution as their antecedent. We habitually look forward to the succession of actions making up the business, etc., of the day, and resolve to perform them in due order as circumstances occur. And the subordination of action to ruling ends implies, as hinted above, a habitual state of resolution, that is preparedness to act in certain ways in certain circumstances."

Exercise No. 11. Make it a rule of life to learn some new and useful thing every day. Especially go outside of your business for such information. This will test the Will and store the memory.

Exercise No. 12. Frequently commit to memory lists of dates, and review often enough to hold in memory.

Make groupings of historic dates and commit to memory. Link each group as a group with other groups from time to time. Frequently review.

Exercise No. 13. Make lists of objects of public interest in your community, with skeletons of information concerning them. Commit, and frequently review.

Exercise No. 14. Commit and frequently review lists of names, as United States Presidents, English Monarchs, United States Navy Vessels, etc.

Exercise No. 15. Determine thoroughly to study some subject which lies outside your business. Keep at it. Remember, growth of mind and Will!

Exercise No. 16. Make the following a perpetual régime:

1. Never be content with any partial acquaintance with things.
2. Learn to refer items of knowledge to general principals.
3. Employ all aids suggested by any particular study.
4. Follow some natural or logical order in fixing facts, propositions, etc., in memory.
5. Cultivate attentive observation wherever you are placed.
6. Stand squarely and conscientiously on the side of truth.

MEMORY CHARACTERISTICS

"In a very general way," as remarked in "*Business Power*," a volume in the Power-Book Library, "the mental characteristics in the matter of memory may be indicated by the following analysis:

"Mind and memory especially occupied with objectively induced sensations.

"Mind and memory especially given to emotions of pleasures and pains.

"Mind and memory especially running to mental pictures.

"Mind and memory especially good in the matter of dates and figures.

"Mind and memory especially attentive to abstract ideas.

"Mind and memory especially interested in principles.

"Mind and memory especially elaborative of laws.

"Mind and memory especially given to details.

"Mind and memory especially given to construction of wholes.

"Now, all minds and memories of average intelligence possess all the characteristics thus indicated in some degree, but none of us possesses them in any all-round equal degree. The type of mind is determined by the prevailing characteristic. Thus also with memories. If your type of memory is shown above, and if you require improvement in some one or more of the particular types portrayed, the method consists in persistent attention and the formation of habits in the desired direction by constant practice and the constant use of associations. You are urged especially to observe that the words: *Resolution — Attention — Per-*

sistence — *Repetition* — *Association* — *Habit*, represent the amount and kind of effort demanded.

"Take, for example, the memory of details. Are you lacking in ability to recall in that respect? You are urged to *resolve* on improvement, to *attend* to all details with all your mind, to *persist* in such labor, to *repeat* the attention, to *associate* the details with recollective 'signs' of any sort that you may invent, to *form the habit* of doing all this in regard to details.

"The trouble with people who forget is in part the fact that they fail to fore-get. In some cases the fore-getting is actual, but it is too easy and quick, for one thing, so that a good rule will be found in this remark: 'My work really begins when I think it is finished.' With most of us it is there that we close the work. In other words, when you are sure that you have a thing, proceed to hammer it into mind, so to speak, for safe-keeping. But always should the fore-getting be assimilated by association with something already possessed in the mind. In the process of fore-getting, repetition is also required because this habituates the mind or the brain-cells in certain ways so that accompanying mental actions or associations are developed which assist in memory."

It is well to bear in mind that it is the art of observing which gathers the materials which memory stores in mind. Speaking on this subject W. H. Groves says: "Robert Houdin and son immortalized themselves in legerdemain by the cultivation of the power of observation. They did things which bordered on the miraculous because their eyes had been trained to observe closely. They would pass through a room, or by a shop window, and take a mental inventory of everything they saw, and then compare notes. At first they observed only a few things, but finally they could see quickly and remember accurately everything.

"A splendid idea is to take a bird's eye view of a room and its articles. Then shut your eyes and recall all you saw,— the appearance and size of the room and articles, their number, nature, color — the chairs, carpet, pictures, etc. At first you may not remember accurately, but practice and perseverance will enable you to take in at a glance everything you see.

"Enumerate at night the persons and things you have seen through the day. Thurlow Weed made his mind 'wax to receive and marble to retain.' A man, who was a wonder, studied a map of the place he was approaching in travel, then shut his eyes and recalled

He did this for about fifteen minutes, and had it clearly stamped in his memory."

All such exercises are of great value and should be practised as time allows. Even when on the street or in company you can be increasing your skill in remembering.

Always, in striving to cultivate the memory, call up and sustain the Mood of strong and confident personality. Resolve: "I shall acquire a great memory for the purpose of increasing the power of my Will."

HOW CAME IMAGINATION?

QUESTION

How came imagination to the brain,
Stirring the fibered cells till nerves alert
Sped messages of life to flesh inert,
And all the marvelous things of joy or pain
Filled mind and body? Came it by the main
Method and law old Nature must assert —
As the blue lotus or the ruby's stain —
Or, by sheer accident law failed t' avert?

ANSWER

Came it that love might fear and fearless die.
Came it that blood might steal Promethean fires.
Came it that thought might drain the fount of truth.
Came it that self, the spirit-lark, might fly
With the great sun, and sing as night expires.
Came it that soul might know and win immortal youth.

— The Author.

CHAPTER XXII

EXERCISES IN IMAGINATION

"WHENEVER a person wills, or, rather, professes to will, to imagine, he has in fact already imagined; and, consequently, there can be no such thing as imaginations which are exclusively the result of a direct act of the Will."—*Professor Upham.*

"I am inclined to think it was his practice, when engaged in the composition of any work, to excite his vein by the perusal of others on the same subject or plan, from which the slightest hint caught by his imagination, as he read, was sufficient to kindle there such a train of thought as, but for that spark (and that direction of the Will) had never been awakened."—*Sir Thomas Moore, " Life of Lord Byron."*

THEORY OF CHAPTER

The highest imagination involves all the powers of the mind;

Willed culture of imagination secures its greatest efficiency;

The steadfast application of imagination highly cultured to the concerns of life requires the strongest and best-regulated exercise of Will-power;

That means the mighty Will developed all round.

"All the leaders in the world's life have been men of imagination."

It is in the action of the imagination that the question is presented, whether a man's life shall be governed by the subconscious mind to take him where it may, or by the conscious Will in control of that great servant. The imagination should be cultivated because it has so important a place in all our affairs, but its cultivation should always have reference to the sway of reason in conjunction with a reasonable Will. "The subjective mind," well said Olston in "Mind Power and Privileges," "will feed upon, and create, from the material given it by the Will. Schopenhauer said, 'My mind draws its food from the medium of intelligence and thought; this nourishment gives body to my work.' He, however, directed the course of his reading and thought to such things as would bear upon his general theme."

Our task in imagination, then, involves not only action of Will, but as well education of the deepest self in the interest of reason, judgment and right motives in life.

Preliminary

Without dwelling upon the various kinds of imagination, as, the scientific, the mathematical, the inventive, the philosophical, the artistic, it is to be observed that the ethical imagination is by far the most important. The imaginative power is indispensable to Will, because willing involves motives and consequences, and the mind requires ability to *see* motives and consequences clearly, vividly, and in proper relation.

"*In action as in reasoning, the great thing is the quest of right conception.*"

Many persons will badly because they cannot perceive the full force of antagonizing motives, and they possess small facility for calling up the possible outcomes of actions or courses of conduct. Hence development of Will demands exercise in consideration of desires, reasons and purposes and in forepicturing of consequences.

"*It may be said in general,*" remarks Professor James, "*that a great part of every deliberation consists in the turning over of all the possible modes of conceiving the doing or not doing the act in point.*"

RÉGIMES

Exercise No. 1. We begin, first, with simple imaginary sensations. Recall a single rose, and imagine its fragrance. Now place yourself in mind before a hill of roses, and imagine the air to be heavy with their fragrance. What would be the effect upon yourself? What would you do in such a case? Repeat this exercise with a drop of musk. Then think of a lake of musk. Repeat with the notes of a song-bird. Then imagine a forest full of birds, all singing.

These exercises should be conducted in a quiet room. Bring the Will to bear with great power upon the work. Make the imagination as strong and distinct as possible. Repeat until the imaginary sensations become as vivid as in life.

Exercise No. 2. Stand by the side of some running stream, or near a water-fall, or in a factory in operation. Now listen attentively to the sounds that assail your ears. There is one general combination of sound. What is it like? What does it recall to memory? What mood does it bring to your soul? After you have become familiar with the whole effect, proceed to analyze it into as many different notes as you can detect. When you have done this thoroughly — have separated the whole sound into its component parts — imagine clearly and powerfully, a great volume of one of these sounds, making it as loud as possible; then continue with another, and a third, and so on, until the general combination has been exhausted.

Lastly, go away from a source of real sound to a quiet place, and recall, first the general harmony, and then its individual sounds as previously analyzed. Continue until the exercise may be carried on with perfect ease.

Exercise No. 3. Recall to memory some distant and real landscape. The difficulty will consist in bringing up the details, but these must be supplied. Resolute practice will accomplish the result desired. By a supreme effort make the mental picture as real as life. In doing this you should try to reinstate the soul's moods occasioned by the original scene. Place yourself, in thought, on the exact spot where first you saw the landscape, and resolutely compel the view to rise before you with as much of detail as possible. Keep the willful mood, and continue with different landscapes until you can summon a vivid picture of real scenery with the greatest ease.

Exercise No. 4. Recall some experience which has made a lasting impression upon your memory. Pass again in thought through its various phases, slowly, carefully, with great intensity of feeling. Dwell upon its cause, its accessories, and its effect upon you at the time. Was the effect pleasant or otherwise? In either case, state why. What influence had it upon your sub-

Does the Prophet Speak Truly? 271

sequent life? Would you repeat it? If not, why not? If so, may it again be secured — and how? May it be avoided in the future — and how?

Continue with various experiences until the lessons of caution and thoughtful self-interest become permanent factors in your mind.

Exercise No. 5. In a quiet room, construct imaginary pictures, such as you have never seen: — of a bird, grotesque and unreal; of an animal, curious yet beautiful, or perfectly tame but horrible; of a building, magnificent yet mysterious; of a landscape, weird and entrancing or wild but not forbidding. Do not allow the mind to wander into revery. You should preserve the Will-mood as strongly as possible. Continue until control of the imagination has been secured.

Exercise No. 6. Gaze at some large object, and try to discover in or about it a suggestion for the play of imagination. It is a horse? Give it wings, and journey to a distant planet. It is a spool of thread? Make it to be a spider's web wherewith to weave a thousand robes or with which to send messages without unwinding by charging with intensest Will-power as you breathe upon it. Continue with other objects and various fanciful imaginings until Will is master of imagination — to call up, to control or to banish.

Exercise No. 7. Select a sentence from a standard author, which illustrates the celerity of a trained imagination, and then will into the mind the complete picture suggested. Thus, Lowell, in "A Moosehead Journal," writes: "Sometimes a root-fence stretched up its bleaching antlers, like the trophies of a giant hunter." The man who said this tells us that "the divine faculty is to *see* what everybody can *look at*." The "divine faculty" of "*seeing*" should be cultivated. And it may become an Aladdin's Lamp to him whose Will is mighty. Try, now, to picture this rootfence of Lowell's scene in such a way as to suggest bleaching antlers. Why did the writer bleach the antlers? Why did he not see them poised upon a row of deer-heads?

Or, take another sentence from the same author: "A string of five loons was flying back and forth in long, irregular zigzags, uttering at intervals their wild, tremulous cry, which always seems far away, like the last faint pulse of echo dying among the hills, and which is one of those few sounds that, instead of disturbing solitude, only deepen and confirm it." Now, if you have not heard the cry of the loon, try to imagine a sound which reminds you of "the last faint pulse of echo dying among the hills." If you have heard these birds, call up the scene and its impressions as vividly as possible. In either case, make the present impression absolutely real. Keep the mind from wandering, holding it to the mood suggested. Then resolutely banish scene and feeling.

Having ascertained what the imaginative element is in such sentences (you can find similar everywhere), proceed to write some statement in which a like play of fancy is obtained. Do not be discouraged. Throw yourself into the mood of imagination. Practise this entire exercise persistently until you can with ease secure the mood and write a sentence of imaginative beauty.

The old injunction, "Know thyself," is by most people sadly neglected. It is worth a deal of labor to get acquainted with this "unknown land." Lowell writes that "a man should have traveled thoroughly round himself and the great *terra incognita* just outside and inside his own threshold, before he undertakes voyages of discovery to other worlds." This is largely true even of mental voyages. "Who hath sailed about the world of his own heart," quotes Lowell from Thomas Fuller, "sounded every creek, surveyed each corner, but that still there remains much '*terra incognita*' to himself?" It would be well if, before trying to read, we could learn how to read; before trying to study, we could learn how to study. These exercises, therefore, have in view the cultivation of one of the greatest of human faculties. They deal with simple matters because this would seem to be best, and they aim at suggestiveness only; but if they are faithfully followed they will result in a developed imagination and, which is particularly to the point here, an increased power of Will of the greatest value in practical life.

Continue these exercises indefinitely.

Exercise No. 8. Examine a machine of not very complex construction. Know its purpose. Understand all its parts and their mutual relations. When you have thoroughly analyzed the mechanism, close your eyes and summons it before the mind. Persist in this endeavor until you are able to form a vivid mental picture of the whole. Then mentally take it to pieces. Then mentally put the parts together. Now try to suggest some improvement by which some of the parts may be omitted, or by which parts may be better adjusted, or by which the machine may be made to accomplish better or less expensive work. Continue this exercise with various mechanisms until you are able to see into machinery, can call up to mind its inner construction, and can with ease form mental pictures of its wholes and its parts.

Exercise No. 9. Think of some matter in your life or home or place of business where a simple device or mechanism would prove valuable by a saving of time or money. The opportunity being found, proceed to think out a suitable arrangement for the purpose. Do not become absorbed in this effort to the injury of other interests. The object here is not to make inventors, but to develop power of imagination in order that motives of Will and consequences of action may be clearly perceived. Make this exercise, therefore, a study to such end. Above all, keep a strong sense of Will thoroughly in mind. Continue until you have acquired facility in the constructive imagination.

Exercise No. 10. Recall one of your great mistakes in life, review carefully, intensely, the various motives which appealed to you at that time. Think over their relations, their force, their persistence. Judge candidly whether you deliberated sufficiently before acting. Remember distinctly that you did not give all motives or reasons an adequate hearing. Acknowledge exactly why you yielded to some motives and rejected others. Bring all these matters before your mind with the vividness of a present experience. Then review all the consequences of your then choice. In what respect do you now see that you ought to have proceeded differently? Had you so done, what would probably have been the outcome? Suppose you were now to be put back into the former circumstances. How would you decide with present knowledge? To avoid a similar mistake in the future, you must then do what you have failed to do, namely, deliberate carefully, summon all motives into court, hear each plea, give to all adequate consideration and weight, and vividly foresee all consequences of choice as far as possible. The present exercise is designed to assist you to these desired ends. Continue such review work until you have called up for examination all mistakes which you can remember. Meanwhile mightily resolve to forefend the future by giving every important matter utmost careful attention.

Exercise No. 11. Recall to memory some very attractive bit of landscape observed in your travels. Let us say it is a great piece of woods seen in autumn. Picture this scene to the soul: the undulating ground, covered with fallen leaves and dotted by occasional clumps of bushes; the many colors of the foliage still crowning the trees, whose numberless trunks lift into the canopy above and afford sunlit vistas in every direction; the play of the winds upon the gleaming leaves, fallen and drooping and still clinging; the vast quiet which broods over all, save when broken by the sighing of the breeze or the call of birds from the open; the swiftly moving stealth of squirrels along the ground or among the branches; and the strange and pleasurable moods suggested when you stood there in nature's haunt of beauty.

Now invent reflections in connection with this scene. Proceed first, by the law of similarity. Of what does it remind you? You are to make the scene you have imagined the basis and cause of other scenes *similar* in one or more respects; and you are deliberately to analyze the suggestion, the two scenes by comparison, and the moods of thought occasioned by both, with reasons for the same. Do not fall into revery. This is downright work. Its value depends altogether upon the amount of Will which you put into it, and the intelligence with which you control the mind during the labor involved.

Proceed, now, to make this scene the basis and cause of another scene by *contrast*. You are to repeat the above exercise in all respects, except that contrast, and not similarity, is to furnish your material.

Follow these directions daily until their full value is apparent in imagination entirely under control of Will.

Exercise No. 12. The above directions may be repeated by substituting experience for scenery, proceeding, first, by similarity, and then by contrast. In all cases be strongly conscious of the willing sense. Continue the exercise indefinitely.

Exercise No. 13. Read some famous poem of the imagination. It will be better to commit it to memory. Having thoroughly mastered it, by understanding every word, and by vividly picturing in the mind every element of fancy, go on to analyze it, making a clear statement in writing of its consecutive thoughts. Then note carefully every specimen of imagination which it contains. Then determine its faults and its beauties as a work of the imagination. Then observe the relation and dependence of one element upon another. Then ascertain the secret of its beauty and of its power upon thought and feeling. Learn why it has lived and exerts its acknowledged influence. What is that influence? Continue this exercise indefinitely until you have mastered many of the world's great poems.

Exercise No. 14. In a similar manner, read some famous book (not fiction), and treat its imaginative elements as secrets to be discovered and explained. Continue this work with the best in your library.

Exercise No. 15. Take a work of fiction, and give it a similar analysis. You are now dealing with pictures of life and human nature. Read so as to obtain a vivid portrait of each character. Become thoroughly acquainted with all the personages of the book. Study the reasons for their actions. Investigate their motives. Note the influence of ancestry and environment upon them. Observe whether or not they are acting in a manner that is true to life. Would you act differently? And why? Appreciate the fact that they reason falsely and do not adequately consider all reasons involved in choice, and hence, do not give due weight to the best motives that appeal to them. Go on to follow their conduct to consequences. Are these natural — demanded by previous acts and conditions? Could the characters have been improved? Or the plot? Or the general developments of the persons? Or the outcome of their actions and relations?

Make the book a piece of real life, and study it as above suggested, in order, first, that you may thoroughly understand it, and, secondly, that you may apply its lessons to your own life. Continue until you have mastered the best works of fiction in English.

In all this remember that you are cultivating the imagination for the purpose of discovering reasons for or against conduct and of appreciating consequences. By as much as you so discover and appreciate in real life must your Will become strengthened and its determination wiser.

"*The determinate exercise of the Judgment*," says Professor W. B. Carpenter, "*which involves the comparison of ideas, can only take place under the guidance of the Will.*"

Exercise No. 16. Suppose yourself to be about to take a certain step or to perform a certain act. It is a matter of vital importance. You wish to make no mistake, for your happiness and welfare depend upon your decision. But how are you to proceed? You may choose one thing or the other. The wisdom of your choice involves the adequate consideration of two matters — motives and consequences. Apprehended consequences are motives, but this division is convenient. Under motives may be arranged reasons for and against either choice; under consequences all outcomes which you can see as likely or probably to follow your decision. If you have cultivated memory, the recollection of other similar problems which you have been compelled to solve will come to your assistance. If you have cultivated imagination, you will be enabled to see clearly the motives that appeal to you, and you will also have power to imagine yourself as entering upon one course of procedure, passing through possible consequent experiences and reaping ultimate outcomes. Here will appear the values of preceding exercises. But above all, you should bring to this imaginary problem (a real problem will serve better) a vivid sense of its reality and importance, and a feeling of strong resolution to consider it with all your might, and to solve it in the best possible manner.

Let us now suppose the problem. You are not fond of the city or town in which you are living and conducting your business. You wish to change residence and business to another place. But there are difficulties in the way. These difficulties you are now to consider.

First, recall all previous experiences in similar matters, and keep them constantly in mind. Secondly, write in brief every conceivable objection to a change. Example: from your present domicile. All your friends and associates are here. You have here a business standing of say, twenty years. Your trade or clientage is established and certain. The town is growing. Investments are fairly remunerative, and they are safe. Your property is located in this place. Taxes are rather high, but not unreasonable, and they represent improvements. Your home is good and pleasantly situated. Your family enjoy fine social relations and are fond of the town. The children are taking root. They have opportunities of value. Schools are first class. Public opinion is sound. Morals are at least average. The churches are fairly active and progressive. Your age is forty-five.

On the other hand: Climate is not agreeable. Some enemies have been developed. Only a moderate business can be carried on here. Investments do not yield a large return. Taxes are increasing. The population cannot exceed a certain rather low estimate. No new railroad facilities need be expected. Manufacturing interests are not likely to become numerous. The surrounding country is agricultural, and it no longer yields its old crops. There are no mineral resources beneath the surface. The place is far removed from points of interest — the mountains, the sea, the great cities. You have long been conscious of a degree of discontent and restlessness. You believe that a new environment would stir you up to better achievements. You ought to have a larger return for your investments of time and money. You desire the advantages of a larger sphere. Your family might therein find increased opportunities for enjoyment and a start in life. You have known better society than that in which you now move. The church of your choice is not located in the town where you live.

After these imaginary presentations of reason for and against a change, a decision is still difficult. You must now go on to select tentatively some place to which you may possibly transfer your life. There may be several in mind. Each location must receive a full and careful consideration. You are lawyer and judge, and you must plead honestly as the one, and decide impartially as the other.

In each contemplated move, you must call up every possible advantage and disadvantage, especially the latter, which may be likely to accrue from any choice that you may make. After each case, for and against, has been presented, proceed carefully to weigh them as wholes, taking in the general impression of both. Now note the balance of judgment: "To go, or not to go." Then proceed to review each case, and carefully strike out all reasons that offset one another, noting, again, at the last, the general balance of judgment: "To go, or not to go." If the two general judgments disagree, set the matter aside for future consideration. If they agree, hold the matter in abeyance a time, but resolve to decide definitely after sufficient opportunity for final reflection. If then you are in doubt, stay where you are.

Proceed in a similar manner with reference to the place to which you propose to move. If after a full deliberation you are in doubt as to one place, try another. If, having determined to move, you cannot decide upon the place "to which," remain where you are. If you decide to move, stir not until the new residence has been properly determined. If that is fixed, bend every energy to move to your own advantage. When your opportunity arrives, seize it quickly. Then dismiss absolutely all regrets.

Continue these exercises indefinitely.

The above are rough suggestions merely. They set forth what intelligent people always substantially do with reference to matters of importance. They are here offered because many even intelligent men seem wanting in the power clearly to see motives and possible consequences connected with momentous decisions. There are strong Wills which are not wisely exercised because of a simple lack of imaginative thinking. Many Wills are like guns set with hair-triggers — they go off before good aim can be taken. Deliberation is worth gold and stocks, and it forefends against sorrow. But a good deliberation depends largely upon the imaginative power of the soul. Our great trouble in life is that we "didn't know it was loaded." *It is the work of the Will-controlled imagination to know. Here is the great prophet of success.*

"Where the Will is healthy the *vision* must be correct."

Though creative imagination is one of the mind's most wonderful qualities, yet nowhere in school or college do we find systematic instruction in this art. All the way from primeval man — through the swing of the centuries and the upward march of mankind, the imagination has been the basis of progress. As a writer on psychology puts it:

" The products of the constructive imagination have

been the only stepping stones for material progress. The constructive imagination of early man, aided by thought, began to conquer the world. When the winter cold came, the imagination pictured the skin of the animal on the human body. *Will power going out in action merely made that image a reality.* . . . The chimney, the stove, the stage-coach, the locomotive, are successive milestones, showing the progressive march of the imagination.

"Every time we tell a story clearly so as to impress the details on the mind of others, every time we describe a place or a landscape vividly, every time we relate what we have read in a book of travels so as to arouse definite images in the minds of our hearers,— we are cultivating imagination. It is excellent training for a person to attempt to describe to others a meadow, a grove, an orchard, the course of a brook, the sky at sunrise, the starry heavens. If his description is not heavy, like unleavened bread, the liveliness will be due to the activity of his imagination."

The healthy Will is that which is bent on achieving right personal success by right methods, because self is a unit in the world's complex whole, which is slowly evolving the right universal Will.

The law of all this individual evolution is the double law of self-knowledge and adjustment.

That this law may "come good" in your case, you need to cultivate, and rightly use, yourself and your relations with the world. It is here that imagination plays its part. *Who are you?* Find that out. *What is your best adjustment to the world?* Find that out. Learn to see things (in self — in world), first, as they really are; secondly, as they should be for all-round welfare. Then carry out the vision.

The Will must not only be strong; it must also act wisely. Its realest motto is: I RESOLVE TO WILL — WITH POWER, AND FOR THE BEST. THEREFORE, ATTENTION! TO REASONS AND TO CONSEQUENCES!!

WHO HATH WISDOM?

Said a king, one day, to his sober fool,
  "Your name, good friend, is far from fit;
Fling cap and bell into yonder pool,
  And say me nought of your dead-man's wit,
  For a sober fool is the Devil's skit."

Said the grinning fool to the sober king,
  "Your name, good friend, is quite misnamed;
Doff sword and sceptre, stand and sing,
  And say me nought of your kingcraft famed,
  For a foolish king is the Devil shamed."

Now a fool is king when a fool complete,
But a king all fool is a madman's freak: —
I would liefer be the world's great jest
Than a grinning ape in purple dressed.
Yet a saner choice of plan or dream
Is the soul that's king by worth supreme.
— THE AUTHOR.

CHAPTER XXIII

SOME DISEASES OF THE IMAGINATION

"THE underlying cause of all weakness and unhappiness in man, heredity and environment to the contrary notwithstanding, has always been, and is still, *weak habit-of-thought*. This is proven by the observed instances in which *strong habit-of-thought* has invariably made its masters superior to heredity, and to environment, and to illness, and to weakness of all kinds, and has redeemed them from non-success and misery, to the enjoyment of success, honor and happiness."—*Horace Fletcher.*

There are some dangers connected with the imagination which should be avoided, because they are enemies of a good Will. These dangers are apparent in the mental life of the majority of people, "Common sense," says James Sully in "Illusions," "knowing nothing of fine distinctions, is wont to draw a sharp line between the region of illusions and that of sane intelligence. To be the victim of an illusion is, in the popular judgment, to be excluded from the category of rational men." But "most men are sometimes liable to illusion. Hardly anybody is always consistently sober and rational in his perceptions and beliefs. A momentary fatigue of the nerves, a little mental excitement, a relaxation of the effort of attention by which we continually take our bearings with respect to the real world about us, will produce just the same kind of confusion of reality and phantasm which we observe in the insane."

It is to difficulties of this character that the present chapter seeks to turn attention, because it is believed that they are curable by good health and the resolute Will.

One of these enemies of Will is *revery,* which is not of a true imagination because not controlled by the mind. Revery may therefore be banished by the Will, and a true imagination may be made to take its place.

RÉGIMES

Exercise No. 1. Whenever the mind exhibits a tendency to wander aimlessly from one thing to another, instantly check its roving. In order to do this, select from its pictures a single image, and deliberately proceed to elaborate that, making it vivid, building up its various elements into a complete whole. In this work, banish the revery-mood and call up the resolute sense. Or weave the selected image into some train of purposed thought or action involving reasoning and an end to be attained. Consider the various motives and follow out the several consequences to an ultimate. Insist upon seeing vividly every picturable thing in the thought-train. Hold the mind steadily to the line determined on. Continue until the bent for revery is displaced by a habit of definite thinking.

Some minds are troubled with various *hallucinations.* Here, again, imagination is out of control, and feelings are made real and images are rendered objective because such is the case. There are so-called invalids who would now enjoy perfect health had they not deceived themselves originally and thus brought about conditions which would ruin the health of a savage. It is not "Christian Science," but common sense, which teaches that the mind may, by resolute assertion of Will, throw off many physical discomforts. The writer once called upon a woman who had taken to her bed from sheer obstinacy. This was her only real disease. But it was real enough at that. Had she been maltreated, neglected, left to go hungry, or dragged out of her comfortable nest with the injunction to get well or get out, she would have recovered instantly.

Exercise No. 2. For a thousand imaginary ills the remedy is a thoroughly "oxidized" state of mind, a mind saturated with the atmosphere of common sense and good health, and a resolute contradiction by Will of the importance of the disease or pain. The remedy, thus, is not reiterated denial that the ill exists, for that is merely another invitation to insanity, and it often simply intensifies the difficulty; the soul should resolutely assert that the matter has no such importance as is suggested, and then proceed to forget the idea by strenuous engagement in other considerations.

Exercise No. 3. Visual and auditory hallucinations may sometimes be banished by a wise assertion of Will. The soul should intensely insist that itself is master. Conditions underlying the images or sounds should be thoroughly investigated. These may be physical, requiring rest and change of scene and diet for correction. Or they may be mental, in which case the same course may be pursued, with a complete variation of interest, this being found in matters far out of the ordinary habits of life.

Exercise No. 4. In other cases the main thing is to get control of the hallucination. If it appear under certain conditions, compel it to appear under other conditions. Persist in substituting a different image or sound. Then compel it to vanish at will. Finally dismiss it. These directions are more easily given than followed, to be sure; but the truth is that many of our ills are due to a weak and fickle Will, and this may be strengthened and trained by wise application to the difficulties suggested.

These pages do not offer a substitute for medical treatment. They are designed merely for ills of a light and temporary form. When difficulties become more than foolishness of fickle fancy, the science of experts is called for.

Exercise No. 5. There are spirits which do not manifest to the eye, yet are terrible in power. Their arena is the heart. These are the *spirits of fear.* And these also may be banished by the resolute Will. It is first necessary to be an *honest person.* The honest soul need fear nothing. But the honest soul is not always wise, and fears do haunt the life of such; fear of man, fear of ill-luck, fear of failure, fear of misfortune, fear of death, fear of hell, fear of God. The name of fear is legion. It is, therefore, not probable that one who has been terrorized by these devils may banish them instantly, bag and baggage, once and for all; but it is as true as life that the honest soul may in time, by the persistent Will, cast them forth forever.

You *fear men* whom you suppose to be above you. Proceed, now, to build up a perfectly honest life; then meet them at every opportunity; learn their weaknesses as well as their virtues; will incessantly to fear them no more. Remember, especially, that there are other people who, with equal foolishness, fear yourself, and that those whom you fear are very likely troubled with fears in turn for others superior in their thought to themselves. And possibly they fear you as well. It was Grant's belief that the enemy was as much afraid as himself; he would therefore strike first. If, with a politic understanding of the word "strike," you can learn to plunge into the feared atmosphere of those you fear, you will certainly in time banish this imaginary evil.

Similarly with *fear of ill-luck*. This is superstition. The remedy is intelligence — as above. There are few failures with the honest soul and the persistent Will. Failure in the life of such a one is made admonition of experience and lesson for the future. *Fear of misfortune* is a coward's attitude. No misfortune ever befell an honest heart which might not be transformed into a blessing. *Fear of death* is anticipation of an experience which will or may bring its own antidote. If thou art right, fear not now, for thou wilt not then. Nature cares for the upright in that supreme hour. *Fear of hell* is either a ghost of theological making, or a most salutary and truthful incentive to climb out of hell's conditions. So long as you are out of hell now, fear nothing. If there is any danger of hell to-morrow, it is the prophecy of hell to-day.

It is in the power of mind to banish all irrational fears clean out of court. With a normal mind and a resolute Will, all these illusions of the imagination may be destroyed. *Cultivate the sane and resolute mood.*

RESOLVE TO WILL FOR MENTAL BAL-
ANCE. ATTENTION!

"The other day," said Cyrus W. Field, at a banquet given in his honor in New York on the completion of the laying of the Atlantic Cable, "Mr. Lattimer Clark telegraphed from Ireland, across the ocean and back again, WITH A BATTERY FORMED IN A LADY'S THIMBLE! And now Mr. Collett writes me from Heart's Content: 'I have just sent my compliments to Dr. Gould, of Cambridge, who is at Valentia, with a battery composed of a gun-cap, with a strip of zinc, EXCITED BY A DROP OF WATER, THE SIMPLE BULK OF A TEAR.'" That gun-cap battery is the human Will — for compressed energy the wonder of the universe.

Part IV—Destruction of Habit

"WE LIVE BY SACRIFICE ALONE"

All things that toward the heavens grow,
  In the huge struggle earth maintains,
  Are clutched by power that restrains,
As waves by ocean's undertow.
  Yet ever higher life remains,
Or forms decay or death makes moan:
  We mark our way by crimson stains —
We live by sacrifice alone.

Betimes high life must feed the low;
  Betimes the high by lower gains.
  The gnawing mystery ordains
Its cycle of existence so.
  And well for him who self constrains
The lesser powers to dethrone:
  For thus the One Ideal reigns —
We live by sacrifice alone.

The kingdom of the soul comes slow.
  O, long its battles, deep its pains;
  And weak Inertia loud complains
That life a rugged way must go,
  Fooled by the lie, "The struggle drains!"
The struggle makes thy self thine own!
  Builds thee man-high, ne'er saps thy veins: —
We live by sacrifice alone.

ENVOY

Life alway evil's drama feigns,
  Yet shall its crowns all loss atone.
The king his conquered foes disdains —
  We live by sacrifice alone.

CHAPTER XXIV.

DESTRUCTION OF IMMORAL HABITS

"BUT if having been once defeated, thou shalt say, *The next time I will conquer;* and then the same thing over again, be sure that in the end thou wilt be brought to such a sorry and feeble state that henceforth thou wilt not so much as know that thou art sinning; but thou wilt begin to make excuses for the thing, and then confirm that saying of Hesiod to be true:

"'With ills unending strives the putter-off.'"
— *Epictetus.*

PRELIMINARY

Francis Bacon said: "A man's nature runs either to herbs or weeds; therefore let him seasonably water the one, and destroy the other." The first part of this advice we have striven in preceding chapters to follow; destroying weeds of a harmful character is to be the business of the present.

A large portion of our life represents habit. This is not necessarily an evil; indeed, the establishment of habituated action is indispensable to intelligent existence. But the word " habit " often signifies fixed tendencies to action, either physical or mental, which are injurious, or foolish or morally wrong. As the great factor in the formation of all habits is repetition continued until attention is not required, the repeated assault of the Will directed by keenest attention and governed by desire until the fixed tendency is overcome, seems to be the only method for rooting out these obnoxious weeds of body and soul. A strong Will can master many habits at once, if the man genuinely desires that this be done. A continued effort to destroy evil habits must develop the Will. But this effort supposes conflicting desires or impulses — those running to the habit, and those opposing it. Hence the value of mental culture, and especially of strength of memory, imagination and Will, in order that the conflict may be made to turn in the right direction.

The *first difficulty* is a general *want of self-control;* a *second* is a *faint or fickle perception* of motives and consequences; a third is a bad *memory of an evil past;* a last is the *weak desire for cure.*

To overcome habits, then, one must bring his entire attention to the matter, must think intensely of the motives and outcomes involved, and must resolve to do all things necessary to turn the mind away from habit toward freedom. We affirm that we resolve; yet perhaps no resolution has really arisen in the mind. In a time of great sorrow, or of extreme excitement of pleasure, or of intense anger or disgust with self, or of fear of results, resolve sometimes is so deeply cut into the soul that it has opportunity to discover its ability to perform and to suffer, and to become habituated a little to the necessary discomfort of self-denial, and so to take a new hold by Will for a more persistent effort. By this time the "force of habit" and the test of continuance have become slightly less, while the power of Will has correspondingly grown. Perseverance now is sure prophet of reward.

It is a law, probably, that as much Will-power must be consciously expended in curing a habit, as unconsciously has been employed in acquiring it.

The entire matter may be summed up in one word: *All evil habits may be destroyed by the man who really DESIRES to master them.*

Mark Twain declared to his physician, who had accused him of using tobacco and coffee immoderately, together with tea and indigestible food and hot Scotches every night: " I can't make a reduction in these things because I lack the Will-power. I can cut them off entirely, but I can't merely modify them." His idea, to be taken seriously because it is fundamental good sense, is that the cure of bad habits is to be effected by *destruction of desire for their indulgence.* " The desire of course precedes the act, and should have one's attention; it can do but little good to refuse the act over and over again, always leaving the desire unmolested, unconquered; the desire will continue to assert itself, and will be almost sure to win in the long run. When the desire intrudes, it should be at once banished out of the mind. One should be on the watch for it all the time — otherwise it will get *in.* It must be taken in time and not allowed to get a lodgment. A desire constantly repulsed for a fortnight should die, then. The system of refusing the mere act, and leaving the desire in full force, is unintelligent war tactics, it seems to me."

Or, to put the matter in another way, the cure of habit depends upon keeping the right idea before the mind — either that of the goal or that of the consequence of yielding.

" The strong-willed man is the man who hears the still small voice unflinchingly," says Professor James, "and who, when the death-bringing consideration comes, looks at its face, consents to its presence (he is speaking of the cold consideration of reason), clings to it, affirms it, and holds it fast, in spite of the host of exciting mental images which rise in revolt against it and would expel it from the mind. Sustained in this way by a resolute effort of attention, the difficult object ere long begins to call up its own congeries and associates and ends by changing the disposition of the man's consciousness altogether.

"Everywhere, then, the function of the effort is the same; to keep affirming and adopting a thought which, if left to itself, would slip away. It may be cold and flat when the spontaneous mental drift is toward excitement, or great and arduous when the spontaneous drift is toward repose. In the one case the effort has to inhibit an explosion, in the other to arouse an obstructed Will."

Nevertheless, the function of the Will lies underneath the desire; to keep desire for indulgence out, and to make desire for freedom stronger. The latter is the work of right-mindedness, the former of a determined Will. After all, then, people are slaves to habit simply because they consent to be slaves.

"*Moral action is action in the line of the greatest resistance.*"

Before going to the following pages, therefore, it will be well to decide definitely that you honestly wish to eliminate the evils mentioned. You have sought a strong Will. For what purpose, if you must yet remain a slave? Let the motto of all previous exercises now be firmly held in mind: I RESOLVE TO WILL! ATTENTION!!

PROFANITY

This is a mark of low breeding. In the long run the best breeding comes up from plebeian blood and common surroundings. It is the specialization of ordinary materials. You can contribute better than yourself to the fruit of your loins. Here is the golden faith of true Americanism.

Profanity is useless; it ruins spoken language; it causes trouble; it is undignified; it is immoral. Therefore, away with it!

Régimes. 1. Think the whole matter over, and set out to become a gentleman. Resolve to stop, now and forever. Keep the thought in mind: the profane man is a fool. When you slip again into the habit, do not pass the fault lightly, but reprove yourself severely. Resolve with increased fury of Will to banish the evil.

2. Imagine the best woman you have ever known to be present, and then make your apologies to her offended dignity.

3. If you feel that you must indulge, proceed with the foolishness of counting twenty-five, slowly and viciously because of your dish-water weakness; don't think " swear "; think twenty-five.

4. If you are very weak in this respect, substitute at first a code of jargon for your profanity; when this habit is formed, break it according to the above instructions. You can now do this for the reason that you have shown successful Will in one direction, and there are no words quite so satisfactory to a profane person as those which you have ceased to use.

5. Meanwhile, write out a complete list of all the profanity you are in the habit of using. Carry it about

with you. Frequently read it, take in its significance, understand its utter folly. At every reading, resolve to rid your vocabulary of every word. Ten days ought to cure this habit for all time.

EXAGGERATION

A good deal of downright lying is due to a bent for exaggeration. A lively imagination and a vivacious temperament may easily induce enlarged or colored statements without intention to deceive. This fault becomes a habit, the liar is born, unconscious of his talents. The intended lie is probably a rarity. Oftentimes people state as facts what are merely conclusions from their own impressions. This is especially apt to be the case when themselves are involved. They do not intend to utter falsehoods; they do not assert what they consciously know to be untrue; but they do assert what they do not surely know to be the fact. When a man states a thing or truth as fact, it is his business to know that it is certainly not false. We gather from the facts which we do know conclusions which we think must be true. Then we proclaim our conclusions as realities. We do not take the trouble to tell *merely* what we surely know — that is, facts; but we proceed across lots, because it is easier, *and we rather like that way,* to assert our opinions as bald actualities. Here we have the heart of lying — carelessness as to exact truth. Few people relate ordinary matters with naked veracity. "The thing was so and so." "He said." "I said." Etc., etc. He did not say exactly that, but just a trifle less. You did not say exactly that, but just a trifle more. The thing was not absolutely so and so, but just a trifle different. All this you know well enough; but you desire to be interesting, and, before you are aware of it, you are carried along in the zest of anecdote. And you are conscious of this fact, but you thrust the feeling into the background and go on with "picturesque speech." In plain English, you are next thing to a liar.

Régimes. 1. A partial remedy will be suggested under the habit "Garrulousness." The man who strips his statements to the fewest possible words is not often an exaggerator, in the nature of the case, and is seldom a liar. You should therefore cultivate abbreviated speech, however much patience and practice may be required. It might do you a deal of good to conclude, and to say softly to yourself a hundred times a day for a month: "I am a liar! I am a liar!" Confessing this, the next story you tell will not be so funny — the humorist who sticks to absolute truth is a laughing grave-yard — but you will become a great deal "longer" on veracity.

2. Then you should thoroughly free yourself from the fog of impressions. Imagine your mind to be a judge and your tongue to be a witness. The witness must confine himself to facts — to what he has seen and heard, not what he has believed about these matters. Example: The tongue testifies —"The man was running down the street. He had a toothache." "Was he really running?" "Well, no; he was walking rapidly, almost in a run." Now, why didn't you say exactly that? Because you wanted your incident to be lively. "How do you know that the man had a toothache?" "Why, he had his hand on his face, and his expression was distorted." As a matter of fact, the man had bitten his tongue, and his look merely indicated that he had discovered that this member was

not designed for mastication. It was just the regular statutory grimace. But you jumped to the conclusion that his tooth was making chaos of his peace of mind, and hence his appearance was "awful." Thus you proceeded to think, not what you saw, but your impression. You have related an inference for facts. It is necessary, therefore, that you should desperately resolve never to relate as truth what you do not positively know to be naked fact. This resolution must be sunk into the marrow of your soul, and held in mind continuously for months.

3. You should discard your paint-pot. Your fancy idealizes or heightens all colors. A good honest blush is "as red as fire." A pleasant smile is "a yellow grin." "The shade of thought" is "bluer than a whetstone." A sparkling laugh is "a lightning glare of hilarity." Now, you must learn to see things as they are, and to tell them as you really see them. You are telling a story, and in it yourself and a few other people are made to say a dozen things which you know were never said. You paint their language in colors that are too high. If you are not past redemption, you were aware of this fact. During the entire recital an inner god is whispering, "No, no; that is not correct! Tone it down! Speak the truth!" But your rush of speech and interest are like lively fire-works, and everything is doubled and exaggerated. You continue to dash on the paint until at last the sober inner Truth-teller actually joins in the laugh, at the shock. After a little he rises up and shouts: "You are a liar! A liar!" At the end, he dies a perfectly natural death.

In order to overcome this habit, you should first use your senses, to know things just as they exist and occur. And you must practise daily, until it becomes a habit, the art of telling facts as nakedly as possible. For example: recall some incident of yesterday, and proceed to narrate it, coldly and slowly, in the fewest words, and with absolutely no exaggeration. Meanwhile, resolve, and state your resolution aloud, in the briefest and coldest manner:

"*I will henceforth reject impressions and all adjective coloring, and confine myself entirely to actual facts.*" To bring this about, you must determine, and begin now, to employ no adjective word if you can make sense without it, and when the adjective must appear, to use the weakest of its kind. In reality, that word will be the very best, though at first it may look like a featherless bird. The bird will in time get all the feathers required, and a " perfectly wonderful liar " will have become a man of plain but reliable speech, a comfort to himself and a support of " English with a moral quality."

IRRITABILITY AND ANGER

Irritation is the germ of anger. There are those, however, who become irritable without explosions of wrath. Very likely their difficulty is physical. A set of unstrung nerves is often the result of wrong-doing, but nevertheless demands the sympathy of the possessors of good health. Weak and disordered nerves are a misfortune, whatever their cause, and should be so treated.

Régimes. 1. The cure in such a case would seem to be rest and treatment by medical specialists of unquestioned standing. Yet here also the Will may find its opportunity. It can do little without scientific assistance, but, thus aided, it may and does accomplish much. If the sick may wisely be exhorted to a resolute fight, much more those who are irritable because of a "touchy" and fault-finding disposition. With reasonably well people irritability and anger are inexcusable. You may thrust these devils out of your life if you honestly desire to do so. In most cases this may be done by a sheer exercise of Will. Certainly with a little artificial assistance the task is sure to end in success.

2. "Refuse to express a passion and it dies. Count ten before venting your anger, and its occasion seems ridiculous."

3. But you must stop violating physical law, and resolve to live according to the dictates of a sound judgment. The suggestions of the chapter on "General Health" should be observed.

4. Cultivate a cheerful state of mind. You can do this if you will. Entertain only pleasing and elevating views and feelings; all others you must resolutely forego. Don't be foolish and brood over wrongs and unpleasant conditions, whether fancied or real.

5. Don't worry. Whenever you are tempted to do so, play the buffoon, or recall the funniest story you know. You will be out of the mood, but it can be forced. Bury yourself in humor; laugh; assert your Will; shout to your soul: "I will not worry!"

"If you sit all day in a moping posture," remarks Professor James, "sigh and reply to everything with a dismal voice, your melancholy lingers. If we wish to conquer undesirable emotional tendencies in ourselves, we must assiduously, and in the first instance coldbloodedly, go through the outward motions of those contrary dispositions we prefer to cultivate. The reward of persistency will infallibly come, in the fading out of the sullenness or depression and the advent of real cheerfulness and kindliness in their stead."

In plain, untechnical language, Dr. Geo. W. Jacoby has said, " Worry works its irreparable injury through certain cells of the brain, and that delicate mechanism being the nutritive centre of the body, the other organs become gradually affected. Thus, some disease of these organs or a combination of organic maladies arising, death finally ensues.

" Scientifically, but little is known about those subtle senses — perception, thought, judgment and reason — except that they are closeted behind the frontal bones, and that it is here the Will-power is generated to be communicated to every other part of the body. The cells located here, some of them in constant service, others acting only now and then, are the most important in the brain. They are the mental citadel, and it is here the awful malady we call worry makes its first deadly assault.

" Considered as a disease, worry, when it does not kill outright, frequently injures to the extent of inducing sickness, physical discomfort and the inclination to seek relief in suicide. It is, perhaps, one of the worst of ills to which the mind is heir.

" The remedy for the evil lies in the *training of the Will to cast off cares and seek a change of occupation when the first warning is sounded by Nature* in intellectual lassitude and disinterestedness in life. Relaxation is the certain foe of worry, and ' don't fret ' one of the healthiest of maxims."

6. You should resolve to discover some good, some bright side, some pleasing element, in everything and in every situation. *You must make this a real pursuit of your soul.*

7. You should keep before your thought, in relation to all those with whom you come in contact, their virtues and excellence. Cultivate that charity which thinks no ill.

8. You should read only that which is agreeable and useful. Shun the blue book, the yellow journal, tainted fiction, and all that is skeptical toward the wonder and glory of life.

9. So far as feelings are concerned, live only in the present. The past is done for; it is not half so bad as you suppose. Verify this by recalling its pleasures and successes alone, resolutely ignoring its sadness and failures. *Live in the present of a sunny mood.* Anticipate nothing but good in the future. Burn all doleful prophecies; they are lies. Some evil must befall you, but those about which you are certain will never "come true."

10. Companion with cheerful thoughts and people exclusively. Why be friendly with those who are miserable for the sake of their deadly comfort? Let the dead bury their dead. This does not contradict the law of kindness. If your motive is their good, you are then armed against contagion.

11. On the morning of each day, find some pleasant or inspiring thought, blaze it deeply into your mind, and cling to it during the hours. Do not let it escape you a moment. Repeat it when irritable. Repeat it when tempted to anger. Repeat it as you perceive the shadows of melancholy stealing over your soul. Invest it with magical power. Constitute it an amulet or charm.

12. Preserve a daily record of instances in which you have shown irritability or anger or melancholy. Be exact in this; let it be faithful and honest personal

history. At the close of each day, write it; then read it; then resolve to improve. At intervals review that record, and note progress. State the fact in your diary, and remember it for encouragement. Continue until you are master.

13. On no provocation permit yourself to fall into melancholy, or to show irritation or anger, in company with another person. Never forget your self-respect. You must remember that *man is entitled to be happy*. People and things about you are irritating and depressing, no doubt; but observe this fact, that many with whom you become angry will merely exult in your downfall, deriving unworthy pleasure from your weakness. Why should you contribute to such enjoyment while rendering yourself miserable? Why make distress for yourself, whatever other people may do? Here is a kind of living suicide. Resolve to be happy. You are not so when irritated, and you simply give the unkind an unnecessary advantage. Your melancholy may be the sole source of enjoyment for some people who protest, nevertheless, that you are causing them misery; why should you play such a fool's part?

14. *Don't try to be a martyr!* Don't assume the role of suffering innocence! Don't pity yourself! The man who pities himself is lost. Don't nurse your nerves! Don't coddle your whims! Don't "baby" your sins!

15. Stand for your rights, control your feelings, insist on a happy frame of mind, take frequently a moral bath in honest, manful Will-power, and live absolutely above the feeble-minded expletive, the wretched sarcasm, the dastardly fling, the cowardly meanness, the cellar of miasmatic brooding and the psycho-physical poison of anger!

> Brooding o'er ills, the irritable soul
> Creates the evils feared and hugs its pain.—
> See thou some good in every somber whole,
> And, viewing excellence, forget life's dole
> In will the last sweet drop of joy to drain.

Evil Imaginations

Opposed to purity, to cleanliness, to personal dignity, to moral vigor, to health of body and soul, this habit has its roots in a degraded tone of mind.

Two things are therefore observable: desire for evil, and a want of proper mental occupation. The desire can be mastered by improvement in health, and by substitution of worthy thought in the mind.

Régimes. 1. The first general treatment must be physical. Nerves which are out of tone, must be brought back to the full condition of health by the varied activities of inspiring interests. You must coöperate by putting yourself in a healthful régime of daily living. (*a*) You must live regularly, as far as possible. (*b*) You must bring yourself to a plain and simple diet, avoiding alcohol in every form, and, if injurious, tea and coffee. (*c*) You should bathe swiftly every day, rinse in clean and gradually cooling water, and rub thoroughly with coarse towels until you are perfectly dry and all aglow. (*d*) Your thought should immediately be taken up with rugged, active affairs. (*e*) You should resolutely compel yourself to engage in systematic, but not violent, exercise. (*f*) You should absolutely shun every luxury of an enervating nature. (*g*) Your amusements should be entirely free from any unworthy excitement. (*h*) You must cultivate an ideal of womanhood as an ever-present portrait in the gallery of thought—innocent, dignified, saintly.

2. On occasion, recite heroic poetry or exalted prose, which you have learned for the purpose. Or recall some stirring event in your own life, or some humorous incident, driving the soul into healthful moods.

3. You should make it your business to occupy the mind with plans, ideas, trains of reasoning, which are practical, noble and profoundly interesting. It may be well to take up some problem of real life as a daily subject of thought, to assail it with questions, to analyze its difficulties, to discover its relations, to bore steadfastly into it, until you have arrived at a solution which seems to be reasonable or satisfactory. Then go into another subject and treat it in the same manner.

4. Whenever an unworthy thought occurs to you, thrust it aside and replace it by a better.

5. Remember, you are to fight this evil *indirectly,* never directly. So long as your mind is upon it to destroy it, it still remains. Make your main fight by occupying the field of thought with values and nobilities.

6. It is true here as it is with reference to every other habit: If you say, "I cannot," you desire not to conquer. Every habit is rooted in thoughtlessness or desire. Kill the desire. Or better, reverse the desire. Example: "I desire this or that indulgence." Substitute for this, "I desire its opposite; I desire the correlative good; I desire freedom!" There is nothing which a man cannot do, reasonably speaking, if he actually and profoundly desires it.

7. You must deliberately demand improvement. "Brain cells and brain fibres cannot learn better ways from preachers, only your own untiring will can do anything with them."

Tobacco and Liquor Habit

If there is not enough manhood left in you to desire reform, you must consult a physician or a " cure "; and if this will avail nothing, then, to be sure, you must go on as a slave.

Régime 1. But if your manhood is still sufficient for these things, you must waste no time over these habits, as such, or directly considered. You must treat with desire, first, middle, last and directly, leaving habit to take care of itself. Thus, you must banish desire for stimulants by substituting for it desires of other descriptions. Keep the first out of mind. Keep the latter forever in thought.

Illustration: *The Man Who Failed.* One who visits a "Keely Cure" and is reformed, falls, in a few months, into the old habit. It is said his case is hopeless; so it is, but not for anything in the treatment; the man doesn't genuinely desire freedom. He drinks now because he desires indulgence, or because he does *not* desire reform. His appetite is his plea; but his desire lies under his appetite. Were he confronted by a loaded rifle, with the assurance of a court of law that the instant he drank this first glass which he holds to his lips he would be shot to death like a dog, he would defer the indulgence because desiring life better than one drink. The contrary is asserted, but it is simply the exaggeration of deluded martyrdom.

Illustration: *The Man Who Won.* A certain man had put drink in place of wife, family and honor. Awakened in his bed, after a prolonged " spree," with a fiery craving for alcohol, he abjectly begged his wife to fetch him whiskey. She coldly refused. In his torment, he promised that if she would grant this one request, he would forever abjure the use of drink. Thereat she yielded. He drank as a babe drinks milk. But he kept his word. Here was right desire harnessed to Will. *But the wife furnished ready hot coffee every hour of the day and night during months.* Many men continue to drink whose wives or mothers lack wit and the power of — simulating affection. Womanly "coddling" is a divine institution. A reforming drinker is weak in nerves and a baby in soul; let his womanfolk pour wrath upon drink and nurse the man for what he is — a hero with no legs to stand on.

Illustration: *The Man Who Tried Again.* A young man discovered the alternative: drink and a perfect mixture of ruin and disgrace, or total abstinence with large success. He got into his soul, first of all, a mighty desire for freedom, and then a great determination to suffer; he could suffer if he could not stop the use of alcohol. He went into the battle — and fell. He sobered, got a new desire for reform, and went into the fight once again. He suffered torments beyond description. His body was an armed enemy. His nervous system massed itself upon his resolution with persistent assaults which ceased not, day or night, during months. He received assistance from no "cure" and no religious experience, so far as he could determine. Hourly he held conversations with his stomach, saying to that organ with clenched fists and shut teeth, "You cannot and shall not have drink." He never yielded the second time. He triumphed, of course. Here was desire harnessed to Will.

Illustration: *The Man Who Makes Excuses.* "How many excuses does the drunkard find," writes Professor James, like a scientific reformer, " when each new temptation comes! It is a new brand of liquor which the interests of intellectual culture in such matters oblige him to test; moreover it is poured out and it is sin to waste it; or others are drinking and it would be churlishness to refuse; or it is but to enable him to sleep, or just to get through this job of work; or it isn't drinking, it is because he feels so cold; or it is Christmas-day; or it is a means of stimulating him to make a more powerful resolution in favor of abstinence than any he has hitherto made; or it is just this once, and once doesn't count, etc.,— it is, in fact, anything you like except being a drunkard. That is the conception that will not stay before the poor soul's attention. But if he once gets able to pick out that way of conceiving from all the other possible ways of conceiving the various opportunities which occur, if through thick and thin he holds to it that this is being a drunkard and is nothing else, he is not likely to remain one long."

Régime 2. The drink-habit is partly psychic, partly physical. In either case the desire must be displaced by a stronger motive. A mediæval legend illustrates this law. The people of Gubio were terrorized by a wolf, and Saint Francis undertook to tame the animal. He went outside the walls of the town, and, meeting the wolf, said to him: "I wish to make peace between you and these people, Brother Wolf, so that you may offend them no more, and neither they nor their dogs shall attack you." Then, as the wolf laid his paw on the saint's hand, in token of a covenant, he promised that the animal should be fed during the rest of his life. "For well I know that all your evil deeds were caused by hunger."

Régime 3. If the drink-habit is caused by a physical condition, it should be counteracted by a régime of food and innocent drink that shall maintain a state of physical satisfaction. A full meal is a sound foundation for a good Will. If the habit is the result of a psychic desire, the Will must be bolstered by a new psychic ideal, of any character whatever. Anything that will introduce to the soul, and maintain there, a suggestion stronger than that of liquor, will win — and nothing less can win.

Hugh Miller relates that a man-o'-war sailor in an engagement had become so exhausted that he could scarcely lift a marlinspike, but, the enemy renewing the fight, "a thrill like that of an electric shock passed through the frame of the exhausted sailor; his fatigue at once left him; and, vigorous and strong as when the action first began, he found himself able, as before, to run out the one side of a twenty-four pounder."

The habit-conquering Will must be fed.

Régime 4. Some physicians recommend for the tobacco-habit the incessant eating of peanuts, inasmuch as a condition of the stomach seems to be engendered by them which revolts against nicotine. If you can nauseate a man every time he craves tobacco he will cease to desire it. It is said that milk has the same effect in some cases. Every person long addicted to these habits needs some medical assistance, because a physical state is involved which usually requires counteraction. Having then, a genuine desire to reform, follow the directions below:

Régime 5. Procure a tonic prescription from a physician who understands your case. Eat heartily plain food, especially any kind which does not seem to agree with tobacco or alcohol, and keep forever in mind the goal of freedom. Eat peanuts or drink milk instead of indulging your appetite in habit. Fix deeply in your soul the conviction that the difficulty is not insuperable, but will yield in time. This is true, because the entire physical system tends to adapt itself to new conditions. Continue these reform conditions long enough and you are a free man.

Régime 6. Don't talk about your effort. Don't dwell upon your suffering. Keep yourself busy, in out-of-door activity as much as possible. Contrive to get a great amount of sound sleep every day. Take a noon nap daily. Flood your stomach with pure water day after day. If the weather permits, perspire freely. Put tobacco and liquor out of sight. Keep them out of mind. When their thought arises, banish the suggestion instantly. As you do so, and in order to do so, set the mind upon other matters.

Régime 7. Don't suffer yourself to fall into the "dead stare"—that unconscious stand-still of mind which occasionally seizes men who are fighting these battles. Anticipate such "spells," and throw yourself into action requiring no concentration of thought.

Régime 8. Don't pity yourself. Entertain no sympathy for your suffering nor your weakness. Don't play martyr. Don't class yourself with heroic reformers. Don't nurse your egotism. Don't imagine that you are doing some great thing. Forget all these temptations. People have lost track of neuralgia over Mark Twain's "Innocents Abroad," and have fought on in battle with shattered arms. You can absolutely forget tobacco and alcohol, if you determine to do so.

Régime 9. Don't ask the Divine Being to cure these habits. All such "cures" have been psychological. Deity is the author of a true psychology, and religious experience is psychological, to be sure; but the Infinite works through His own laws, one of which, underlying the crowning achievement of moral realms, soul development, is that Divine help is given to no human being in an especial manner or degree who can achieve success by obedience to ordinary principles of right living.

A person once declared that "the Lord had taken away his craving for tobacco." When closely and persistently questioned, he confessed that there had been times at first wherein his throat and mouth had felt "raw," one of the symptoms of tobacco denial. He had forgotten his desire in his intense religious excitement. Here was "Divine assistance," of course, but without any distinctively supernatural element.

Some people can get " cured at the altar." It doesn't matter what notions they entertain, so long as they escape the "beggarly elements." But other people can never quite surrender to the auto-suggestion necessary, and frequently these fail of achieving what is called "victory" because they rely upon mistaken ideas and ignore the true law of these subjects, the curability of habits where there is genuine desire backed by resolute Will and proper mental conditions. Any method which will create desire for reform, foster determination, and occupy the mind with absorbing thought or excitement long enough to enable the system to readjust itself, will realize the happy results of the "converted drunkard" or the "sanctified tobacco user."

A book just published on curing the tobacco habit, by Mac Levy, has among others, the following "dictums":

1. Having decided to quit tobacco, keep your thoughts upon the grand benefit soon to come, and do not allow yourself to be dissuaded from your purpose.

2. Continue with tobacco as usual for two weeks. If you feel that you are making such progress that you can cease the use of tobacco before the fixed time, do not stop completely — reduce the quantity if so inclined.

3. Sip all liquids and other soft foods, allowing them to remain for a brief period in the mouth before swallowing. Chew every mouthful or bite of solid or dry food many times before swallowing.

4. Avoid foods or drinks that disagree with you.

5. Consume eight glasses of liquid, non-alcoholic and non-gaseous, daily, between meals.

6. Practise deep breathing every morning and night.

In conclusion we may quote from "*The Culture of Courage*" suggestions which make for the conquering spirit. "Faith, conceived as the affirmatively expectant attitude of the whole self, is one of the mightiest powers in this world. It is the fundamental element in auto-suggestion. You are therefore invited to make your entire thought and life a suggestion to self that these directions, faithfully carried out, will infallibly eliminate from your nature" the habits indicated.

But remember, "faith without works is merely a 'say-so.' Real faith is confident action toward a goal. The continuation of such action measures the kind and power of faith supposed. You should, therefore, determine to persevere — a thousand years if necessary, for you are yourself everlasting, if you will. But let it be remembered that mere resolution is only one-half of real determination. Some people resolve — and then resolve, never achieving victory. Others put 'bite' into the matter in hand once for all, and do not seem to know how to let go. The only cure for resolution is determination, for determination is just doing the thing resolved upon.

"The soul that says, 'I am going to overcome,' will very likely fail. The leverage runs too far into the future. A valiant Will always acts on a short lever. You should, therefore, declare: 'I am overcoming! The thing is now being accomplished! The matter in hand is mastered.' This may seem a trifle false, but it is more than a trifle true if you really mean it. When a man swears the needed thing now, it is by so much already done in his Will, and a good deal of it, unknown to him, is accomplished in the concrete."

"'TIS WISE SURRENDER CROWNS THE KING."

Our Mother Life her children slays —
  Old earth is but a sepulchre.
Yet has her madness wisdom's ways
  That honor and develop her.
Each death decreed unfolds her praise
  In law of world-wide ministering:
And so, for man the victor bays —
  'Tis wise surrender crowns the king.

True living counts its passing days,
  Not by a globe's diameter,
But by the drama spirit plays
  To London Town from ancient Ur.
And when itself its progress stays
  In weakling loves that fondly cling,
To cherish must the gods amaze —
  'Tis wise surrender crowns the king.

No God-soul after impulse strays
  Through time as 't poor Ophelia were,
Nor like a fickle Hamlet prays
  For power Will may not confer.
Love well thy pains! Achieve the phase
  Of dying which is life at spring;
For if thy self thy self would raise,
  'Tis wise surrender crowns the king.

What evil thing may growth defer
  If life with death has reckoning?
Why, then, to sorry cost demur?
  'Tis wise surrender crowns the king.
                                    — THE AUTHOR.

CHAPTER XXV

CORRECTION OF OTHER HABITS

"IMPURE thought, despondent, hopeless, repining, fault-finding, fretful, slanderous thought, is certain to make the blood impure and fill the system with disease.

"So with certain habits of body consequent on such habits of thought, such as the habit of worry, the habit of laying undue stress on things not the most needful for the hour; the habit of trouble borrowing and many others, which permeate and influence every act of life. Their combined effect is exhaustion, and exhaustion is the real mother of most of the ills flesh is heir to."— *Prentice Mulford.*

"We are continually denying," said Henry Ward Beecher, "that we have habits which we have been practising all our lives. Here is a man who has lived forty or fifty years; and a chance shot sentence or word lances him and reveals to him a trait which he has always possessed, but which, until now, he had not the remotest idea that he possessed. For forty or fifty years he has been fooling himself about a matter as plain as the nose on his face."

We now take up certain habits not regarded as immoral.

SLANG

Perhaps one such unconscious habit is that of slang. Some people are, indeed, slaves to the tyrant, "Correct

Style." There is a golden mean. It is related of a college professor that his usual manner of speaking was so excessively elegant that he really obscured the natural scintillations of a bright mind; he was dull where a slight admixture of the "common parlance" would have imparted vivacity to his otherwise interesting conversation. He stands as a type of the few uncanny and "literary fellows."

One may indulge slightly in slang as an agreeable concession to a work-a-day world, but its habitual use indicates a want of self-control.

"The use of *slang*," said Dr. O. W. Holmes, "or cheap generic terms, as a substitute for differentiated specific expressions, is at once a sign and a cause of mental atrophy. It is the way in which a lazy adult shifts the trouble of finding any exact meaning in his (or her) conversation on the other party. If both talkers are indolent, all their talk lapses into the vague generalities of early childhood, with the disadvantage of a vulgar phraseology. It is a prevalent social vice of the time, as it has been of times that are past."

The habit may be destroyed by following the suggestions relating to profanity and garrulousness.

Remember that slang consisted originally of the "cant words used by thieves, peddlers, beggars, and the vagabond classes generally."

Cultivate the society of the best speech. "If you hear poor English and read poor English," said Richard Grant White, "you will pretty surely speak poor English and write poor English."

HESITATION OF SPEECH

It may be that the stammerer's ancestry could never get well quit of a clear statement. Many people can

Will Masters the Lord of Misrule 319

make no smooth headway through a simple utterance of fact or opinion. With real "stuttering" we have here nothing to do. Those who stammer, without rhyme or reason, are but themselves at fault. Perhaps the difficulty is due to a want of "steam" sufficient to force a clear expression of thought; some people do well when excited or angry, but in calm moments they make sad work of it. Perhaps, again, the trouble is owing to an amount of "steam" which they do not control: they speak smoothly when not disturbed, but excitement causes them to sputter like a fire-hose out of which water is failing. Persistent practice of the suggestions below ought to cure this difficulty, whatever its cause, except in case of physical deformity.

Régime 1. Recall some incident of your experience or observation occurring within the last twenty-four hours. Deliberately and rapidly recite, in an ordinary tone of voice, and as if speaking to some person, a connected account of the entire transaction. Speak as rapidly as possible. Do not permit yourself to pause an instant for want of a proper word; thrust in any word, as nearly right as may be, or even one having no related significance — any word — and go swiftly on to the end.

Régime 2. When you have begun a sentence, plunge straight through it to the close. Then proceed in the same manner with the next, and drive yourself to the finish of your account.

Régime 3. Now repeat the process, resolving to employ better language with each sentence; but do not pause an instant; force yourself to say what you desire *in some way,* no matter whether elegant or not.

Continue daily practice of these directions until your difficulty is overcome.

Régime 4. But meanwhile, one fault in your speech is this: you do not consciously think your thought in actual words. This you must learn to do. Recall, then, some subject of thought on which you have an opinion. Proceed, now, to state that opinion exactly to yourself and in an ordinary tone of voice. The exercise may be varied by pronouncing the words mentally, but do not fall into that imbecile habit of moving the lips. Your opinion must be uttered rapidly, the Will compelling the thought to march on without hesitation, no matter what an occasional word may chance to be. You have two things to learn: to think exact thoughts in actual words; and to think them with the greatest speed.

Régime 5. It will assist you, now, if you will begin to write the opinion or account as swiftly as you can dash the pen across the page. Work here also with fierce energy, never pausing an instant, but always, when tempted to hesitate, writing the best word of which you can think — or throwing in a dash or any word coming to mind. When this is done, sentence after sentence, read the whole, and proceed to criticise and correct: then rewrite in a better manner but with all possible speed.

Régime 6. Commit to memory and keep in mind the following rules:
I will speak rapidly — or slowly, as required.
I will never stop for a word.
I will never pause to correct a word or a phrase.

I will never leave a sentence unfinished.
I will never turn back in a sentence.
I will use the best possible language.

I will not speak in two styles — one for common life, and one for uncommon occasions. I will adopt a good style and always employ this.

I will not speak loosely, and I will not converse like a prig or a pedant. I will be correct, yet simple; elegant, yet unaffected.

Mind-Wandering

Elsewhere, in Chapter XVIII, will be found other pertinent remarks on this fault. The importance of the topic cannot be overestimated, and it will therefore bear further suggestions.

The wandering mind is the thoughtless mind. Thought loves the highway; notions climb the fences. Thoughts are trained hounds; fancies are puppies — off for every scent. It would weary the intellect of a Newton to follow the wanderings of a young dog. Wandering thoughts waste the brain and they get no "game." The uncontrolled brain is a fool's paradise. Nothing comes of the mind which cannot stick. The cure of mind-wandering is control by the Will. The practice here suggested will cure this senseless fault, and at the same time strengthen the Will itself.

Régime 1. In reading, always proceed slowly, until you have acquired the power of rapid comprehension. Select some good sentence for reading. Read it, slowly carefully, understanding every word. Ten notions have flitted across the field of thought. Resolve to keep that field clear. Read the sentence again, proceeding as before, and willing intensely to hold to its thought and nothing else. Continue to read that sentence until you can attend absolutely without a single failure to what it says. When you can read it, with nothing whatever save its own thought in mind, take your eyes from the page and repeat it — the thought not the words — in the best possible manner. Your mental action has now "wandered." Go back and read the sentence again, giving it exclusive attention; then state in mental words its thought, holding yourself to complete absorption in the matter.

Régime 2. Continue the above exercise until you can confine the mind to that thought with not the shadow of another idea. Then proceed with further reading in exactly the same way. You will not make much progress at the start. Your habit is of long standing, and it will require great patience and perseverance to destroy it. But the thing can certainly be done. Remember! For what are you reading at all? Really to read — genuinely to think. Here are goals which are worth untiring labor and unlimited time. A page a day which the soul bores its way into is better than a book read carelessly in one hour.

Régime 3. When about to read, ask yourself: "Why am I to read this matter?" Find that out; then insist upon getting what you are after. Read the first sentence, and ask: "What did that sentence mean and say?" Read the sentence until you know and can tell the fact or truth in your own words. Proceed thus to the close of the first paragraph, and ask: "Exactly what does this paragraph declare?" Persist in reading the same paragraph until you can relate its thought. Continue these exercises to the complete mastery of thoughtful reading. You will find your mind-wandering slowly vanishing.

Régime 4. While engaged in business or other matters, pause frequently to note what you are thinking about. You will meet with many surprises. Catch yourself indulging some train of fancy, and then ask: "Has this any value to me? Am I thinking out the matter in which I am physically engaged, or on which I set out, or am I merely running about in it like a puppy in a new field?" Keep the mind upon thoughts of value. They need not relate to death and the judgment; pleasant thoughts are not unlawful. Compel your mind to think, not only thoughts of value, but in a connected way as well. Stand guard over your own mind. Dispel every fleeting fancy and uncalled notion not germane to the thing in hand, as far as possible. Cultivate a reliable and purposeful intellect. Commit the following lines to memory, and make the verse a talisman against wandering thoughts:

> A wandering mind is like a shooting star:
> With orbit none, it yields a transient light.—
> The mind God launched across Creation's bar
> Hath His omnipotence — great Reason's might.

Garrulousness

The majority of people talk too much, often saying nothing, or what is perhaps, the worse for themselves, uttering words which they afterwards wish had been left unsaid. There are others who are as uncommunicative as the oyster — and not always, when they open their mouths, does a pearl fall to your prize. In social life they are fallen logs, against which the stream of conversation dashes and from which it turns aside in sparkling agitation. In business they are enigmas, perennial objects of suspicion. They do not, as a rule, make many friends, although when they do, these stand by to the death.

The opposite class are numerous, and, because they talk too much, are objects of a fellow-feeling among men and are believed to be amenable to improvement. The following rules will cure garrulousness, if obeyed to the letter.

Régime 1. At the beginning of each day for, say, three months, run over in your mind all matters that are of vital importance to your social and business life. You will discover some things which you ought to keep to yourself. Make an iron-clad resolution to reveal them to no human being. *Remember! Remember! Remember!* When in conversation with others, recall that resolution. *Remember! yes, remember!!* If you fail during the day, *remember! remember!* and renew the resolution on the next day. Stand by it! Carry it in mind every hour. In the evening review your success or failure, and saturate your thought with condemnation and with fiercer determination to reform. Do not yield until you can instantly repress any impulse to speak on any subject. In three months you will be master of your tongue.

Régime 2. You are using too many words at all times. This fault can be corrected. You must, in order to improvement, cultivate terseness of speech. Practise every day for a year the following. This is labor, but the result will amply repay you.

Régime 3. Think a fairly long statement concerning some object, person or event. You must deliberately think in words, making an intelligible sentence. Now write it out in full. We will call this statement " A." Repeat it, attending to your own voice. How does it sound? Is the sentence the best that you can make? If not, improve it. Now reduce it to its lowest possible terms as a clear, definite and complete statement. Write it on another sheet of paper. Repeat it, noting its sound. Then determine to cut it down one-third, or even one-half. Persevere until this is done. Write the result on a third sheet of paper. Now compare the three statements. Compute the per cent. of reduction. You will be astonished to observe the waste of breath and language in your ordinary conversation.

Régime 4. Resolve to carry out the idea of condensation in all your speech. In the course of a few months you will discover two things: first, your vocabulary will have become larger and better, because this effort requires the use of dictionaries and thoughtful practice with words; secondly, your manner of speaking will have become surprisingly condensed and intelligent.

Régime 5. Select, further, some author whose style is chaste and condensed. Read his works carefully, a little every day. Following the rules for memory, commit some of your author's best sentences and paragraphs. A small book which is a condensation of a larger one may be used in connection with the preceding suggestion. In time, this practice will, without any special effort on your part, greatly modify your general style of speech.

Régime 6. No one will affirm that Carlyle's tumultuous chaos of words is a finished globe of conventional economy in the matter of language; but this Thunderer has thoughts and is recognized as a wizard with our mighty English. Read the following, therefore; cut it deeply into memory, and live in the atmosphere of its suggestion:

"The great *silent* men! Looking around on the noisy inanity of the world, words with little meaning, actions with little worth, one loves to reflect on the great Empire of *Silence*. The noble, silent men, scattered here and there, each in his department; silently thinking, silently working; whom no Morning Newspaper makes mention of! They are the salt of the Earth. A country that has none or few of these is in a bad way. Like a forest which had no *roots;* which had all turned into leaves and boughs; — which must soon wither and be no forest. Woe for us if we had nothing but what we can *show* or speak. *Silence, the great Empire of* SILENCE; *higher than the stars; deeper than the Kingdoms of Death! It alone is great; all else is small.*"

THOUGHTLESSNESS

This is the habit which causes one to miss his train, forget his wife's message, send an important letter without signature, rush to keep an engagement an hour late, omit to carry his pocket-book to church, dress for an evening party without a necktie, leave the comb in her hair, and cry, when the house is afire: "Where is the baby?" It may and ought to be cured. The main secret of remedy is, of course, the resolute Will. Every habit which men confess can be broken, if it be thoroughly willed that the thing must and shall be done.

Régime 1 You should resolve every day until it ceases to be necessary, as soon as you rise, to remember whatever you ought to remember during that day. It would be better to so resolve at morning and at noon. At the close of the time limited, you should recall wherein you have failed, and spend a few moments in deliberate thought on the folly of this fault.

Régime 2. You should ask yourself concerning any particular matter requiring attention: "Why do I wish to remember this thing? Who will suffer if I fail? Who will be benefited if I succeed?"

Régime 3. You should make up your mind absolutely never to defer what ought to be done at some time, and may be done immediately. The moment you think of a matter which you wish to attend to, proceed instantly to do it. If it is impossible at the time, charge your mind with it again, state why it must be done, and when you will give it attention. Do it then at almost any cost. You are fixing a habit of recollection, and this is worth all inconvenience.

Régime 4. You should begin now to give your whole mind to whatever you undertake. Do nothing without full thought. Repeat to yourself: "I know what I am doing and why. This one thing I do." When the matter is finished, and before you allow yourself to think of anything else, review it carefully. Is it all complete? Is it exactly to your satisfaction? If not, go back and do it over again, following the above directions. This develops the habit of thinking on what you are doing.

Régime 5. You should never think of one thing while trying to do another — except in certain habituated tasks.

Régime 6. You should put yourself to inconvenience to make good any carelessness.

Régime 7. You should never allow yourself to become excited.

Practise daily, for three months, making a different route which you will follow in going to and returning from your place of business, and never fail.

Régime 8. Determine every day until unnecessary, to recall, at a certain exact hour, some particular matter to which you will then attend. Keep the same hour for many days; then change the hour; continue until you are master in this respect. This will build up a habit of obeying your own orders.

Régime 9. At frequent intervals, during each day until unnecessary, stop all active work, and recall any particular matter which you ought to have attended to. Then recall any matter to which you must yet attend. Do not be hurried. Give your whole thought to these efforts. Immediately make good your negligence.

Régime 10. Never trust mere note-books for matters which a fair memory ought to retain. Never trust anything else for dates and important business transactions. Put no confidence in mnemonics; tie no strings to your fingers; make no associations (unless of the simplest kind) as helps. Use your Will. Compel yourself to obey that power.

INDECISION

There are those whose Will-power is very good when they have decided what they will do. But they find it difficult to arrive at decision. They balance the *pros and cons* to weariness, and cannot settle the matter in hand. That is to say, they believe themselves to be engaged as indicated. The truth is, their minds are confused, and it is but vaguely that they think at all. If this is your habit — that of indecision — you must summon your entire strength to its destruction. The difficulty is more or less constitutional; nevertheless it may be overcome.

Régime 1. Carry always with you a strong sense of resolution.

Régime 2. Cultivate consciousness of self and self-possession.

Régime 3. Remember always where you are and what you are doing.

Régime 4. Under no circumstances permit yourself to become excited or confused. If you find either of these conditions obtaining, defer the matter until calmness returns. If it cannot be deferred, summons tremendous Will; remember, "I must be calm!" and decide as best you can. At the next emergency profit by this experience. But waste no energy in useless reviews of mistakes. Store away the mood of coolness for future use.

Régime 5. Learn to think of but one thing at a time. When engaged with any matter, put the whole mind upon that alone.

Régime 6. Make the difficulty and discomfort of indecision cause for immediate resolution.

Régime 7. When in doubt attend to motives singly. Think of one at a time clearly and forcibly. Do not become distracted by many considerations. In examining motives force a vivid conception of each, and then of all together. Then rapidly review all reasons, for and against, as nearly at once as possible. Then act! Decide! Take some chances. All men must do so more or less. Waste no time with consequent regrets.

Régime 8. For at least three months resolve every morning as to how you will dress. Do this quickly. Fix the exact order of procedure. Adhere strictly to your plan. Never yield; never hesitate. Dress as rapidly as possible. Vary the order each day, as far as may be done with your combination.

Régime 9. Resolve, when you start for your office, or any objective point, that you will keep in mind what you are doing until you arrive. Do not plan the way at the start. Proceed on your way; think that you are going; at the first opportunity for varying the course, pause an instant, think of reasons for one way or another, and immediately decide — to take this car or to follow that street; at the next opportunity, repeat the process. Continue until facility in quick decision in the matter is acquired.

Régime 10. You should cultivate the habit of acting in a rapid, energetic manner. Do everything you undertake with keen thought and a strong feeling of power.

Régime 11. You should above all learn promptness. Meet every engagement on the minute. Fulfil each duty exactly on time. Never dawdle in any matter. Be decisive in all things.

Régime 12. In addition to hours and dates ordinarily fixed in your life, make many artificial resolutions relating to time and manner, and religiously carry them out to the letter. Keep forever in mind the necessity of promptness, energy, quickness of action, strength of Will.

WANT OF OPINION

The fundamental difficulty here is lack of thought. People who think have opinions. Thought can be cultivated only by exercise of Will, and in three ways: by *forced efforts,* which require Will; by *reading,* which requires intelligent comprehension, and by *observation,* which requires attention.

Régime 1. You do not observe keenly and clearly what is going on about you. You should resolve and instantly begin to *see things.* It is a great art, that of seeing correctly. The wise man is he who *sees* what other people are *merely looking at*. You should determine to see things as they are. This means that you are to find out what they are. You can begin upon any common object: the ground; the grass; household furniture. After a time you will become interested, and you will then find yourself thinking. Then you will have opinions, because you will believe or know many matters.

Régime 2. You need to discover wherein you are ignorant. That will be comparatively easy. Then you must set about finding all that you can discover upon some particular subject. Look around; ask questions; read papers, magazines, books. Keep the end in view, to know this subject to the bottom. Do not allow yourself to be diverted from this purpose. Become a walking encyclopedia on this one thing. When you have exhausted the matter as far as possible, you will possess genuine opinions. And you will then be eager to take another subject, and will follow it to the last farthing of value. The result will be — more opinions.

Régime 3. In the meantime, you will have discovered the luxury of *intelligent* opinions, and of the habit of forming your own. People accept the opinions of others because they are aware of their own ignorance. So soon as they become themselves informed, they decline this sort of superiority. Want of opinion and want of knowledge are equivalent. The latter is the sole right remedy for the former. But there is no cure for want of brains. Without brains so-called opinions are fools' quips. At the brainless person Nature wrings her helpless hands. It is a finality of despair.

OPINIONATIVENESS

This habit is the outcome of a stubborn Will exercised by a blind soul. The opinionated man sees himself only. His Volitions are not so much strong and active as set and inert. The Will is here more or less diseased, because the self has no proper outlook upon life. The self supposes that it understands things, events and persons, but its real understanding is vague and partial. Could it know more, it would arrive at different views. It looks at the silver side of the shield; it ought to discover the other side; but it cannot do this. Certain aspects of events are presented; it cannot penetrate to additional phases. Views of people give it notions which are not real ideas because true motives of conduct are hidden. The opinionated person is usually wrong. As woman depends largely upon intuitions, when she betrays the fault here under consideration it is well-nigh incurable, for intuitions are not amenable to reason. They are divine when right, but the despair of man when wrong. The difficulty here lies in the fact that the opinionated soul views all things through itself, and magnifies its own personality to enormous proportions. It is ruled by subjective conditions which shut out the relations and perspective of the world.

> Who ne'er concedes the law of truth,
>   That truth transcends his mind,
> Mistakes himself for God, and, sooth,
>   With open eyes — stands blind:
> His soul a world, great "views" he spawns,
> While humans laugh and Nature yawns.

Such a conception of self can only be corrected by a true realization of the personality of other people.

There are those who never actually appreciate the fact that their fellows are genuine existences. To them human beings are little more than phantoms, presenting various unsubstantial phenomena of life; they are never *bona-fide* persons possessed of hearts and brains, and engaged in concrete realities. Why should phantoms have opinions? Themselves are real; themselves discover reasons for views; themselves are therefore entitled to opinions. This right is not universal because other minds are not by them apprehended as actual. Hence the remedy for this species of "insanity" must go to the root of the difficulty. These people must learn to realize their fellows. If the habit of opinionativeness is to be cured, humanity must be made concrete and real in thought.

In order to this, let the following suggestions be practised during life. After death your happiness will largely depend upon your power to concede to your fellows a legitimate place in the universe.

Régime 1. Select one of your friends or acquaintances, and study that soul with no reference whatever to yourself. Learn his ways, his sentiments and emotions, his thoughts and motives. No matter whether these elements of his life are proper or improper, right or wrong; you are not to sit in judgment upon him, but merely to become thoroughly acquainted with his nature and character. In time you will discover that he thinks he has various reasons for his opinions, which you are not to condemn, because that is not the thing in hand, but which you are vividly to realize as facts in his life. Above all, you will gradually find yourself thinking of him as a real being in a real body and engaged in a real life.

Régime 2. Continue this study with reference to other people about you, until you have formed the habit of feeling thoroughly the fact that you are dealing with living men and women.

Régime 3. When you have ceased to think of them as phantoms, a curious thing will occur; you will regard some of your old-time opinions as more or less confused, inadequate and baseless.

Régime 4. At all times you should remember with whom you are coming in contact. If your idea of human life is justifiable, you need look upon no one as your inferior. Many people may be so, indeed, but it isn't worth while considering. You have, perhaps, been accustomed to deference and obedience from your employees. Such a relation demands politeness on your part for the sake of your own dignity. The person who is not polite to servants surrenders moral values. Yet politeness is merely the veneer of the Golden Rule. That rule, in all respects, should be practised toward those with whom you deal. When it governs a man's life, the "maid," the "man," the employee comes to be regarded as a human being in an exalted sense. Such an habitual regard transfers from the ranks of servants to those of fellows. You have fallen into the habit of hurling your opinions at people to whom you pay no wages because you have had authority over those who receive the means of living at your hands. Were you to look upon your "help" as real beings, sensitive and possessed of rights, you would not arrogate to your opinions sole legality and exclusive value. Whatever you do as to "hands," you do not own the rest of mankind. It is not "good policy" to forget this trifling fact.

Régime 5. You should forever strive exactly to understand opinions opposite to your own. You cannot thrust them aside as wrong unless you know what they really are. The opinionated person seldom understands what he contradicts. A thorough knowledge of another man's thought will bring you nearer to him, and your ideas, being then compared with his, will probably not seem so huge and so unquestionably correct.

Régime 6. The study of opposite opinions involves the study of reasons. There is a possibility that, when you fully discover another person's reasons for opinions, your own reasons may undergo some alteration. It would diminish your infallibility if you could see the force with which reasons other than your own make for differing views.

Régime 7. You should occasionally recall your errors in judgment. It may be ventured with some assurance that you will be able to recollect at least one such error. If once in error, possibly many times. Burn that into your soul.

Régime 8. You should also recall the mistakes of your life. You have thus suffered injury. If you can write this on the retina of your eye, perhaps you may reform a little of your cocksure attitude. Some of your mistakes have injured others. If you do not care about this, close the present book and " gang your ain gait." The pig-pen has one remedy — fire and the sword.

CONCLUSION OF PART IV

In conclusion of the two preceding chapters, it would be well for every person occasionally to submit to self-examination as to the reign of habits, whether immoral or otherwise. Beware of the "devil's palsy of self-approbation." Let a list of personal faults be carefully and deliberately made. They should be scrutinized severely to ascertain their power and results. Then resolve to destroy them, root and branch. Begin at once. Carry the list with you. Frequently read it. Determine, again and again, to be rid of them. Give each a definite time for extirpation. Preserve a record of success and failure in this respect. Read this at the close of each day of battle. Continue until free.

Meanwhile, in all things, cultivate the resolute, conquering Mood of Will. *You can be free!*

RESOLVE! "ATTENTION TO THE KING ON HIS THRONE!!"

SPEECH

All objects of creative power have speech;
Else how her laws might Earth her children teach
How might the vaster Mother, Universe,
Her ancient Vedas with Lord Time rehearse,
Till Psyche waked and dared life's endless reach?

The countless atoms threaten or beseech,
In forest, mountain, valley, ocean, beach —
All objects speak in language clear and terse.

Such speech is aye for better, ne'er for worse,
Till man evolves his blessing or his curse.
Yet man with heart afire may beauty preach —
To him the gift of eloquence in speech!

The words of kings do largesses disburse;
The gifts of kings do but their kingdoms nurse:
Let nought unmeet thy sovran word impeach!
— The Author.

PART V—CONTACT WITH OTHER PEOPLE

ELOQUENCE

With self the soul companions through the night,
Mayhap with friends beyond etheric sight,
Nor holds the speech of earth in lust and might,
But language born for service and delight.

Now when the world returns to day and toil,
And life is huge activity and moil,
Our words betray our blindness and the soil,
And so we fain must ape them or recoil.

Supreme the task to utter gracious thought,
Diviner yet to have it nobly sought;
And only when high passions, swiftly wrought,
Sublime the soul, is power's secret caught.

From labor patient comes the godlike art
Of thought's conveyance, but the burning heart
In eloquence of life plays chiefest part —
The master aye of cloister or of mart.

Who craves the golden tongue must lift and climb,
Know lairs of eagles and the look sublime,
Yet fires that purge the valley's dust and grime,
Vast solitudes and yet the mob of time.

With self must he companion through the night,
And with high friends who own the larger sight,
Drink youth's eternal waters of delight,
And win the human soul for truth and right.
— THE AUTHOR.

CHAPTER XXVI

THE WILL IN PUBLIC SPEAKING

"WHILE engaged in the composition of my 'Elements of Chemistry,' I perceived, better than I had ever done before, the truth of an observation of Condillac, that we think only through the medium of words; and that languages are true analytic methods. The art of reasoning is nothing more than a language well arranged."—*Lavoisier.*

"In a thousand emergencies men have been obliged to act with quickness, and, at the same time, with caution; in other words, to examine subjects, and to do it with expedition. The consequence of this is, that the numerous minute circumstances, involved more or less in all subjects of difficult inquiry, are *passed in review with such rapidity, and are made in so small a degree the objects of separate attention, that they vanish and are forgotten.*"—*Professor Upham.*

The design of this chapter is suggestive only to the author's elaborate and practical work, "*Power For Success.*" Power of Will is here the central consideration, and the following pages have mainly to do with that factor.

The *chief difficulties* of public speaking relate to *thought, language and imagination.* Those who lack one or the other of these talents can, therefore, never acquire the art. But such talents may exist without discovery, merely requiring proper cultivation. And the word "talent" must not be exaggerated. It is not necessary to possess great abilities in order to speak well before others. Many who would probably fail in presence of an audience express themselves with clearness, and sometimes with eloquence, in ordinary conversation. The difference between conversation and public speaking is largely the power of sustained effort. As Professor George H. Palmer remarks: "Talking moves in sentences, and rarely demands a paragraph. I make my little remark — a dozen or two words — then wait for my friend to hand me back as many more. . . . The brief groupings of words which we make up in our talk furnish capital practice in precision, boldness, and variety; but they do not contain room enough for exercising our constructive faculties." The constructive faculties must therefore be cultivated. Any person of average brains can acquire thought and extend his vocabulary; and if he has persistent determination and opportunity, can force his ideas to put on the orderly clothing of vocal utterance.

Régimes

1. *Acquiring Thought.* Brains count immensely in this matter. Your first source of trouble consists in a *lack of sufficient thought.* For this deficiency there is but one practical remedy. *You should read, study, think, for the purpose of accumulating facts, acquiring opinions, furnishing the mind with thought. It is not enough to have ideas; these must be woven into some actual fabric by real thinking.* When you know and

think on any given subject, you can talk about it before an audience, other things being equal.

2. *Developing Language.* But other things seldom are equal. Hence, the next difficulty consists in a *lack of language.* You should first of all, now, accumulate a good stock of words — words — words — as the raw material of expression. If you are pursuing the directions previously suggested as to attention in reading and development of the power of thought, you are storing up in memory many words which are not heard in the average conversation. You should make it your business to enlarge your vocabulary by a large number of unpretentious and sober-minded words. In order to this, while accumulating thought, keep a good dictionary convenient for reference, and permit no word which you do not clearly understand to escape your zeal as collector. But avoid as much as possible odd words, long words, pedantic words.

3. *Exercising Expression.* Meanwhile you should seize every opportunity for practising the art of expression. Begin with every-day conversation. Refer to directions as to hesitation and exaggeration. Do not try to talk like a magazine article. Avoid the stilted style as strenuously as the slovenly. Above all, study and strive for natural, easy expression. At the same time you must employ your enriched store of words in the utterance of your increased fund of thought. This demands courage and Will. "We fall into the way of thinking that the wealthy words are for others, and that they do not belong to us." " When we use a word for the first time we are startled, as if a fire-cracker went off in our neighborhood. We look

about hastily to see if any one has noticed. But finding that no one has, we may be emboldened. A word used three times slips off the tongue with entire naturalness. Then it is ours forever, and with it some phase of life which had been lacking hitherto." You should cultivate, therefore, the courage of a speech which is unusual to some of your circles. But always should you hold in mind the effort to state with freedom the exact truth or fact in the least redundant manner. Make this a goal, never for a moment to be forgotten.

4. *Mental Speaking.* In the next place, you should practise thinking in terms of words. Do not be content with mere notions about things. Think matters out verbally. When alone, think a sentence through, and then speak it aloud. Proceed immediately to improve the statement. Go on with another related thought; work it out mentally in words; then repeat and improve, as before. Become accustomed to your own voice under conscious conditions. In public speaking you are conscious of your own voice and gesture, and this disturbs you. You should cease to be aware of self before an audience. To do so, you should become perfectly familiar with yourself in the labor of preparation.

5. *The Plow of Mental Word-Using.* Vary the above frequently by thinking your way through an entire subject without the practice of speaking. Do not be content with supposing that you know an item or phase of the subject well enough, and may therefore pass it by. You will often be surprised to discover in public speaking that the thing has suddenly

become as dense as granite, and at that point you will hesitate and lose control of your thought. Let this be a rigid rule in all your preparation: Plow up every inch of ground by the actual use in mind of words put together to express your thought as you wish to deliver it on the public occasion. But do not try to memorize the words employed in preparatory thinking. This would unsettle your public thinking and rob your speech of ease, vivacity and force. There is a dangerous middle between memoriter speaking and prepared extemporaneous utterance; the mind labors to recall words not thoroughly memorized, and at the same time, strives for the freedom of the moment, and it thus lacks the exactness of the one thing and the force of the other. Think in words to prepare, but memorize nothing except the thought. Recollection of thought, however, must follow as a result of your labor in thinking, and especially of some sort of logical association, rather than of deliberate effort to commit to memory.

6. *Making Connecting Links.* It may be well to fasten in the mind a few catch-words, or connecting links, which come up naturally in thought, as a means of guidance when before an audience. But it is better, after all, to make your arrangement of thought such that, to yourself at least, one thing suggests another. Nevertheless, you should, in preparation, look well to your connections and transitions. Frequently one paragraph follows another naturally enough, but you find difficulty in letting go of one and in getting into the other. This is because you have not thought your way through the *transitions,* and you do not on the spur of the moment know how to do it. Make sure,

then, before you begin to speak, that you are familiar with the links between thoughts and paragraphs.

7. *Actual Practice.* Seize every opportunity for public speaking that comes in your way. Practice in prepared utterance will be of invaluable service to you. Be equally on the alert for opportunities to speak on the spur of the moment. Resolve to learn to think on your feet with your voice in your ears.

8. *Cultivating Imagination.* A further difficulty relates to the *imagination.* You should cultivate this faculty, according to directions given for that purpose. You have now an opportunity for its exercise. Professor Palmer well says: "Most of us are grievously lacking in imagination, which is the ability to go outside of ourselves and take on the conditions of another mind." In your plowing-up process of thought you should strive always to perceive in the mind every detail on which you are to speak. You must not only think matters out in words, but also realize all your subjects of discussion. If truth — feel it; if love — experience it; if joy — possess its emotions; and thus with all elements of the thing in hand, except evil.

9. *Working up Illustration.* This rule is especially applicable to illustrations. Do not try to talk about an incident in life without becoming part of it — without seeing it clearly and vividly. But you must not be content with such a realization of the incident — can you relate it? You are to think it all out, not to memorize, but to assure yourself that you have the ability to describe it as seen in mind. Do not be content with a vague picture of nature, but call up before the mind all

The Orator is One Who Knows 347

necessary details and state them in words. Only thus may you know that you can describe that scene. When you have gotten it clearly into language, determine what salient points you will suggest to your audience. Avoid the photographic style; remember that those to whom you are speaking possess some imagination; they resent an opposite assumption; they delight in painting, with lightning strokes, a reality which you have merely sketched.

These suggestions as to thought-preparation in words may be illustrated in the following manner: Let us suppose your audience to be a woodland lake, with various objects upon its surface, such as leaves, twigs, pieces of bark, etc. You wish to set its surface in motion, in waves and ripples, by striking one of these objects here and there. But you have no materials with which to do this. The shore is a clean slope of sand, and not a throwable thing upon it. You therefore gather such material from any distant source, making a mound ready for use. Now, you have not said: "This stone I gather for the purpose of hurling in a certain direction; that piece of bark to toss upon a given leaf; and that clump of soil to cause a particular kind of wave." You do not arrange these details beforehand. You gather abundance of material, with a given general purpose in view. You then manipulate that material in the manner best adapted to the end sought, leaving particulars to be determined by the demands of the occasion.

Observe. In thought-preparation for public speaking, you are not to memorize in any arbitrary way; you are simply to assure yourself that you know and can express thought on a given subject. On the public occasion you find thought and language ready for use because you have gathered them and they are separated from surrounding materials, loosely placed, so to speak, for instant employment.

Many speakers cease preparation with a general outline of the subject in hand. This is slovenliness, and they fail of reaching the highest mark of eloquence because they are poor in material. As a matter of fact they have at that point merely gotten ready for honest, hard work in preparatory thinking. Make sure, therefore, of details, look well to your illustrations, have a care for the connections, and, above all, fill the mind with abundance of thought which has been thoroughly cast into words and sentences.

"When Nestor stood before the Greek generals and counseled attack upon Troy, he said: 'The secret of victory is in getting a good ready.' Wendell Phillips was once asked how he acquired his skill in the oratory of the Lost Arts. The answer was: 'By getting a hundred nights of delivery back of me.'"

10. *Overcoming Stage-Fright.* The difficulty which seems most prevalent, however, is that of *fear of the audience*. Here is a curious thing. You are not afraid of any particular individual in the audience, perhaps, but the multitude of ordinary men and women shortens your breath, causes your heart to pound in your breast, and dries up the secretions of your mouth, till you are compelled to fashion words, as it were, out of raw cotton.

The *difficulty is three-fold.*

First, you do not become *familiar with your audience prior to facing it.* You must keep it and the coming occasion constantly in mind while making preparation. See that crowd of people, here and now; see it clearly and vividly. Then think out your subject in words addressed mentally to that sea of upturned faces. Remember forever that you don't look half as much frightened as you are; that the people do not gaze into your skull; that if you fling in a word with meaningless desperation now and then they will not, ninety-nine cases in the hundred, know the fact; and that, if you do not absolutely fail and fall flat (and you will not if you fiercely will otherwise), you will be doing vastly better than seventy-five per cent. of your auditors could do.

Secondly, you are *not in good practice.* You must avail yourself of every opportunity for public speaking. The more difficult the occasion the better. Never let a chance slip. Forefend against surprises by preparing for all occasions wherein you may be called out or secure the floor. Don't be a bore — if it is possible to avoid it; but, continue this practice, whether or no. Whenever you fail, laugh the discomfiture off — people will not remember it forever — and seize the next opportunity. Discover why you failed, and profit by experience. Analyze your success, and make sure of your forte. Follow with the persistence of the foxhound the determination to win.

Thirdly, you are *lacking in good Will-power.* You must summons Will to the mastery of all difficulties. Changeless resolution is necessary in all preparation. This is merely a matter of sticking to a purpose. But the latter does not exhaust the difficulties. You suppose yourself ready for the trial, and, in a sense, you are. It is in the concrete act of speaking that your trouble begins. You are afraid of man. Your Will suddenly becomes flabby, your force of spirit evaporates, and you cannot command your preparation. At this point bull-dog determination is required. Do not deserve defeat before uttering a word. Don't permit a feeling of collapse at the start. Put Will at the fore. Mentally defy the entire crowd. Fetch up all the egotism you possess. Fiercely challenge all foes. Keep cool at the outset. Take time to get a good send-off — it is your occasion. Put your thought into carefully chosen words; be in no hurry; proceed with deliberation enough to gain self-control and keep it. If you get on the track nicely, you will warm up after a little, and your audience will come to your assistance. Look the people straight in the eyes. Will to stand to it then and there. Will to keep your mental vision on a thought ahead. Resolutely appropriate the occasion as your own, and willfully use it as such. If the right word fails you, throw in another as nearly right as may be, or as meaningless as printers' "pie." If any one looks weary, ignore that person as an imbecile. Cleave to the friendly face, though it be that of a fool. Remember, everybody desires that you should do well, for an audience suffers under a public collapse. Believe that fact. Keep faith in yourself. Storm the situation. Resolve to win on the spot.

If you are called upon to speak at a late hour, when the people are weary and your enthusiasm is low — don't speak.

11. *Confidence in Audience.* Both in preparation and in delivery, the speaker should have confidence in and respect for his audience. Austin Phelps, Professor of Sacred Rhetoric in Andover Theological Seminary, wrote: "When President Lincoln was once inquired of what was the secret of his success as a popular debater, he replied, ' I always assume that

my audience are in many things wiser than I am, and I say the most sensible thing I can to them.' Two things here were all that Mr. Lincoln was conscious of — respect for the intellect of his audience, and the effort to say the most *sensible* thing. He could not know how these two things affected the respect of his audience for *him*, their trust in him as their superior, and their inclination to obey him on the instant when they felt the magnetism of his voice. But he saw that, say what he might in that mood, he got a hearing, he was understood, he was obeyed."

12. *Courage.* The mind that would influence others by public speech must be fearless. In the author's work "*The Culture of Courage,*" will be found practical directions for the development of a courageous spirit. Said the Emperor of Austria to Baron Wesselenyi, a Hungarian patriot, "Take care, Baron Wesselenyi, take care what you are about. Recollect that many of your family have been unfortunate." "Unfortunate, your majesty, they have been, but ever undeserving of their misfortunes." And the Baron would not apologize for this bold defense of his family's honor, even when attacked by his sovereign.

13. *Profound Convictions.* If you have great feeling in the beliefs you present, you inspire others with at least similar emotions. Could anything be more effective than the following from Louis Kossuth's description of his own appeal to his people:

"Reluctant to present the neck of the realm to the deadly stroke which aimed at its very life, and anxious to bear up against the horrors of fate, and manfully to fight the battle of legitimate defence, scarcely had I spoken the word — scarcely had I added that the defence would require 200,000 men, and 80,000,000 of florins, when the spirit of freedom moved through the hall, and nearly 400 representatives rose as one man, and lifting their right arms towards God, solemnly said, 'We grant it, freedom or death!' Thus they spoke, and there they stood in calm and silent majesty, awaiting what further word might fall from my lips. And for myself; it was my duty to speak, but the grandeur of the moment and the rushing waves of sentiment benumbed my tongue. A burning tear fell from my eyes, a sigh of adoration to the Almighty Lord fluttered on my lips; and, bowing low before the majesty of my people, as I bow now before you, gentlemen, I left the tribunal silently, speechless, mute. Pardon me my emotion — the shadows of our martyrs passed before my eyes; I heard the millions of my native land once more shouting 'liberty or death!'"

14. *Holding the Audience.* A popular instructor in public speaking, Grenville Kleiser, says on this subject: "A public speaker should cultivate a conversational style of address. The day of stilted and bombastic oratory is passed. Audiences like and demand the most direct kind of speaking possible. . . . A speaker of real power must learn to emphasize his important thoughts, not by mere loudness of voice, nodding of the head, or slapping the hands loudly together, but rather by inflection, change of pitch, judicious pausing, and by other *intellectual* means. . . . The successful speaker should have force in his style. Not merely the force of loudness, but the force of earnestness and sincerity. It is the power behind the man that makes for effective oratory, the power 'speaking on the tongue, beaming from the eye, in-

The Orator is One Who Knows 353

forming every feature, and urging the whole man onward, right onward to his object.'"

You can make your every day affairs — your contact with individuals or with groups — precisely the training ground you seek for acquiring this power to hold men while you are addressing them.

In the entire subject, from first to last, keep at the fore the strong Mood of Will, the sense of resolute personality. Hold the mind steadily upon the motto of these pages: " I RESOLVE TO WILL! ATTENTION!! "

KNIGHTED.

Oh, life's perennial Knight, Sir Any Man,
  Trust thou nor Opportunity nor Fate:
The one, a mere detail in Nature's Plan,
  The other, error's name for Best Estate.
Complainer! Know'st thou not the oath, " I can,"
  Shall win brave Kingdoms to thy Will elate
If Good Soul do but scorn their wizard ban?
  On thee, the Master, see, they fawn and wait!

I sing no Law of Accident or Birth,
  No Gift of Fortune by Divine Decree.
I sing the Call of Courage, Honor, Worth,
The world-wide Call of our old Mother, Earth.
  Heed thou, Sir Knight, this Golden Prophecy:
  The Throne to him who forces Destiny!
                              — THE AUTHOR.

CHAPTER XXVII

CONTROL OF OTHERS

"IF you would work on any man, you must either know his nature and fashions, and so lead him; or his ends, and so persuade him; or his weaknesses and disadvantages, and so awe him; or those that have interest in him, and so govern him." — *Francis Bacon.*

The preceding directions and illustrations relate to the control of one's self. Will-power is constantly shown to embrace others as well. Here is one of the most interesting of modern subjects of inquiry.

This chapter deals with plain matters. Its subject will be treated further in the volume on "*The Personal Atmosphere.*" There are many things in our life that are not elucidated by what some are pleased to call "Common Sense," and these will in part appear in the discussion of that work.

At the outset we may observe certain broad principles. Without exception, these principles are possible to the large and determined Will. According to your Will-faith, so be it!

GENERAL PRINCIPLES

First Principle — Belief. Genuine belief in the thing in hand makes mightily for success in the contact with others. Said Emerson: "I have heard an experienced counsellor say, that he never feared the effect upon a jury of a lawyer who does not believe in his heart that his client ought to have a verdict. If he does not believe it, his unbelief will appear to the jury, despite all his protestations, and will become their unbelief. This is that law whereby a work of art, of whatever kind, sets us in the same state of mind wherein the artist was when he made it. That which we do not believe, we cannot adequately say though we may repeat the words never so often. It was this conviction which Swedenborg expressed, when he described a group of persons in the spiritual world endeavoring in vain to articulate a proposition which they did not believe; but they could not, though they twisted and folded their lips even to indignation."

Second Principle — Confidence. A prime element in personal influence is confidence. Pizarro, the Spanish adventurer, left with one vessel and a few followers on the island of Gallo, where the greatest dangers and suffering had been endured, was offered relief by an expedition from Panama. "Drawing his sword, he traced a line with it on the sand from east to west. Then, turning towards the south, 'Friends and comrades!' he said, 'on that side are toil, hunger, nakedness, the drenching storm, desertion and death; on this side, ease and pleasure. There lies Peru with its riches; here Panama and its poverty. Choose, each man, what best becomes a brave Castilian. For my part, I go to the south.' So saying, he stepped across the line." And they followed him.

Third Principle — Enthusiasm. Enthusiasm is also a large factor in the matter. Samuel Smiles wrote very practically: "There is a contagiousness in every example of energetic conduct. The brave man is an inspiration to the weak, and compels them, as it were, to follow him. Thus Napier relates that at the combat of Vera, when the Spanish centre was broken and in flight, a young officer, named Havelock, sprang forward, and, waving his hat, called upon the Spaniards to follow him. Putting spurs to his horse, he leaped the abattis which protected the French front, and went headlong against them. The Spaniards were electrified; in a moment they dashed after him, cheering for ' *El chico blanco!* ' (the fair boy), and with one shock they broke through the French and sent them flying down hill."

Fourth Principle — Self-Mastery. Hence the *secret of a large control of others is found in the moral mastery of self.*

It has been well written: "Keep cool, and you command everybody." A recent author quotes a good remark of Clarendon, who said of Hampden: "He was supreme governor over his passions, and he had thereby great power over other men's." Man may be controlled in an ignoble way by studying and ministering to his weaknesses, but a noble use of self-mastery has sublime privilege in exerting good influence over the weak spot and the foible of humanity. In either instance the strong man is that one whose Will is steady and purposeful. Sooner or later, however, men discover their degradation in manipulated weakness, and, resenting the imposition, throw off the yoke, whenever the motive of fear ceases to restrain them.

Fifth Principle — Motives. The character of man's influence over his fellows depends upon the motives which he suggests for their action.

One may dominate multitudes by fear — Nero ruled Rome as a buffoon and a madman. Or, love may become the controlling force in personal loyalty — Jesus swayed thousands by the inspiration of His Divine goodness. In the one case influence is coercion, ceasing so soon as fear disappears, or assuming such power as to break in desperation with its own dictates; in the other case motives of fidelity are multiplied, and they become stronger as love's gracious spell continues.

Sixth Principle — Insight. The control of others demands ability to penetrate their motives and discover their plans. Of Mirabeau it was said: "It was by the same instinctive penetration that Mirabeau so easily detected the feelings of the assembly, and so often embarrassed his opponents by revealing their secret motives, and laying open that which they were most anxious to conceal. There seemed to exist no political enigma which he could not solve. He came at once to the most intimate secrets, and his sagacity alone was of more use to him than a multitude of spies in the enemy's camp.... He detected in a moment every shade of character; and, to express the result of his observations, he had invented a language scarcely intelligible to any one but himself; had terms to indicate fractions of talents, qualities, virtues, or vices — halves and quarters — and, at a glance, he could perceive every real or apparent contradiction. No form of vanity, disguised ambition, or tortuous proceedings could escape his penetration; but he could also perceive good qualities, and no man had a higher esteem for energetic and virtuous characters." *This ability may be successfully cultivated.*

Seventh Principle — Coöperation. Permanent influence over others flows from the enlistment of their strength. The supremest individual power in this respect is gauged by the pleasure which it offers as inducement to surrender, or by the sense of right to which appeal is made for alliance, or by suggestion of highest self-interest as a reason for loyalty. The best rule in the control of others is the Golden Rule. In the long run, life reciprocates with those who do unto others as they would that others should do unto them. That power of Will which can compel one to be polite, considerate, patient, helpful, luminously cheerful, is sure to cast a large and agreeable spell upon our fellows.

It is not to be understood that these suggestions seek to put a premium upon what is called "policy." Men are not all selfishness. There is a divine reason in humanity which makes it amenable to the kingly sway of sincerity, reality and righteousness. Not a few individuals in high positions to-day there are whose chief capital is their unblemished manliness. The native vigor of down-right honesty creates a current of attraction which it is hard to resist. The people put faith in Grant, because, no doubt, of manifest ability, but also for the reason that they saw in the silent commander an actual man. When a soul succeeds in convincing others that it is genuinely possessed by an eternal truth or principle, the Infinite steps in and accords him a public coronation as leader. Saul among the Jews was simply fantastic; David was a real argument for a king and a throne. Stephen A. Douglas, with culture and political machinery behind him, was no match for Lincoln, because in this man burned the unquenchable fires which blazed in the heart of the

North. It was the "Little Giant" against "Honest Old Abe" and the great slavery-hating States. Here the Will, that years before had shaken its clenched fist at the "Institution," rose to grandeur and assumed the robes of prophet and deliverer.

Eighth Principle — Will-Power. The resolute Will is leader by Nature's choice. If itself is throned in righteousness, its sway is certain and permanent — in a modified sense at times, to be sure, but not infrequently with limits outlasting the span of its possessor's life. Cromwell's Will made him "Ironsides." William of Orange competed with the subtlety, patience and tireless pertinacity of Philip the Second, and won a lasting influence which the Spanish king could not destroy by power of wealth, position or ecclesiastical backing. These historic dramas are huge representations of smaller affairs in every community. In the fullest sense, *a strong Will for control of others is a right Will.*

Yet it seems true that not all such control is explicable on the theory of plain means and methods. What is the secret of the power which cowes the wild beast, compelling its eye to wander from the steady gaze of man? What bows the stubborn purpose of the would-be criminal when confronted by the resolute fearless gaze of his victim —" in that deadly Indian hug in which men wrestle with eyes"? What maintains the mastery of family, school, prison, when some quiet spirit walks among their inmates? It is not always fear, for his punishments may not be unduly severe. It is not always love, for he sometimes fails to inspire affection. It is personality centered in unyielding Will-power. Other elements of explanation are frequently possible, but there are dominant minds whose only explanation is — themselves.

Mirabeau, speaking at Marseilles, was called " calumniator, liar, assassin, scoundrel." He said, "I wait, Messieurs, till these amenities be exhausted." The Will of Mirabeau was phenomenal. "His whole person gave you the idea of an irregular power, but a power such as you would figure as a Tribune of the People."

Of Wellington, Victor Hugo remarked: "The battle of Waterloo was won by a captain of the second class." But, Hugo, who set out to be the greatest man of his time, and who wrote the greatest work of prose fiction that has been produced for an hundred years, was here biased by the Napoleonic tradition. Wellington's campaigns were skillfully planned and carried out with a pertinacious patience calculated to wear to shreds the hostilities of many Bonapartes. When asked, during Waterloo, what should be done in case of his death, he replied: "Do as I am doing." Here was the culmination of that spirit which could say to a madman coming into his presence with the remark, "I am sent to kill you," "Kill me? Very odd." In such men the static Will exhibits the Gibraltar on which mind is fortified in action. It is a power seemingly capable of achievements by means that are superior to ordinary appeals. It discharges, as it may be said, like a battery, either to overwhelm or to win, by sheer resolution. Unseen, without gesture, it speaks: "I am your master. I claim you for my friendship, my following, my uses." And the thing is even so.

The phenomena of hypnotism are familiar. It is now distinctly asserted that "no one can be hypnotized against his Will; no one can be hypnotized without he complies with certain conditions and does his part to bring about the subjective state. To be hypnotized in no respect shows a weakness; weak-minded people (contrary to the opinion of some) do not make good sensitives; the most susceptible subjects are intelligent people having strong minds and Will-power, with the ability to maintain a certain passivity as to results; hypnotism is not a conflict of Will-powers in which the stronger overcomes the weaker. The person hypnotized may have a very much stronger Will than the operator."

Hypnotism thus seems to depend largely at least upon prearranged conditions. But here is the secret of "personal magnetism." One is truly magnetic who establishes the best condition of mind among those with whom he comes in contact. Here arises the necessity for a good personal address, a right personal atmosphere, a plausibility of argument, dexterity in avoiding disagreeable matters, the ability to present pleasing motives for action by others, and qualifications of the like kind. The real secrets of results of "personal magnetism" are to be found not only in yourself, but as well in the "other fellow"; if you can readily make him feel as you feel and think as you think, without suggesting the fact to him that you are doing so, you are "magnetic." Hence the precepts of average social and business success, together with indomitable Will not to lose control of self and forever to keep success in mind, constitute a source of real personal magnetism which has its illustrations everywhere in our life. "Every thought created by our mind is a force of greater or lesser intensity, varying in strength according to the impetus imparted to it at the time of its creation."

Suggestions

The great subject of personal magnetism is elaborately and practically set forth in the author's work, "*Power for Success,*" to which the student is referred.

If you will make the following suggestions a part of your working capital, you are on the highway of agreeable and satisfactory relations with your fellows. Though the matter seems simple enough in theory, it will tax your perseverance to the utmost to carry it out to practical results:

1. Never show temper.
2. Never betray envy or jealousy.
3. Indulge in no sarcasms.
4. Keep unpleasant opinions to yourself.
5. Tell no man an uncomfortable truth, if this can with honesty be avoided, and make sure that you disclose the motive of a well-wisher if you must utter the facts.
6. Make no remark about others which you would not instantly make in their presence.
7. Make no remark about others which you must know will, if instantly reported to them, cause enmity against you or injure their interests.
8. Never criticise to a man his wife, to a wife her husband, to a parent the child, to the child its parent, nor to any person a relative or friend.
9. When conversing with others make sure with whom you are talking in these respects, and in regard to all social, business, political and religious matters.
10. Never make a joke that hurts any one present or absent.
11. Never relate anything which might not with propriety be repeated to a lady just introduced to you.

12. Make no promise without knowing that you can fulfill it. Then fail not.
13. Make your word good promptly. If you cannot, explain to the person involved.
14. Never dodge a creditor.
15. Don't be a bore.
16. Ride your hobby in the back yard.
17. Permit other people to have views.
18. See things as they are; tell them as you see them — when good sense and kindness allow.
19. Put a heart into your handshake.
20. Be as courteous to "low" as to "high."
21. Be considerate of the rights and feelings of others. How about your barking dog? your thrumming piano? your lusty boy?
22. Carry the Golden Rule on your sleeve.
23. Never rub a man the wrong way.
24. Never contradict an irritated person.
25. Never get into an argument in a parlor nor on the street.
26. Never ridicule a man's pet theory nor a woman's foible.
27. Never ridicule a person's walk, dress, habit, speech.
28. Never laugh at weakness.
29. Permit yourself to sneer at nothing. The sneer is the devil's laugh.
30. Never hold any one in contempt. At least conceal the feeling like a death's-head.
31. Never order people about. Your clerk is no dog.
32. Be absolutely honest everywhere.
33. Be gracious and accommodating.
34. Cultivate generosity of pocket and of thought.

35. On sixty dollars a month don't browbeat the people. You are only a ticket-agent, a steamboat purser, a hotel clerk, a bank teller. Not much, after all, if you are to treat the public as though you were a lord. A good deal if you are decent.

36. Don't stalk along the street as though you were superfine, angelic, distilled wonder of imperial blue-blood. You are exceedingly lovely, to be sure; yet just a woman — bones, fat, blood, nerves, weaknesses and blunders — like the rest of womankind.

37. Never antagonize others unless principle demands. And then, hold the purpose in view, "To win, not to alienate."

38. Never pass judgment upon others without first mentally "putting yourself in his place."

39. Never utter that judgment unless you are convinced that this will accomplish some good or satisfy the reasonable demands of a definite principle.

40. Never permit your general opinion of a person to blind you to his good qualities.

41. In discussions, never interrupt a speaker, nor talk in a loud tone of voice. If you cannot speak without interruption, go away, or keep silence. One who will not hear your views is not worth the trouble of excited conversation.

42. Preface all statement of difference of opinion with a conciliatory word.

43. Never insist upon doing business with a person who evidently does not wish to see you — unless you are a policeman, a sheriff, a tax-collector, a lawyer's clerk, a physician or a messenger of death.

44. If your man is busy, yet makes an effort to be polite, get out of his presence as quickly and pleasantly as possible. Go again when he feels better.

45. Don't try to do business with a madman.
46. Don't try to conciliate a pig; it is always best to let him alone.
47. Don't sell a man what he doesn't want.
48. Don't sell a man an inferior article which he believes to be a superior.
49. Don't ask a favor from a person whom you haven't treated properly.
50. Don't try to fool people whose business it is to know people.
51. Always grant a favor if reasonably possible.
52. Don't try to down a man who knows more about a subject than you do.
53. Don't criticise or condemn matters into which you have never delved to discover merits or demerits. How can you say whether it is right or wrong when you don't know its real or pretended principles?
54. Bear in mind that a friend is always worth more than an enemy. "Grudges" and ill-feelings toward other men wreck havoc in the brain substance.
55. Be above petty jealousies, or a continual fretting about what somebody said or did.
56. Cultivate the ability, in dealing with others, to turn aside cutting remarks, either real or fancied. Don't have super-sensitive feelings that are cut by every zephyr of jest.
57. Remember Carlyle's "great silent men"— don't tell everything you know, either concerning others or relating to your own affairs
58. Don't tell things "before they are ripe." Oftentimes green may-be-so's later cause mental indigestion.
59. Don't launch a project until you have looked on every possible side of it. Sometimes the unobserved side is the one where the cave-in starts.

60. Always use pleasant words; this is not expensive, and you know not when the boomerang may return. A bad word is like a mule's hind feet; it will wait years for its one chance — and it usually gets that chance.

61. Treat every man, woman and child as though you were just about to confer a great favor — but avoid all condescension.

62. Make sure that your way is best before insisting upon it. Defer such insisting until you have won over the other person.

THE WILL OF THE CHILD

O, the will of a child is the wings of a bird,
  And the fragrance and color of flowers,
And the light of a star, and the love-song heard
  In a life's most miraculous hours.
Would you banish from air all the wonder of flight?
  Would you exile all beautiful things?
Would you make of youth's morning a Stygian night?
  Would you plunder love's crystalline springs?

O, the will of a child is a god in the soul,
  And a woe to the world if you vanquish;
When the gods that are human surrender control
  All that's human in living shall languish.
Woo the deity well with your love and your truth,
  Give it freedom to come to its own,
And the man shall have power's perennial youth,
  And the woman shall honor her throne.

For the will is the self, and the self is a breath
  Of the Infinite Breather outgoing.
On the day when the will topples down to its death
  Comes disaster surpassing all knowing.
But the self as a sovereign power reveals
  By so much of the God undefiled
As it selfhood perceives, as it liberty feels —
  O, be wise with the will of a child.

— The Author.

CHAPTER XXVIII

THE CHILD'S WILL

"WE are all born to be educators, to be parents, as we are not born to be engineers, or sculptors, or musicians, or painters. Native capacity for teaching is therefore more common than native capacity for any other calling. . . . But in most people this native sympathy is either dormant or blind or irregular in its action; it needs to be awakened, to be cultivated, and above all to be intelligently directed. . . . The very fact that this instinct is so very strong, and all but universal, and that the happiness of the individual and of the race so largely depends upon its development and intelligent guidance, gives greater force to the demand that its growth may be fostered by favorable conditions; and that it may be made certain and reasonable in its action, instead of being left blind and faltering, as it surely will be without rational cultivation."—*Principal James A. McClellan.*

The thought of the present chapter is not juvenile education, but the culture of the child's Will.

In this, the aim is suggestion rather than exhaustive discussion.

In its actual life the young child is little more than an animal.

It is endowed with a Will because it is an animal.

It is endowed with reason because it is a moral animal.

The Will of the human animal finds sole explanation in its moral intelligence.

Without moral nature, reason has no purpose. Without reason, or instinct, the Will has no significance. Without the Will, reason is impossible.

Man is justified in his moral nature, and the moral nature becomes possible in the self-disposing Will.

The first, middle and last idea in all Will-training of the child, therefore, is the permanent welfare of a moral being.

At the outset, then, certain basal requirements are to be noted:

That the parent or teacher understand at least somewhat of child-nature in general.

That the parent or teacher understand as far as possible the particular child in hand.

That the parent or teacher possess a right Will.

That correct methods be employed in culturing the child's Will.

It is, moreover, to be remembered that treatment of the child's Will cannot be reduced to prescribed and specific rules. This for two reasons:

Child-nature and child-Will are individual.

Specific rules would obscure rather than settle the problems involved.

At this point appear some

COMMON ERRORS

First Error: That the child's Will should be conformed to a certain standard set up by parent or teacher. This implies a making over of original nature. Original nature can be cultivated and improved, but it always determines the final results.

The true question is this: What is the peculiar Will-character of this particular child? Or how can this particular Will be improved? The child's individual Will is its personal motive-power. It is not like a boiler in a factory, connected with a good or bad set of machinery, and to be replaced by a better, or remodeled, if not satisfactory. It is a living thing, and is indissolubly related to its mental mechanism; it is the mind's power — this mind's power — to determine, and therefore cannot be conformed to any standard not indicated by itself.

Second Error: That the child's Will should be broken. "Breaking the Will" is a heresy against the nature of things and a crime against man. The future adult's success depends upon his own kind of Will, and upon some power of that Will as a human function. To "break the Will" is to destroy the soul's power of self-direction; that is, to wreck at the start the child's chances of success. If the Will is properly understood, no one will wish to "break" it.

Teaching the child obedience does not demand an *assault* upon its Will, either with the calm resistlessness of an iceberg or the fierce clash of arms in battle. The sole intrinsic value of obedience is found in the child's Will; it does not reside in obedience itself, nor in the results of obedience disconnected from Will. The one justifiable goal of enforced obedience is the Will in the child taught to will the right thing. A Will that is merely coerced is not with you, and, so long as coercion lasts, cannot be with you. In other words, enforced obedience does not in itself strengthen Will, except in the spirit of resistance. Enforced obedience may lead to reflection and discovery of the rightfulness of commands, and thus strengthen the Will indirectly. If it does not, or may not, lead to such discovery, it is worse than useless; it is then a positive injury to the child. The child should be taught the nature of law, but a greater lesson is the nature and value of reason.

Here may be given

THE MAXIM OF BEST CHILD TRAINING

Force, physical or other, sparing; reason, abundant, patient and kind.

The application of this maxim must always depend upon the nature of the individual child. The more difficult the case, nevertheless, the more urgent the maxim, and the greater the demand that grows out of its application, to wit:

The parent or teacher must possess reason — be reasonable — and be able and willing to show the same with self-control and confidence in reason's power.

Do not, then, attempt to conform the child's Will; patiently train it.

Do not try to break the child's Will; seek its intelligent development.

Do not leave the child's Will-action to its own impulses; culture it to symmetrical conditions.

Always regard the child's Will as an unspeakably holy thing.

Do not relegate the child's Will to chance methods; give it a thoughtful and deliberate education — the education of a Prince Royal of the Blood. Such an education involves

Three Fundamental Processes

First, the training process;
Second, the developing process;
Third, the process of symmetry.

First Process of Will-culture — Training

This branch of Will-culture has reference to the power of Will as now possessed. It is not an abstract problem; it is concrete.

Such problem involves two basic principles, Reason and Interest.

The first basic principle is Reason, or Judgment.

The child's Will requires for its perfect training an atmosphere of reason, so that its own judgments may be saturated with the feeling of reasonableness and may impel corresponding volitions.

This principle of reasonableness attaching to Will-acts comes, on analysis, to be broken up into certain questions, which should be kept constantly before the child's mind, but in a way to encourage rather than to harass it: —

1. Is this act *correct?* Is this the correct way to do the thing in hand? Example — handling a saw or a needle.

2. Is this act *complete?* Have you left nothing undone? Example — making a toy or stitching an apron.

3. Is this act *your best?* Example — your best recitation, or your best manner.

4. Is this act *wise?* Is it likely to be followed by satisfactory consequences to yourself? Example — the desired picnic, or tardiness at school.

5. Is this act *understood?* Example — the lesson, or the way of doing a particular thing.

It is primary that arousing the child's understanding enlists its Will. The average child is an animated and creative ganglion of interrogations. Here is a huge opportunity. It may be seized by means of a few familiar questions — *Why, How, Where, When, What, Whose* — all sharp openers to the young intellect, because perfectly in harmony with its own activities.

Example: A command has been given; the child's mind proceeds to enquire —"*Why* must I do this?" "Why must I do this in a particular *manner?*" "Why must I do this at a prescribed *time?*." "Why must I do this at some particular *place?*"

Similarly in a different series, as the following: "*How* must I do this?" "*Where* must I do this?" "*When* must I do this?" "*What* must I do?" "At *Whose* desire or for whose interest must I do this?" "*What* will be the consequences of this act?" "*What* will be the consequences of omitting this act?" "*What* experience have I had in similar cases?"

This general suggestion may also be employed by the teacher. It will astonish you to discover how the child's intellect can be electrified by the touch of the interrogative. It will unearth ignorance thus seen to be unnecessary both in the child and in the parent or teacher. Try the following questions as to any common object:

What is this thing?
How is this thing?
Where is this thing?
When is this thing?
Whose is this thing?

Why is this thing?

The fact is, the child is too largely compelled to discover for itself the necessity for such questions, is left to its own impulses for their asking and their answers. This is the rough-and-tumble education of life.

The amount of unintelligent teaching with which the child has to contend, at home and at school, is enormous. Adults do not understand or think; why should the child understand and think? The teacher does not draw all the water out of the well; why should the child be expected to do so, or to know what is at the bottom?

I asked a child how she would ascertain the number of square feet in a certain wall. She repeated the rule. Then I asked, "Why do you multiply the number of feet on one side by the number of feet on the other or longer side?" She did not know. It had never occurred to the teacher to go beyond the rule with the child.

I asked another child why summer is warmer than winter, notwithstanding the greater distance of the sun. She answered, "Because in summer the sun's rays are direct." "But why does that fact make the weather warmer?" She did not know. It had never occurred to the teacher to ask that question.

"A friend of mine," says Professor James, "visiting a school, was asked to examine a young class in geography. Glancing at the book, he said: 'Suppose you should dig a hole in the ground, hundreds of feet deep, how should you find it at the bottom — warmer or colder than at the top?' None of the class replying, the teacher said: 'I'm sure they know, but I think you don't ask the question quite rightly. Let me try.' So, taking the book, she asked: 'In what condition is the interior of the globe?' and received the immediate answer from half the class at once: 'The interior of the globe is in a condition of igneous fusion.'"

In this case the prime fault lay with the writer of the geography — or the school committee. But a teacher or a parent ought to break into pieces the usual forms of instruction that come the child's way. No marvel that tasks set to the child's Will train it only imperfectly.

Make doubly sure that the child understands the nature of things as taught and their main purpose. Understanding involves action of the reason, and thus, without direct effort, trains the Will.

6. Is this act *right?* Is it right because I have suggested it, or because of a higher law? Example — the use of certain words, or of exaggeration.

It is imperative that Will-training be conducted on the lines of morality. The absence of ethical quality in Will-culture, on the part of the parent or teacher, and of the child, destroys confidence, undermines the foundation of commands, leaves the child without a sense of authority other than that of force, and confuses the whole question of any right use of the Will.

If, now, the basis of Will-training in the child is reason or understanding, *certain attitudes common at home and in the school require condemnation.*

Never dominate the child with that inexcusable tyranny —"Do as I tell you." "Because I say so."

If the command has no better support, it is a species of bullying.

If you have better reasons, but will not kindly declare them, your command is a sure bidder for future anarchy. The child's reason is an acute questioner and judge. It obeys, but inwardly rebels because its master is arbitrary, and its Will is thus demoralized by nursed and secret resistance. Its power has become hostile both to yourself and to the child's welfare.

Never put off an answer to the child's questioning for the reasons connected with a command. The child ought never to be compelled to act or Will blindly. Your reasonableness will develop its faith, always a prime factor of the right Will.

Seldom draw on the child's Will in the form of a command. In the long run, if other things are equal, expressed desire will be doubly efficient. Even when the direct command seems necessary, the reasons which make it your desire can be urged upon the child's attention, and will ultimately win the thing you ought to wish — a willed obedience.

Throughout all engagements of the child's reason, the element of interest plays an important part. In the main it is inevitable, for an awakened mind is an interested mind. The child, may, however, perceive the correctness of an act, its ideal, its present possibility as an ideal, its wisdom and its moral rightness, yet be altogether lacking in the Will-attitude which expends itself in Will-culture. Such Will-attitude must either be forced, or won. If it is forced, nothing is directly gained for the Will. If it is won, it is by so much strengthened and trained. To win the child's Will, its interest must be excited. This requires infinite trouble and patience, but the method is sure to justify in a better power and quality of Will-action. A Will trained through interest becomes finally a Will that can plod at the goading of necessity or dreary duty, and hold to purpose after all interest save that of duty has waned.

The second basic principle, then, is Interest.

The child's interest, now, responds to *certain appeals:*

To the feeling of curiosity.
To the desire to imitate.
To the desire to emulate.
To the desire to know.
To the desire to benefit itself.
To the desire to please others.
To the desire for independence.

These feelings and desires are incessantly active in every normal child. They may be turned hither and thither, always causing the child to will with that Will it possesses.

It is *curious* — and wills to discover.

It wishes to *imitate* — and wills thought, action, speech.

It wishes to *emulate* — and wills to equal others.

It wishes to *know*, to possess serious knowledge — and wills the exercise of its faculties.

It wishes to *benefit itself* — and wills the discovery and use of means appropriate.

It wishes to *please others* — and wills its conduct into line.

It wishes to be *independent* — and wills judgment and freedom.

The lessons for parent and teacher are evident:

1. *Keep the child's curiosity* vigorously alert.

2. *Train the imitative desires* wisely, in the matter of selection, avoidance, discrimination and manner of imitating. Is it merely aping? Repress. Is it imitating poorly? Improve. Is it imitating unwisely? Repress. Is it imitating in a beneficial manner? En-

courage. See that it has the best possible examples, and incite interest to do its own best.

3. *Imitation may lead to emulation.* All the suggestions in regard to imitation apply here. But imitation may be spontaneous, and if right, should be made voluntary. Emulation always involves the Will. The difference between imitation and emulation may be illustrated. John repeats the language used by his father, as a parrot might do, without any act of the Will beyond that required for the proper control of his vocal organs. This is imitation. But John may be taught to admire his father's ways, principles, purposes; to think about them, and to desire that they may appear in himself. His imitation has now become emulation.

Is the child emulating a bad example? Turn the capacity in another direction. Is it emulating a good example incompletely? Improve. Is it emulating for an inferior purpose? Direct its attention to a higher. Bring to its mind matters and persons worthy of emulation, and invest the idea of emulation with every possible interest. You are seeking to train the child's Will; noble emulation is one of nature's great provisions.

4. *Cultivate the desire to know.* Ask a thousand questions about the child's affairs. Encourage it to bombard you with questions of its own inventing. This thing has its limit, to be sure, but the limit is large. Questions are the crackling noises of an opening brain.

Never reply to questions, "Oh, because!" "Oh, never mind!" "Oh, don't bother me!"

If you are too busy to answer just now, make a future engagement to attend to the matters, and keep the appointment.

If the child cannot now understand, promise to answer its questions when it can, and fulfil that promise.

If you do not know, honestly confess. Then look up that matter as a thing of first importance, and give the child the desired information.

Secure interest in all tasks. The uninteresting is the unwilled. Example: Sewing aprons merely to keep busy will very likely be poor work; sewing on the next party dress is an intensely interesting thing securing good work, and is therefore an education. Or, again: The study of the geography of Spain-ruled Cuba a few years ago was a dull task poorly performed. "What's the use!" Studying that Cuba where your brother had gone to fight Spain's tyranny and plant the Stars and Stripes was "just fun." The "fun of the thing" awakened the Will and illuminated geography.

5. *Cultivate the child's desire to please and benefit itself.* This desire is one of nature's strongest motors in man, and should be intelligently developed and regulated. It works injury only when misunderstood or wrongly applied. Analyzed, it divides into two impulses, that of self-interest and that of selfishness. A few characteristics will reveal the difference between these forms of personal motive.

Self-interest seeks the best interest of self; Selfishness seeks a false benefit which ultimately injures self.

Self-interest is ascertained by a study of law; selfishness is conceived in indifference to law. The one is represented by liberty; the other by license.

Self-interest respects the consensus of opinion; selfishness ignores the general opinion.

Self-interest is always concerned with the highest welfare of others; for man's life is a community-organism, and his highest interest is realized through law-

Let the Child Prophesy Fair

abiding independence subordinated to service; selfishness isolates itself from the demands of relations to others, and realizes in law-defying independence requiring service for self regardless of others.

Self-interest is an eternal reality; selfishness is eternally a denial of that reality.

Self-interest forever fulfils itself and creates larger capacities and huger worlds of opportunity; selfishness forever defeats itself, destroys capacity for welfare, and ultimates in the world of the infinitely little.

Hence, to cultivate the child's desire for its own benefit and pleasure is to cultivate true ideals of happiness and welfare. This means a reasonable and kind process of education resulting in the elimination of selfishness from life and the substitution therefor of a true self-interest.

How, then, shall the child's desire to please and benefit itself be trained?

By appeal to *experience*. The child has sought to please itself selfishly; see to it that disagreeable consequences are emphasized in its thought and memory. If none are likely to be apparent, bring them about, not necessarily as punishments, but as natural consequences and wholesome lessons.

If the child has subordinated itself, bring out clearly the beneficial results. If none are apparent, manage the matter in such a way as to secure them, even if artificially.

Always must the child's Will be kept in mind. The will to do for a real pleasure or benefit will certainly be stronger after proper experience duly emphasized than the will to do for fancied happiness or welfare shown in experience to lead to unhappiness.

By appeal to the *love of reward*. Reward is a fruit

of the nature of things. It should have a large but regulated place in the child's life. Here is perfect stimulation to right exercise of Will. Hence,— Do not reduce the child's life to the plane of mere duty.

Do not compel it to perform an act simply because you order it. Suggest rewards of some sort — gifts, or pleasure promised, or benefits upheld as certain to come about naturally.

Do not seek to dominate the child's conduct by remote or abstract ideas. Teach the remote through the present, the abstract through the concrete.

By appeal to *theory*. Theory builds on the practical for the practical. It must be made to appear to the child in a concrete form as a concrete value. If the child does not perceive such value, its interest ceases and the Will flags. If it suspects that theories are mere visions and personal notions, it loses respect for your teaching. It must in some way be made to get hold of principles and their reality, so that it may intuitively apply them to various practical cases. The circles called home, street, school or playground, neighborhood, village or city, are all ramified by certain general principles which guarantee welfare. We may suggest them in the word "respect."

Respect for the *feelings* of others.
Respect for the *rights* of others.
Respect for the *opinions* of others.
Respect for the *customs* of others.
Respect for the *beliefs* of others.
Respect for the *opportunities* of others.
Respect for the *liberty* of others.
Respect for the *destiny* of others.
Such principles may be thrown into ideals or maxims

and made incessantly prominent in all the child's relations to the various circles of life.

6. *Cultivate the child's desire for the happiness and welfare of others.* The preceding suggestions inevitably make for these ends. But life ought at times to forget even self-interest. Encourage, therefore, action for others which does not think of self. A thousand opportunities are afforded for this effort. Certain simple rules may be indicated:

Request the child; do not order it.
On compliance, express your thankfulness.
For unusual obedience, manifest appreciation.
For voluntary service, exhibit a lively gratification.
Occasionally provide some unexpected pleasure.
For exceptional thoughtfulness, indicate corresponding approbation.

7. *Cultivate the child's desire for independence.* With all safeguards thrown around it, the child must, in countless ways, think, determine, act for itself. The more frequently and fully it does so, under wise supervision, the more surely will its Will-power be trained, and its future be mortgaged for the largest success. A right spirit of independence may be cultivated,—

By appeal to the *love of ownership.* The child ought to own many things in " fee simple," as it were. Its ownership should be thoroughly respected, and seldom overshadowed by any superior claim. In addition to possession in the ordinary run of life, it should also be made owner of special things with responsibilities or unusual opportunities connected therewith, as a piece of land, an animal, a boat, a set of tools, some kind of mechanism for making various articles, materials to be worked over, etc.

By the appeal of the *practical in society*. Under proper restrictions, stores, shops, factories, farms, public buildings, and the like, afford fine opportunities to acquire familiarity with common objects and common ways of doing things which inevitably minister to the child's sense and power of independence in times of special need.

By throwing the child upon its *own resources and judgment,* as far as may, in any given case, be wise. This requires that it be given as large a measure of liberty as is compatible with a long-headed view of its best welfare. Sooner or later it must depend upon itself. The present question is, shall its future freedom be that of liberty or that of license? The man's liberty must grow out of the child's law-governed independence.

Do not smother independence, therefore, but regulate it.

Do not tie the child to your tether of personal notion. Cut the apron-string, or get a long rope. This increases your care, but it builds the child's Will.

If the child gets hurt in its freedom — experience is a good teacher. If it falls into error — there is your opportunity to preach an illustrated sermon like a story-teller, with all points suggested above for divisions, and self-regulated independence as the main lesson.

Never say "No" to a child merely to relieve yourself of trouble.

Never say "No" to a child without stopping to think.

Do your first thinking silently. If favorable, repeat the process to the child. If unfavorable, and you wish to give the child a lesson in experience, repeat the process aloud and say, "Yes." If you are found to have been mistaken, reason the matter out to the preservation of the child's respect for you, notwithstanding. If you were right, abstain from gloating, but impress the lesson handsomely. If your judgment is unfavorable to the child's desires, and you do not wish to chance the lesson of experience, repeat the process of thought and say " No."

Always make the " No " as easy as possible.

Never say a reasonable " No " and change to a thoughtless " Yes."

Never say " No " when " Yes " would be exactly as wise. Avoid the habit of senseless objection.

Never say " Yes " and change to a thoughtless " No."

Never say, " Oh, I don't care! " This shows that you rule or permit without thought.

If the problem will not resolve itself to your thought, state the case fairly, and win the child's assent to your doubt. Cultivate independence, again,—

By inducing the child to *launch out,* now and then, in some heroic venture, always forefended and watched over.

By encouraging *heroic endurance* of consequences.

By encouraging frank and *heroic assumption of blame* for mistakes of its own.

By encouraging *modest appropriation of legitimate praise* and satisfaction for favorable outcomes of independent decisions, conduct and ventures.

These suggestions will readily recall to mind various illustrations as to means and methods, and need not be further elaborated.

Now, the child's interest is usually spontaneous and natural. But nature constantly indicates that spontaneous interest may be invented. It is the possibility of invented interest that enables Professor James to state the following

LAWS OF INTEREST: —

First law of interest: "*Any object not interesting in itself may become interesting through becoming associated with an object in which an interest already exists. The two associated ideas grow, as it were; the interesting portion sheds its quality over the whole; and thus things not interesting in their own right borrow an interest which becomes as real and as strong as that of any natively interesting thing.*"

This law suggests three practical rules:

1. Associate in the child's life interesting things with uninteresting things; or, cause the uninteresting things to borrow interest from things that are in any way possessed of interest to the child. As this rule may be divided,—

2. "Begin with the line of his native interests, and offer him objects that have some immediate connection with these.

3. "Step by step connect with these first objects and experiences the later objects and ideas which you wish to instil. Associate the new with the old in some natural and telling way, so that the interest, being shed along from point to point, finally suffuses the entire system of objects of thought."

In a few words, get hold of the child's interest in some way, immediate or remote, in the subject or task in hand; then connect its interest, as it exists, by any roundabout way, with the thing or act desired.

Second law of interest: "*Voluntary attention cannot be continuously sustained; it comes in beats.*"

This is true in the adult mind. Voluntary attention in the child's mind is much more fickle; hence the value of the prescription:

Let the Child Prophesy Fair 387

"The subject must be made to show new aspects of itself; to prompt new questions; in a word, to change.

"From an unchanging subject the attention inevitably wanders away. You can test this by the simplest possible case of sensorial attention. Try to attend steadfastly to a dot on the paper or on the wall. You presently find that one or the other of two things has happened: either your field of vision has become blurred, so that you now see nothing distinct at all, or else you have involuntarily ceased to look at the dot in question and are looking at something else. But, if you ask yourself successive questions about the dot — how big it is, how far, of what shape, what shade of color, etc.; in other words, if you turn it over, if you think of it in various ways, and along with various kinds of associations — you can keep your mind upon it for a comparatively long time."

Third law of interest. In the child's life the concrete is always the realest and the most interesting.

All is things. The mind constantly concretes the abstract. It is this fact that gives life an enormous fictitious interest; examples: units = apples, dolls, etc.; freedom = eating all the jam you want; God = a huge man who is invisible, but, because He is omnipresent, can be caught in an old shoe and tied up — a real case in the family of a religious professor of physics.

Make the child's Will, therefore, a mover of concrete realities.

Always is it to be remembered that the child is pre-eminently a subject of education. And what education is, let Professor James tell us:

"It cannot be better described than by calling it

the organization of acquired habits of conduct and tendencies to behavior."

At home or school, this process of "organizing acquired habits" involves a great aphorism:

"*No reception without reaction, no impression without correlative expression.*"

The preceding basic principles of reason and of interest, with the suggestions noted, simply mean that whatever properly goes into the child's mind should be worked over, by itself, in its concrete life. All such reactions tend to train the Will. Right reaction equals right Will-exercise. Similarly, all right impressions upon the child's mind are to be returned in some kind of expression in action. If you arouse judgment or reason and interest, you inevitably secure reaction and expression in life. The rule is infallible.

SECOND PROCESS OF WILL-CULTURE — DEVELOPMENT

Right training of the child's Will must, in the nature of the case, result in more or less increase of its power. But the specific end, a stronger Will in the child, becomes now the larger goal.

The Will is merely the mind's ability to put forth volitions.

The mind, willing repeatedly in any given direction, acquires greater ability to will in some directions.

The mind, willing readily and strongly in one direction, may be so trained in that direction as to will readily and strongly in other directions. This has been disputed, but it seems obvious. He who acquires facility in performing a certain kind of mental task may thereby acquire power for other tasks. He who successfully resists one temptation prepares himself for successful resistance of another temptation. A will trained in the use of reason and by appeals to a true interest, becomes a better and stronger Will for response to the naked call of duty. It is not necessary to acquire power for all different kinds of acts; the soul stores power adequate to untried cases. Any general faculty of the mind may be developed as a general faculty.

Development of Will regards, indirectly its present state, but primarily the increase of power wherein the mind lacks. The mind possesses a certain ability to will at present; it may be educated, unfolded, so as to acquire power to put forth volitions more strongly for any purpose.

For such development of Will-power the basic principle is now practice.

SIR ANYMAN

Oh, Life's perennial Knight — Sir Anyman
Trust thru nor Opportunity nor Fate:
The one, a mere detail in Nature's Plan,
The other, Error's name for Best Estate.
Complainer! Know'st thou not the oath, I Can,
Shall win brave kingdoms to thy will elate
If Good Soul do but scorn their wizard ban?
On thee, the Master, see! they fawn and wait!

I sing no Law of Accident or Birth,
No Gift of Fortune by Divine Decree.
I sing the Call of Courage, Honor, Worth!
The world-wide Call of our old Mother, Earth.
Heed thou, Sir Knight, this Golden Prophecy:
The Throne to him who forces Destiny!
— THE AUTHOR.

CHAPTER XXIX

CONCLUSION. THE SYMMETRICAL EXISTENCE.

OUR labors are now nearly concluded. Henceforth it only remains to carry out in daily life the ideas of the preceding pages. The book is not a treatise; it seeks to be a teacher, and thus leaves much to the intelligence of the reader. If it prove suggestive and lead to practical efforts for culture of the Will, the devotion of the long period required for its mastery will surely be justified.

As M. Guizot said to his class in lecturing on the "History of Civilization":

"The good fortune to have all the faculties called into action, so as to ensure a full and free development of the various powers both of mind and body, is an advantage not too dearly paid for by the labor and pain with which it is attended."

It is hoped that the following are among the *results achieved:*

The fundamentals of the mental constitution have been more fully disclosed.

The reader has been introduced to his own centre of power, the Will, and has perceived some of the tests and secrets of success in life.

A neglected fact has been made plain, that the Will may be cured when defective, and thus trained and developed.

Recognition of the reader's self has been aroused —

as a psychic power possessed of two psychic instruments, body and mind.

Certain more specific results follow these considerations:

First. *The body and the senses are better understood and controlled.*

Life demands clear *soul-windows.*

Correct *hearing* allies with genius.

In the sense of *smell* the chemistry of instinct prepares for intelligent mastery.

The sense of *taste* foreruns the discriminations of a purposeful art.

The sense of *touch* advance-guards the soul's progress.

The *nervous* values of existence are measured by the degree of restraint imposed upon the nerve-system.

The *hands* should be the great art-servants of the mind.

Nerves and muscles act rightly together as they are mastered by *determined intelligence.*

The Will enjoins *health;* and its power depends upon the amount of order obtaining within its kingdom.

The labor which involves these discoveries originates indomitable *Will-power.*

Second. *The mind has become a new kingdom, surveyed and given government.*

The mind that can master *attention,* achieves.

The gift of *reading* depends for value upon the focusing Will.

The attribute of *thought* is kingly according to the degree of concentrated personality behind it.

Masterful personality anticipates the future as its *memory* realizes the past.

The pioneer of life, which is the *imagination,* makes or destroys by as much as personality has willed *moral* or immoral *purpose.*

Willed moral purpose has absolute power over all *habituated action.*

Man's *relations with his fellows* is rightly masterful if the reasonable Will is dominant.

The ability to *converse with the voiceless crowd,* any ordinary audience, is not a gift nor a trick, but is an extension of usual communication by the magnetic personality laboriously acquired.

The subtle secret of *true magnetism* is a mighty Will morally determined.

The *Personal Atmosphere* is a vibrant centre to be given moral quality by high-purposed Will.

The *child* may become the supreme benefactor of the man.

The labor which involves these discoveries originates self-conscious and indomitable *power of Will.*

Third. A deathless interest in such and further important discoveries appears.

Interest awakened in self — hitherto largely unknown.

A wonderful domain has opened, causing astonishment that it should have been so long neglected.

Do educated people know themselves? Literature and schools abundant! Meanwhile, the psychic self pores and bores, unmindful and uninstructed that it is psychic or has a power of Will, and that this is given to be grown, and nurtured, and trained for ultimate destiny.

For, observe!

Nowhere, to-day, probably, exists a college or university wherein the individual shall study and master himself to a degree, before engaging in the smaller conquest of infinite worlds.

But what history so valuable as that of a man's own growing soul?

What science so imperative as that of a man's own bones, nerves, muscles, limbs, organs, senses, functions?

What psychology so important to know as your own?

What power so needful to understand as the electric nerve-force, the secreting and expanding dynamics of thought, the sovereign energy of Will?

Discovery of the value of systematic labor in the fundamental fields of self for its own improvement.

Is it not largely true that prevailing educational methods set minds at work upon tasks concerning ten thousand matters, more or less remotely related to the growth of mind, rather than upon matters in the mind directly related to these multitudinous facts, so-called?

It is like trying to improve a machine by working it on inconceivable miscellanies of tasks, when reason would suggest the definite understanding and improvement of the mechanism preparatory to its adapted work.

Man's education should first concern his own fundamental powers and possibilities.

This requires more than one régime with every department of his constitution.

The value, therefore, of systematic labor on as well as with the senses and the various mental powers cannot be overestimated.

This value should be directly and deliberately sought

— in the man's self, not merely in an universe, the worth of which, to him, depends wholly upon what he knows and masters of himself.

The universe, as a field of endeavor, reacts upon the individual, to be sure. But the true goal is to get the man to react rightly upon the universe. This requires self-development, sought by direct methods, as well as by the roundabout methods of objective analysis and attack.

The direct and conscious development of Will, understood as within, as the man's master or his servant, as his maker or his destroyer.

If this book has been worked into the student, he has emerged from its pages a joyous, conquering Will; — a masterful personality. He ought now to decide with the prompt and compelling power of a rifle-shot. He ought now to "brake his wheels" with divine authority. He ought now to persist and sleuth-hound his purposes with the tenacity of nature's laws.

He will not have transcended his original endowments, but his true possibilities will certainly have come to the fore. That is his whole measure of responsibility and success.

If he has become self-reliant — a man who can stand alone or go alone, as his real interest may demand, he has achieved the Mood of the gods, confidence in his own throne and dominion.

The book has undoubtedly suggested many possible exercises not found in its pages. This is a value; it implies power in the reader. All such suggestions should be tried, tested, and, if practicable and useful, adopted, for temporary purposes or for permanent régime.

Some additional chapters might have been written, as, for example, on the relation of the Will to knowledge, the place of Will in belief, the Will and the beautiful. But such chapters would prove afield of the end in view — a great Will. All exercises given tend to this end. Only in a secondary manner, probably, would practice in willing for belief or the cultivation of taste have so resulted.

It is a commonplace, however, that knowledge, in itself and as to its kind, demands willed purpose and willed selection; that right beliefs are legitimately within the province of a healthy and determined Will, in the way of forcing honest investigation and true methods, etc.; and that intelligent Will has much to do with the appropriation of art and the beautiful in general.

Will may determine æsthetics, either for a high or a low type, either for a purpose or an influence that is essentially moral or morally indifferent. Transform an artist's or a people's moral character, and note the function of Will in the elevation of art.

A final prime result should now be perceived:

Fourth. The goal of the Symmetrical Life.
Let us observe:
The Symmetrical Existence is the ultimate of the perfected Will.

Man is a kind of personality. Personality is body plus sensation plus consciousness plus sensibilities plus intellect plus reason plus conscience plus moral judgment plus spiritual states plus environment plus Will.

These facts outline for us the following *synopsis:*

I. *Every human possesses:* —

All Radii Equal

Physical life: Body, organs, muscles, nerves, functions;

Mental life: Consciousness, sense-perception, sensibilities, memory, imagination, reason, intuitions, Will, consciousness;

Moral life: Conscience, spiritual states, and perceptions, faith, affections, hope.

II. *Every human acquires:* —
Defects;
Development or improvement;
Consciousness of the same;
Enjoyment or suffering from the same.

III. *Every human works with:* —
Heredity;
Environment.

IV. *Every human unfolds:* —
Character;
Conduct.

Hence, there are to be noted the Symmetrical and the Unsymmetrical Existences.

Examine these in the reverse order.

FIRST, THE UNSYMMETRICAL LIFE

The Unsymmetrical Life is always individual, not typical. In other words, it is more or less blameworthy.

I. *It is burdened with defects of* POSSESSION,— curable, incurable.

1. Of the *Physical life*. The *incurable* must be borne by Will. The *curable* must by Will be sought out and eliminated.

Examination: Put yourself under the most rigid scrutiny as to curable defects,—

Of body; examples — stoop-shoulders, toe-in, etc.;

Of senses; examples — near-sightedness, dull hearing, etc.;

Of organs; examples — indigestion, weak lungs, etc.;

Of muscles; examples — flabby, unequally developed, etc.;

Of nerves; examples — weak, "touchy," etc.;

Of functions; example — slow hearing due to dull mind.

Resolve to cure all these defects! Begin the work now, desperately, with a high hand.

2. Of the *Mental life*. The *incurable* should be reluctantly recognized, then made the most of by indomitable Will. The *curable* must immediately be discovered.

Examination: As before, rigidly cross-examine the mind for these curable defects,—

Of perception; example — scant and slow observation;

Of consciousness; examples — vague, confused, not studied;

Of the sensibilities; examples — unfeeling, too humorous;

Of memory; examples — for names, faces, dates;

Of imagination; examples — with past experiences, with future contingencies;

Of reason; example — hasty judgments;

Of Will; example — indecision;

Of "intuitions"; example — personal antipathies.

3. Of the *Moral life*. The *incurable should never be admitted*. The moral always involves the Will. All defects, therefore, are curable. The Will must set about the task with the desperation of life battling against death.

Examination: Here, particularly, search out unceasingly, in body and mind, minutest defects,—

Of conscience; example — in trade details;

Of spiritual states and perceptions; examples — indifference to human interests or to Deity, imperfect ideas as to right and wrong in conduct;

Of belief and faith; examples — inadequate consideration of evidence, willful persistence in belief or disbelief in spite of alleged evidence; lack of confidence in an overruling Power;

Of the affections; examples — little thought as to the Golden Rule, ill-will freely entertained;

Of hope; examples — indifference to moral consequences, mental lethargy as to a future existence.

II. *The Unsymmetrical Life represents, further, wrong* ACQUISITIONS.

If the Will is right, what has been evilly acquired can be eliminated. If the Will is not right, it must be trained and developed. *All acquired defects are curable*. It is, first, a question of desire, and secondly a matter of Will.

Examination: Search every field of personality with minutest scrutiny for acquired defects. You enjoy them, it may be, and are not willing to perceive them. Look, hence, with the eyes of other people. Pass under honest review,—

Each factor of the body which is under the control of Will;

Every department of the mind for inequalities and wrong habits;

The moral nature, for wrong beliefs, dispositions, tendencies, etc.;

The whole sphere of self-control, for indifference and acknowledged weakness, for vagaries and want of practical tone and balance;

Erroneous and misleading "intuitions" or notions;

Consciousness of abilities and growth, for lack of same, for undue recognition of, for inadequate appreciation of self;

Enjoyment derived from such consciousness, for selfishness and the threat of sloth or arrogant pride;

Suffering caused by consciousness of defects, for reasonableness and relation to improvement;

Antipathies as to persons and things, groundless and uncontrolled.

III. *The Unsymmetrical Life involves defects of* HEREDITY *and* ENVIRONMENT.

Of Heredity. The *incurable* must be borne by Will, and may often be utilized for self-benefit. Example: the blind develop extraordinary acuteness in the other senses. The *curable* may be brought to light with proper labor and care. They are handicaps,—

Of body; examples — consumptive tendencies, left-handedness;

Of mind; examples — peculiar habits and traits which indicate abnormality;

Of morals; example — natural sharp bent in money matters.

Of Environment. The *incurable* must be made means for personal welfare in spite of their existence. This can be done only by the indomitable Will. The *curable* must be cautiously handled when discovered.

Examination: Be fair as to defects of family, of house, of neighborhood, of town, of society, of church, of climate, of state.

Four questions here appear:

How can you contribute to the *reform* of these environments?

How can you best *adjust yourself* to them, after such contribution?

How can you best secure *different* environments?

How can you *make the most* of your environments which cannot be reformed or changed?

IV. *The Unsymmetrical Life stands for wrong* UNFOLDMENTS.

Your character is what you have made yourself. Of this, conduct is the truest expression. This book has had in view the growth of a power with which alone character can put forth right conduct and develop by its expression. Whatever you are, aside from incurable heredity, is due to your use of the Will. If character is weak, wrong, etc., it is because, with your original make-up, you have permitted it to become or remain so. Your standard is not some abstract ideal, but it is just this first nature and what you can make of it under all the circumstances of your life. Hence, all defects of character and conduct are curable.

Orison Swett Marden remarks suggestively: "How many of us rank high in most respects, but our average is cut down very low by some contemptible weakness or some vicious habit. How easy it is to forget that the strength of the chain lies in its weakest, not the strongest link; that a small leak will sink a ship as surely as a large one, it being only a question of time."

IN THE SECOND PLACE, THE SYMMETRICAL LIFE.

The Symmetrical Life is, now, with the Unsymmetrical, always individual, not typical. In other words, the ideal is relative rather than absolute. With divisions as before, observe:—

I. *As to* POSSESSIONS.—

1. Here the possessions of the *Physical Life* require,—

That all the laws of health shall be obeyed;

That intelligent exercise shall be carried on;

That a rational control of the body shall be maintained;

That all defects shall be remedied as far as possible;

That a noble use of all powers shall characterize all movements.

2. The possessions of the *Mental Life* require,—

That all powers shall be cultivated for their own sake;

That they shall be coördinated in the best possible manner;

That the reason shall dominate;

That the Will shall be conscious, intelligent and strong, yet judicious in exercise;

That the whole mind shall be rightly related to the surrounding life;

That life's abilities shall be enjoyed for the highest personal welfare;

And that the mind shall always be open to the truth, and nothing but the truth.

3. The possessions of the *Moral Life* require,—

That the conscience shall be enlightened, quick and healthy;

That its dictates shall always be obeyed;

That it shall be nourished by the highest thought and action;

That spiritual states shall be taught, classified, intensified and used;

That belief and faith shall be founded in reason, developed by search for light and encouraged by right relations with, and reliance on, appropriate objects;

That the affections shall follow, carefully, intelligently and persistently the Golden Rule and the sublimest axioms of religion;

That hope shall be quickened by sensitive apprehension of moral qualities in things, ideas and actions, and rationally based in the nature of things as reverentially studied and ethically understood.

II. *As to* Acquisitions.—

The *acquisitions* of the Symmetrical Life require,—

That defects shall be discovered and immediately eliminated;

That every power of mind and body shall be assiduously developed;

That every faculty of the entire self shall be controlled by supreme Will according to the dictates of morality and reason;

That antipathies shall be banished if possible, and always regulated;

That consciousness shall embrace the sum total of

acquirements in order to best use, and be enjoyed, not merely in appreciation of the present, but as well in expectation of greater developments to come;

That "intuitions" shall be disciplined by sound common sense.

III. *As to* HEREDITY.—

In the Symmetrical Life, *heredity*, if favorable, is to be utilized to the utmost; if unfavorable, overcome.

IV. *As to* ENVIRONMENT.—

In the Symmetrical Life, *environment*, if indifferent to progress, is to be dominated by positive qualities; if hostile, is to be conquered, or reformed, or given up for better; if favorable, is to be taken with all advantages, not to be permitted mastery, which is always the tendency of propitious surroundings, but to be seized and controlled with the masterful Will.

In nature, environment is the workshop of heredity; in man, environment ought to be the Throne Room of Will.

V. *As to* CHARACTER.—

Character, in the Symmetrical Life, if based upon heredity, is to be improved, corrected, or suppressed; if based upon right Will, is to be valued, studied, cherished and nourished, as eternal good;

VI. *As to* CONDUCT.—

Conduct, in the Symmetrical Life must be right toward self, right toward man, right toward truth and Deity.

This outline sets forth a gigantic task. But life that is a failure involves gigantic toil, and it is an unspeakable ruin because it is Will-power regnant amid anarchy.

Let it, then, appear:

That the Will is not the man entire;

That the perfect Will is the man matured;

That personality complete is the Will centering and ruling the maturing man — body, emotions, intellect, conscience, and all religious faculties.

All higher powers inhere in the Will. They are nothing without the Will.

They come to perfection through the Will. Their development involves culture of Will-power.

The Will is the centre from which all powers radiate to the circle of the perfected personality.

Hence, there can be no Symmetrical Life that is not determined, sought and secured by Will.

The Unsymmetrical Life is one in which Will fails, either to seek self-discovery and development, or to improve where defects and better possibilities are known. Here the radii of powers fail to extend out to the perfect circle of personality.

The majority of men are unnecessarily ignorant of their own defects and possibilities. The Will does not, thus, centre their selfhood.

A multitude of people recognize defects, but ignore them because of lack of Will to set about correction.

Discovery of fault should be instantly followed by remedy. This is often prevented by sloth, by fear of consequences, by dread of cost, by indifference to a true personality.

The Unsymmetrical Life is largely inexcusable.

It is a promise of ultimate bankruptcy.

It is the threat of culpable suicide.

In the Symmetrical Life the man seeks to improve all powers to the utmost. He gives due regard to each, carefully, persistently. He strives to bring out each radius to the perfect circle. He endeavors to fill up every depression in the sphere of his being.

The Symmetrical Life, therefore, is independent of heredity; this is true because symmetry is not an abstract matter determined by reference to some universal standard, without regard to individuality, but is a concrete thing having reference to the man as originally endowed.

A rose is concrete symmetry, although it lacks the abstract symmetry of a glass imitation.

The Symmetrical Life starts with its own endowments, builds on its own foundation, develops according to its own laws.

Hence, there are grades in symmetry. Each grade has perfect value by as much as it is determined by intelligent Will.

The law and the privilege of life are that a man shall make the most of himself as heredity has really endowed him. He can develop symmetry in himself, however imperfect this may be as compared with others or an abstract ideal which is indifferent to his nature.

Superior beings and ideals merely assist in inspiring his symmetrical growth — the bringing out of his own powers. Such beings and ideals must never be regarded as discouraging standards.

The intelligent Will does not attempt the impossible.

The Symmetrical Life is, also, in a true sense, independent of environment. It cannot be destroyed, nor prevented by surroundings, provided its Will holds good.

A good Will *adjusts* to environment, and grows in its mastery.

A good Will *conquers* environment, and thus thrives on difficulty.

A good Will *makes* environment, and thus unfolds in triumph.

A good Will — at the last resort — *forsakes* old for new environment, and thus strengthens itself by a rational persistence.

Civilization attests all the above propositions.

Every truly successful man is an epitome of the civilization of his own time.

The secret of the Will's power over self, over heredity and environment, lies in the fact that it is active, that it is intelligent, that it is individual, that it is a law unto itself and thus subject to law, and that, therefore, it is free.

But the ideally free Will is the ideally perfect Will.

And the ideally perfected Will is the Symmetrical Existence.

In "Raja Yoga" there is this legend: A great God-sage, travelling everywhere, found a man who had been meditating until an ant-hill had been built up around his body. The man begged the sage to ask God to give him his ultimate freedom. Further on the traveler saw another man who was dancing and singing, and who begged him to ask the same boon. Later, the sage, returning, met the first petitioner, to whom he brought the message from heaven: "The Lord told me that you would attain freedom in four more births." And then the man began to mourn. But the sage met the second petitioner, to whom he said: "I have to tell you that as many leaves as there are on that Tamarind tree, so many times you will be born, and then you will attain your freedom." And the second man shouted: "I will have freedom after so short a time!" But a voice came, "My child, you will have freedom this minute."

The Symmetrical and the Unsymmetrical Existence are near or far according to the persistence and energy of the Will.

The following chart, which does not aim to be exhaustive, is now suggested for study and comparison with yourself. It should be read, again and again. "Know thyself." Indicate in writing on the chart your own photographic details, and resolutely set about the correction of defects, the improvement of excellences, and the bringing of all powers to a better condition and a greater harmony among themselves.

Permit no defect to continue.
Cultivate neglected faculties and capacities.
Make the best use of good qualities.
Compel your strong points to assist your weaker.
Overcome hostile heredity.
Master environment.
Seek the circle of individual perfection.
Resolve on the ideal in character and conduct.
The Symmetrical Existence is your ideal.

The ideal is absolute and relative.
The absolute ideal is never realized.
But the absolute ideal is the inspiration of the relative ideal.
The relative ideal is that of attainment just beyond and of high purpose now steadfastly entertained.
The ideal of purpose is always shifting. So soon as

it is realized in attainment, a substitution appears; it is no longer ideal, but is actual, and the true ideal is discovered as a new goal.

The relative ideal of purpose is thus the impelling power of growth and progress. It is both the despair and the inspiration of the Symmetrical Life.

The reason why men are so unsymmetrical is largely the fact that the ideal is so seldom studied or sought.

The study and search for symmetry makes great demands on the Will.

Endeavors to attain symmetry become by all odds the supremest instructors and developers of Willpower.

If you will honestly study the suggestions of this chapter, and resolutely and persistently devote your life to attainment of the Symmetrical Existence, you will fare on as a hero, a constantly growing soul and a creator of highest Will.

Your want of symmetry shows your need of alliance with the nature of things, with all noble spirits among men, and with that ruling "Power not ourselves that makes for righteousness."

The man who attempts to live without this is an anarchist. He contemns and disregards the law of best estate. He lives without the essence of life. He sluices out of himself all that guarantees and develops his human reality. He is slowly committing suicide.

You exist to help. This requires that you seek to know what the nature of things has designed for you. This is your goal — none other — your life, your immortality.

Said Wilhelm von Humboldt: "The end of man, or that which is prescribed by the eternal or immutable dictates of reason, and not suggested by vague and transient desires, is the highest and most harmonious development of his powers to a complete and consistent whole; the object towards which every human being must ceaselessly direct his efforts, and on which especially those who design to influence their fellowmen must ever keep their eyes, is the individuality of power and development."

John Stuart Mill, in comment, said: "Human nature is not a machine to be built after a model, and set to do exactly the work prescribed for it, but a tree, which requires to grow and develop itself on all sides, according to the tendency of the inward forces which make it a living thing."

And now, in all our work, it is best to remember that life is not a judgment to drudgery. It is a glory, a dignity, an opportunity, a prelude and a reward. The true life has deep content; —
In itself,
    In its worlds,
        In its brotherhood,
            In its death-swallowing hope.

And it is for the body to rest, as well as to toil.

And it is for mind to relax and change, as well as to concentrate.

And it is for the man to play, to rejoice with the hills, to throb with the sea, to laugh with nature, as well as to struggle and pile up victories.

But it is for the Will to slumber not, to relax never, to go forth day and night, in the full majesty of conquest.

FOR, TO THIS END CAME THE KING TO HIS THRONE.

Milton Keynes UK
Ingram Content Group UK Ltd.
UKHW051104250324
439991UK00007B/767